AGING
Volume 1

Aging
Volume 1

Clinical, Morphologic, and Neurochemical Aspects in the Aging Central Nervous System

Editors:

H. Brody, Ph.D., M.D.
Professor and Chairman
Department of Anatomical Sciences
State University of New York at Buffalo
School of Medicine
Buffalo, New York

D. Harman, M.D., Ph.D.
Millard Professor of Medicine
Professor of Biochemistry
University of Nebraska
College of Medicine
Omaha, Nebraska

J. Mark Ordy, Ph.D.
Head, Neurobiology
Delta Regional Primate Research Center
Tulane University
Covington, Louisiana

1976

EXCERPTA MEDICA, AMSTERDAM · OXFORD
AMERICAN ELSEVIER PUBLISHING COMPANY, INC., NEW YORK

International Standard Book Number 0-89004-023-0
Library of Congress Catalog Card Number 74-15666

Foreword

Aging is now our number one health problem. The aging process has nullified all attempts since 1955 to increase our average life expectancy, a rough measure of our healthy life span, beyond 70 years. Future significant increases in the period of vigorous life will most likely be achieved through aging inhibition.

To assist in the effort to survey as well as stimulate research in this vital area, a new series of books, *Aging,* has been initiated. This initial volume was organized under the auspices of the American Aging Association. Each volume in the series will be concerned with current studies in some area of biomedical gerontology. There will be subseries within *Aging.* Thus the topic of *Aging in the Central Nervous System,* the subject of Volume 1, will be covered again at intervals dictated by research advances to provide material for future volumes of *Aging.*

Denham Harman

Preface

The purpose of this volume is to present studies from several basic and clinical disciplines demonstrating the relationship of aging to changes in the central nervous system. The contributions were the product of the fourth annual meeting of the American Aging Association held in Los Angeles in September 1974. Since the problems of aging in the brain could benefit from an interdisciplinary approach, the presentations deal with anatomical, chemical, pathological, and clinical aspects of aging, reviewing the present state of knowledge in the respective area, major unsolved problems, and possible directions for future research. Although the primary interest was in human aging, findings from animal studies were also included to gain a broader comparative insight into structural and functional changes.

It seems inevitable that all aspects of aging will receive increasing attention in basic and clinical biomedical research. Since many of the human problems of aging include mental impairment and a high incidence of brain disorders, development of a neurobiology of aging may contribute significantly to a clarification of normal aging as well as providing some understanding of the mechanisms involved in diseases of the central nervous system.

Harold Brody
Denham Harman
J. Mark Ordy

Contents

Contributors

Herbert Barden
Department of Neurotoxicology
New York State Psychiatric Institute
New York, New York 10032

Kenneth R. Brizzee
Delta Regional Primate Center
Tulane University
Covington, Louisiana 70433
and
Department of Anatomy
Tulane University School of Medicine
New Orleans, Louisiana 70112

Govind A. Dhopeshwarker
Laboratory of Nuclear Radiation
  and Radiobiology
and Division of Environmental and
  Nutritional Sciences
University of California
School of Medicine
Los Angeles, California 90024

James C. Harkin
Department of Pathology
Tulane University School of Medicine
New Orleans, Louisiana 70112

Lissy F. Jarvik
Psychogenetics Unit
Brentwood Veterans Administration
  Hospital
Los Angeles, California 90024

Bernice Kaack
Delta Regional Primate Center
Tulane University
Covington, Louisiana 70433

James F. Mead
Laboratory of Nuclear Medicine and
  Radiation Biology
and Department of Biological Chemistry
University of California
School of Medicine
Los Angeles, California 90024

J. Mark Ordy
Delta Regional Primate Research Center
Tulane University
Covington, Louisiana 70433

Thaddeus Samorajski
Biology and Gerontology Section
Texas Research Institute of
  Mental Sciences
1300 Moursund Avenue
Houston, Texas 77025

Arnold B. Scheibel
Departments of Anatomy and Psychiatry
and Brain Research Institute
University of California
School of Medicine
Los Angeles, California 90024

Madge E. Scheibel
Departments of Anatomy and Psychiatry
and Brain Research Institute
University of California
School of Medicine
Los Angeles, California 90024

Jean C. Shih
School of Pharmacy
University of Southern California
Los Angeles, California 90033
and
Department of Psychiatry
University of California
School of Medicine
Los Angeles, California 90024

Aging. Volume 1, edited by H. Brody,
D. Harman, and J. M. Ordy. Raven
Press, New York © 1975.

The Aging Central Nervous System: Clinical Aspects

Lissy F. Jarvik

*Psychogenetics Unit, Brentwood Veterans Administration Hospital, Los Angeles, California
90025, and Department of Psychiatry, School of Medicine, University of California at Los
Angeles, California 90024*

To many of us, the most frightening aspect of the aging central nervous system is the image that it brings to mind of a doddering, demented, and dispirited old man who can control neither his drooling saliva nor his disoriented babblings. Truly, were it not "for the special physical, emotional and social burdens imposed by mental decay in later life, the geriatric problem would be of a far less formidable and quite different character" (Roth, 1972, p. 110). Is this mental decay the clinical expression of an aging central nervous system?

Until the early part of this century, the answer would have been positive. It was unquestioningly assumed — on the basis of then available pathological evidence — that senile mental changes were indeed the result of morphological changes in the brain. In the 1930s, however, emphasis began to be placed on the poor correlation between morphological changes and clinical status. In particular, some cases of far advanced senile psychosis failed to show the characteristic brain pathology, while some persons with unimpaired mental functioning exhibited marked pathology on postmortem examination. By the 1950s it was generally taught that the brain of nearly every old person showed senile plaques and some neurofibrillary tangles, and that there was no relationship between morphological changes and mental functioning.

By the 1960s the pendulum began to swing back, thanks largely to the work of Corsellis (1962), Simon and Malamud (1965), and Roth, Tomlinson, and Blessed (1967). They reported significant correlations between degree of morphological change and severity of mental deterioration. Roth and colleagues suggest that a certain level of cerebral damage has to be reached before the progressive intellectual and personality deterioration associated with dementia, whether senile or arteriosclerotic, becomes manifest. According to Roth (1972) this "'threshold effect' might explain the rapid step-like deterioration often observed in elderly persons after years of little more than a mild, slowly progressive, or stationary defect of memory for recent events, together with some accentuation of life-long personality features" (p. 118).

The "threshold" model is an attractive one because it offers hope of successful intervention and prevention. According to the threshold model, morphological changes occur slowly, so that there is adequate time to detect their behavioral consequences before a critical level, or "threshold," is reached and to intervene therapeutically early enough to prevent clinically irreversible damage. Unfortunately, at this point in time we lack the means for successful intervention. Hopefully, we will discover either the relevant pathological mechanisms or an effective therapeutic agent.

We must remember, however, that even in the hands of the staunchest advocates, the relationship between cerebral pathology and mental deterioration rests on correlations which, though statistically significant, are far from perfect (ranging at best between 0.59 and 0.77). Roth (1972) points to the "obscure and indirect" relationship between the measures of brain pathology used by him and his colleagues "with what is almost certainly the crucial variable, namely, the outfall of neurons" and suggests that the actual relationships are probably even stronger (p. 121). Not only do we need more data concerning neuronal outfall in man, but such data need to be procured separately for the various regions of the brain. As Brody (1973) has shown, cell loss is not uniform and may range from a high of nearly one-half of neurons lost in the superior frontal gyrus between the fifth and ninth decades to no demonstrable cell loss at all in the inferior olivary nucleus. Attempts to correlate loss of neurons in specific cerebral regions with impairments of mental functioning will be more meaningful than the gross approximations on which current opinions are based.

It is likely, as Malamud (1972) suggests, that some of the individuals classified as normal and later shown to have mild cerebral pathology were not really psychologically unimpaired when placed in the normal category, but exhibited behavioral defects too subtle to be detected in the type of testing generally employed. Conversely, some persons who suffered from memory loss, confusion, and disorientation while alive and in whom very little, if any, brain pathology was seen post-mortem, might actually have had pathological brain changes but not of the type detectable by the usual post-mortem examination.

One mechanism by which such functional impairment might occur without concomitantly observable morphological changes is through chromosomal changes in dividing neuroglial cells which would impair the optimal functioning of the cells in question, and either directly, or indirectly, through alterations in homeostasis with consequent impairment of neuronal functioning, lead to mental deterioration. The evidence for this possibility is preliminary, inferential, and in need of confirmation. It stems from the only two laboratories reporting on investigations of chromosomes in relation to the mental functioning of older persons. Both laboratories found an increased frequency of chromosome loss (hypodiploidy) in the cultures of peripheral leukocytes from women with senile psychosis or organic brain syndrome (OBS) as compared to women with arteriosclerotic mental change or age-matched normals (Jarvik, Yen, and Moralishvili, 1974; Nielsen, 1970). From a subsequent study (Cohen and Jarvik, *in preparation*), in which the relationship between chromosome loss and cognitive impairment was less clear cut, it appears that at advanced ages chromosomal changes may also be associated with mild memory defects and ordinarily imperceptible cognitive changes.

The hypothesis has been proposed (Jarvik, 1967) that peripheral leukocytes can be taken as a model for other dividing cellular systems, like neuroglial cells, and that hypodiploidy occurring in neuroglial cells is associated with senile mental changes. This hypothesis, however, applies to women only, since men do not show the association between chromosome loss and mental decline. Indeed, chromosome loss as such is no more frequent in old men than it is in young men, although it occurs significantly more often in old than in young women (see review in Jarvik, Yen, and Goldstein, 1974). This sex difference may also be in line with the differential frequencies of senile dementia in older men and women. Gruenberg (1961), for example, has stressed the rarity of senile, as distinguished from arteriosclerotic, psychosis in men and its relative frequency in women. Our own clinical experience parallels his, but, unfortunately, lacks the crucial autopsy data. Indeed, one of the explanations for the lack of a relationship between chromosome changes and mental changes in men is the fact that the male sample may be heavily contaminated by persons with cerebral arteriosclerosis despite efforts to screen them out. The unreliability of the antemortem diagnosis, based upon the usual clinical examination and laboratory tests in ambulatory patients, is notorious. The more frequent occurrence of arteriosclerotic disease in males than in females would lead to more heavy contamination of male than female sample with persons whose arteriosclerotic disease had been overlooked.

In addition to arteriosclerosis, an important differential diagnosis in the elderly is that of depression. In our own chromosome studies care was taken to detect signs and symptoms of depression, since depression is frequent in the elderly and may either accompany organic brain syndrome and aggravate it, or mimic its symptoms. In the United States, for example, 80% of first admissions over the age of 65 years receive a diagnosis of organic brain syndrome and only 8.5% are diagnosed as suffering from functional psychiatric disturbances (Simon, 1971). In the United Kingdom, by contrast, 43% are diagnosed as suffering from organic brain syndrome and 46% from functional disorders. From the studies of Zubin and collaborators (Gurland, *in preparation*) we know that the difference is not due to differential frequencies of the disorders in the two populations but rather to cross-national differences in diagnostic styles. Even in the United States, however, between 37 and 52% of diagnoses in elderly patients were those of affective disorders (primarily depressive illness) for patients admitted to voluntary nonprofit or private psychiatric facilities, or seen in geriatric outpatient services (Pfeiffer and Busse, 1973).

Whether in the United Kingdom or in the United States, depression is one of the most serious psychiatric problems associated with aging. Even though the peak incidence of depression seems to lie between the ages of 40 and 65 years, the frequency after the age of 65 is still considerable. Varying with the type of survey, a prevalence of 4 to 8% appears to be common at least up to the age of 70, and there is general agreement on decline in prevalence after the age of 70 even though new cases of depression have been reported even in the age groups over 75 years. There is a distinct sex difference in all studies, women showing higher rates of depression than men throughout the age span, although the difference between the sexes tends to decline somewhat after the age of 70 (Gurland, *in preparation*). The above data are based on the diagnosis of depression as made by psychiatrists. If depressive symptoms, rather than psychiatric diagnosis of depression, are taken as a basis for estimating the prevalence of depression, they are found to be highest in the age group above 65 (Gaitz and Scott, 1972; Busse, 1961).

The uncertainties concerning the incidence and prevalence of depressive illness reflect in part our ignorance when it comes to etiologic considerations. Etiology of depression at any age remains largely undetermined, and there are no clues at present to indicate whether or not depressions seen in the elderly are qualitatively different from those seen in younger age groups. It is difficult, therefore, to know to which extent, if any, affective disorders in the elderly are a function of the aging central nervous system. The most generally accepted hypothesis of the organic component in depression is the "biogenic amine hypothesis." The age-related changes in the biogenic amines and the key enzyme, monoamine oxidase, are discussed in subsequent chapters (Shih; Samorajski, *this volume*).

Whatever the biochemical factors, depression is usually precipitated by psychological stresses, and psychological stresses are known to increase with advancing chronological age. There are the losses of significant persons through separation or death, the loss of income after retirement with a consequent decline in the standard of living, the loss of occupational identity with the resultant reduction in status, the loss of physical vitality together with the onset of a variety of physical illnesses, as well as social isolation concomitantly with poverty and physical debility. Epstein summed up the situation very well: "Whether functional illness arising in old age is predominantly a reaction to an aging process, the culmination of life-long conflicts in particularly vulnerable individuals, or is a combination of these, remains an open question" (Epstein, *in preparation*). Since, as described in subsequent chapters (Ordy, Kaack, and Brizzee; Shih; Samorajski, *this volume*) the age-related changes in biogenic amines tend in a direction conducive to depressive illness, it is surprising that such illness does not occur even more frequently than it does, particularly in view of the stresses accumulating with age.

In reviewing the biochemical aspects of age differentiation in depression,

Lipton (*in preparation*) concludes that data on both the biology of depression and the biology of aging are largely controversial: "It would appear, however, a simple biochemical explanation is inadequate. Aging has associated with it a high level of psycho-social and physical stress and it calls for a high level of coping psychologically and a high level of biological adaptation. All of this occurs at a time when adaptive capacities are increasingly limited physically and psychologically, and depression ensues when these devices fail."

The preceding discussion of depression might create the impression that there really is such an entity as depression. In actuality, the term subsumes what are probably a variety of etiologically distinct entities. At present, however, there is no fully satisfactory way of distinguishing the group of syndromes "in which there are abnormal, persistent affective changes associated with feelings of worthlessness and guilt, impaired capacity to perform everyday social functions; and hypochondriasis, accompanied by such physical alterations as anorexia, weight change, constipation, psychomotor retardation, or agitation, headache, and other bodily complaints. Even to the untrained observer, most depressive states are pathological by virtue of their intensity, pervasiveness and persistence, and their interference with the patients usual social and physiological functioning. All these symptoms seldom occur in any one individual patient. Varying combinations are observed and numerous attempts have been undertaken to reduce the heterogeneity by identifying groups, typologies and symptom classes" (Klerman, *in preparation*). If the most popular division—that into endogenous and reactive forms of depressive illness—is utilized, then the majority of depressions in the elderly fall into the endogenous group (internally evoked), while in the young, more of them tend to be reactive (externally provoked). In both young and old, most episodes are unipolar (i.e., cycles of depression only), rather than bipolar (cycles of depression alternating with mania). Unfortunately, little is known of the natural history of depressive illness, be it unipolar or bipolar, with advancing age.

We do know that in the upper age groups interdependence of physical and mental illness becomes prominent. Physical illness frequently precipitates or aggravates organic brain syndrome and, of course, depressive illness in the aged. Conversely, according to Harris (1972) physical ailments severe enough to interfere with functioning have been reported in 80 to 90% of geriatric mentally ill patients in the United States and the United Kingdom. It is difficult, therefore, to distinguish between those mental changes which are the result of intervening physical illness and those which may be considered the normal accompaniments of increasing chronological age.

We do know that cognitive decline can be one of the earliest indicators of morbidity and mortality. Emanating from the first longitudinal studies of aged individuals (Jarvik, Kallmann, Falek, and Klaber, 1957; Kleemeier, 1962), the positive association between mortality and decline on selected psychological tests has been confirmed by every longitudinal study of aging reported since (see Jarvik, Eisdorfer, and Blum, 1973). In all of these studies, and there are close to a dozen now, those persons who survived to be retested some years later had had the higher scores initially, when compared to those who died during the interim. Since the most common causes of death in the age group above 60 are arteriosclerotic cardiovascular or cerebrovascular disease, we may infer that the lowered cognitive performance reflects subclinical cerebral changes. From our own 20 year follow-up of a group of aged twins, it emerged that a "critical loss" in cognitive functioning, defined as a specified rate of annual decline on certain psychological tests, differentiated not only the groups of survivors and decedents, but proved to be an accurate predictor of mortality in individual twin pairs. In 10 of 11 pairs discordant for "critical loss," the partner showing the "critical loss" was the first to die, and in the 11th pair, the partner with the "critical loss," though still alive at last report, showed marked physical and mental deterioration, while his co-twin had remained in good health (Jarvik and Blum, 1971).

In contrast to cognitive declines, decreasing scores on speeded psychomotor tasks appeared to be normal concommitants of aging and not indicative of impending mortality.

Indeed, a decline in speed may be the only inevitable accompaniment of advancing chronological age. This slowing is characteristic not only of mental activities but of physical activities as well; champion athletes are rarely beyond their twenties in sports placing a premium on speed. If behavioral slowing is the hallmark of old age, then it seems logical to search for the key to this basic phenomenon within the aging central nervous system. After all, it is the nervous system which integrates behavior. And, indeed, behavioral slowing has been associated, not with general health status, but with respiratory functioning, EEG slowing, evoked potential amplitude and decreased flicker-fusion frequency (Jarvik and Cohen, 1973). The slowing of the alpha frequency of the EEG and its role as a central timing mechanism for the central nervous system remains to be elucidated. Changes in circadian rhythms have been noted with age and temporal disorganization, as a compensatory mechanism for biological changes has been proposed as one reason for the behavioral slowing with age (Samis, 1968). Even though such compensation would be a healthy adaptive response, it would induce, as an undesirable side effect, a desynchronization of activity, which in turn might result in slowing of organizational functioning. Decreased sensory input, possibly due to reduced central inhibitory influences, together with impaired receptors are again conducive to a decline in speed of behavior. Further, the decrease in autonomic activity with age, the loss of neurons (particularly those with fast-conducting fibers), and the slight slowdown in peripheral nerve conduction, tend to reduce the speed of behavior. It is likely, however, that the decreased speed of synaptic transmission, possibly due to the accumulation of lipofuscin postsynaptically, is an even more important contributor to behavioral slowing.

Even if the decline in speed may be considered as the main, or only, consequence of advancing chronological age, there still are marked individual variations in rate of decline. One woman in our study, for example, was tested three times between the ages of 60 and 80 years, scoring 90, 97, and 91, respectively, out of a possible 100 points. Unfortunately, we do not have scores for her at the ages of 20, 30, or even 40. She is a rare exception to the trend toward marked declines in speed during the last decades of life, but her case illustrates the tremendous variability we find between aging persons and, together with the examples of actively functioning long-lived persons in some parts of the world, offers the hope that age-related deterioration can be postponed far beyond the ages with which it is now commonly associated (Jarvik, 1975).

It is well to point out before closing that the clinical aspects of the aging central nervous system which I have been discussing really apply to only a small portion of our population. Even those of us familiar with the fact that less than 5% of all persons over the age of 65 suffer the severe mental deterioration we associate with the term "senility," find it difficult to divorce the term "old age" from that of "senility." If we add to the 5% of persons over age 65 years who are institutionalized in this country, another 5% in the community who are as sick as the hospitalized population (Lowenthal, Berkman, Brissette, Buehler, Pierce, Robinson, and Trier, 1967), we are still left with 90% of the population over the age of 65 who are able to function more or less adequately in the community. We must be cautious, however, because the age group over 65 includes people we would really not consider old today. Neugarten (1974) has advocated the division of the age group above 65 into the "young-old" and the "old-old." Unfortunately, it is difficult to find data separately for age groups above 65 in published statistical reports. Occasionally those over 75 are listed separately, as, for example, in Simon's background paper for the White House Conference on Aging (1971) where he gives data for the resident population of the U.S. state and county mental hospitals in 1963. The rate for persons 65 to 74 years old was 0.7%, and for those over 75 years it was 1%, one-third of the latter carrying the lable of "functional" disorders. We need more data for the age groups above 75, preferably by 5-year periods. Only in that way can we determine what the risks are that any given individual will develop senile mental changes sufficiently severe to require either institutionalization or comparable care on the outside.

The picture I painted for the age group above 65 years, as a whole, might conceivably be unduly optimistic—analagous to the "4% fallacy" described by Kastenbaum. Taking off from the statistic that there are only 4 to 5% of persons over the age of 65 who reside in homes for the aged, nursing homes, mental hospitals, and other extended-care facilities, Kastenbaum argued that this statistic did not tell us how many people will have resided in such facilities at some time during their lives. Working backwards from death certificates, Kastenbaum and Candy (1973) found that 24 instead of 4% of individuals over the age of 65 had died in an extended-care facility. Thus, we may yet find that by the age of 90 only 10% of us will remain free of severe senile mental changes, instead of the reverse. Lest there be too much pessimism, let me hasten to say that our own 25-year follow-up data show that out of the group of 18 twins who were reexamined at an average age of 90 years (age range 79 to 100 years), five resided in extended-care facilities and two of these five showed no signs of organic brain syndrome whatever on careful psychiatric examination.

We also have the example of Dr. Karl Menninger, co-founder of the Menninger Clinic, Dr. Morris Fishbein, long-time editor of the *Journal of the American Medical Association,* and Dr. Walter C. Alvarez, physician, clinician, and prolific author for professional and lay journals. The three of them were photographed together at the ages of 81, 85, and 90 years, respectively, on the occasion of their common birthday. Their histories demonstrate that even if most of life is spent in public prominence, with all the stresses that connotes, it is possible to remain active, productive, and alert at an advanced age, far from the incapacitating senility we usually associate with octogenarians. Indeed, it is perhaps because they have continued to remain active throughout their lives that we see them as they are today.

From our own longitudinal study we have some evidence that maintenance of mental as well as physical activities characterized those who aged successfully (De Carlo, 1971). We have all been taught that "the brain is not a muscle." When it comes to the effects of inactivity, however, perhaps the brain is like a muscle after all. And possibly, much of what we consider today to be clinical aspects of an aging central nervous system, will turn out to be clinical aspects of atrophy of disuse. If this be so, prevention and intervention would become feasible along well-practiced lines.

REFERENCES

Brody, H. (1973): Aging of the vertebrate brain. In: *Development and Aging of the Nervous System,* edited by M. Rockstein, pp. 121–133. Academic Press, New York.
Busse, E. W. (1961): Psychoneurotic reactions and defense mechanisms in the aged. In: *Psychopathology of Aging,* edited by P. H. Hoch and J. Zubin, pp. 274–284. Grune and Stratton, New York.
Corsellis, J. A. N. (1962): *Mental Illness and the Ageing Brain.* Institute of Psychiatry Maudsley Monograph No. 9. Oxford University Press, London.
DeCarlo, T. (1971): Recreation, participation patterns, and successful aging. Doctoral Dissertation, Teachers College, Columbia University, New York.
Epstein, L. Depression in the elderly. (*In preparation.*)
Gaitz, C., and Scott, J. (1972): Age and the measurement of mental health. *J. Health Soc. Behav.,* 13:55–67.
Gruenberg, E. M. (1961): A mental health survey of older persons. In: *Comparative Epi-*

demiology of the Mental Disorders, edited by P. H. Hoch and J. Zubin, pp. 13–23. Grune & Stratton, New York.

Gurland, B. J. The comparative frequencies and types of depression in various adult age groups. (*In preparation.*)

Gurland, B., Sharpe, L., Simon, R. J., Kuriansky, J., and Stiller, P. (1972): On the use of psychiatric populations. *Psychiat. Quart.*, 46:461–473.

Harris, R. (1972): The relationship between organic brain disease and physical status. In: *Aging and the Brain*, edited by Charles M. Gaitz, pp. 163–177. Plenum Press, New York.

Jarvik, L. F. (1967): Survival and psychological aspects of aging in man. In: *Aspects of the Biology of Aging*, pp. 463–482. 21st Symposium of the Society for Experimental Biology, Sheffield, England.

Jarvik, L. F. (1975): Some thoughts on the psychobiology of aging. *Amer. Psychol.*, 30:576–583.

Jarvik, L. F., and Blum, J. E. (1971): Cognitive declines as predictors of mortality in twin pairs: A twenty-year longitudinal study of aging. In: *Prediction of Life Span*, edited by E. Palmore and F. C. Jeffers. D. C. Heath and Co., Lexington, Massachusetts.

Jarvik, L. F., and Cohen, D. (1973): A biobehavioral approach to intellectual changes with aging. In: *Psychology of Adult Development and Aging*, edited by C. Eisdorfer and M. P. Lawton, pp. 220–280. American Psychological Association, Washington, D.C.

Jarvik, L. F., Eisdorfer, C., and Blum, J. E., editors. (1973): *Intellectual Functioning in Adults*, Springer Publishing Company, New York.

Jarvik, L. F., Kallmann, F. J., Falek, A., and Klaber, M. M. (1957): Changing intellectual functions in senescent twins. *Acta Genet. Statist. Med.*, 7:421–430.

Jarvik, L. F., Yen, F. S., and Goldstein, F. (1974): Chromosomes and mental status. *Arch. Gen. Psychiatry*, 30:86–190.

Jarvik, L. F., Yen, F. S., and Moralishvili, E. (1974): Chromosome examinations in aging institutionalized women. *J. Gerontol.*, 29:269–276.

Kastenbaum, R., and Candy, S. (1973): The four-percent fallacy. *Int. J. Aging Hum. Dev.*, 4:15–21.

Kleemeier, R. W. (1962): Intellectual change in the senium. Proceedings of the Social Statistics Section of the American Statistics Association, pp. 290–295.

Klerman, G. Age and clinical depression: Today's youth in the 21st century. (*In preparation.*)

Lipton, M. Age differentiation in depression: Biochemical aspects. (*In preparation.*)

Lowenthal, M. F., Berkman, P. L., Brisette, G. G., Buehler, J. A., Pierce, R. C., Robinson, B. C., and Trier, M. L. (1967): Aging and mental disorder in San Francisco: A social psychiatric study. Jossey-Bass, San Francisco.

Malamud, N. (1972): Neuropathology of organic brain syndromes associated with aging. In: *Aging and the Brain*, edited by C. M. Gaitz, pp. 63–87. Plenum Press, New York.

Neugarten, B. (1974): Age-groups in American society and the rise of the young-old. In: *Political Consequences of Aging*, edited by F. Eisele. *Ann. Amer. Acad. Polit. Soc. Sci.*, 415:187–198.

Nielsen, J. (1970): Chromosomes in senile, presenile and arteriosclerotic dementia. *J. Gerontol.*, 25:312–315.

Pfeiffer, E., and Busse, E. W. (1973): Mental disorders in later life — affective disorders; paranoid, neurotic and situation reactions. Chapter 7. In: *Mental Illness in Later Life*, edited by E. W. Busse and E. Pfeiffer. American Psychiatric Association, Washington, D.C.

Roth, M. (1972): Recent progress in the psychiatry of old age and its bearing on certain problems of psychiatry in earlier life. *Biol. Psychiatry*, 5 (No. 2.):103–125.

Roth, M., Tomlinson, B. E., and Blessed, G. (1967): The relationship between quantitative measures and degenerative changes in the cerebral gray matter of elderly subjects. *Proc. R. Soc. Med.*, 60:254–260.

Samis, H. V. (1968): Aging: The loss of temporal organization. *Perspect. Biol. Med.*, 12:95–102.

Simon, A. (1971): Background paper on mental health for White House Conference on Aging. Government Printing Office, Washington, D.C.

Simon, A., and Malamud, N. (1965): Comparison of clinical and neuropathological findings in geriatric mental illness. In: *Psychiatric Disorders in the Aged*, p. 322. Geigy, Manchester, United Kingdom.

Aging. Volume 1, edited by H. Brody, D. Harman, and J. M. Ordy. Raven Press, New York ® 1975.

Structural Changes in the Aging Brain

Madge E. Scheibel and Arnold B. Scheibel

Departments of Anatomy and Psychiatry and the Brain Research Institute, University of California, School of Medicine, Center for the Health Sciences, Los Angeles, California 90024

> *The heart grows heavy and remembers not yesterday.*
> (Ebers papyrus, ca. 1550 B.C.)

Inexorably the wear of daily life takes its toll on the brain. As evidence, most aging brains show a group of structural changes which are progressive and which mimic in less intensive fashion the more catastrophic pathology of the acute and chronic dementing diseases. Some of these changes, both gross and microscopic, have been known for a century or more, and an extensive literature bears witness to man's concern with this part of the biosocial experience. The histopathology revealed over the years by light microscopy, though well known, offers remarkably little in the way of definitive clues to etiology and pathogenesis. Newer analytic methods and electron microscopy have added significantly to our knowledge of what happens within the cyton as life proceeds, but remarkably little more as to ways, means, and ends. Few investigators doubt that definitive answers, insofar as they exist, must be sought at the molecular level, a threshold we are already beginning to cross, as evidenced by many of the chapters in this volume.

However, there may still be much to learn at levels that demand less resolution. Despite the number of histologically oriented papers, there are virtually no descriptions of neuropil in the senescing brain. Little has been said about dendrites, axons, and collaterals as seen with the light microscope, and the type of circuit relations maintained among neurons in old age; and it is virtually impossible to approach such a problem with the electron microscope. However, the chrome-silver methods initially developed by Golgi (1886), and their more recent modifications, are well suited to this task, even though they have seldom been applied to neuropathological specimens.

Our present purpose is to review, very briefly, some of the structural changes which have been described in the brains of aged individuals, using both low and high resolution techniques. We then summarize the results of our own Golgi observations, emphasizing a putative relationship between selective loss of horizontal dendritic systems in the cortex and the aging process.

THE BACKGROUND

Gross changes in the brains of aged persons were described in the literature almost 150 years ago. Esquirol (1838) noted marked atrophy of gyri and widening of sulci when the leptomeninges were removed from the surface of the hemisphere. The enveloping tissues themselves have long since been noted to be opaque, thickened, and variably adherent to underlying brain tissue. The ventricular system is frequently dilated and the cortical gray and white matter often perceptibly shrunken. Gyral atrophy is usually most marked over the frontal lobes (Grinker and Bucy, 1949) although temporal and parietal changes are also noted, especially in the presenile dementia of Alzheimer.

A number of microscopic changes are also well known through a massive literature. However, despite the amount of available neurohistological data, it remains difficult to correlate specific histological changes with the age of the subject or the degree of apparent intellectual intactness or sensecence. The pathogenesis and mechanisms of each of the more obvious histological changes also remain largely unknown. Such uncertainties undoubtedly reflect our lack of understanding of the aging process as a whole, and may hopefully begin to resolve as the physiological meanings of senescence become clearer.

Lipochromes

The most constant histological finding in the aging brain is the intracellular presence of yellow, green, or brown fluorescing pigments called lipochromes or lipofuscin. In humans, they are commonly found in the cells of many, although not all, neural centers, at varying ages. Vogt and Vogt (1946) hypothesized that a specific sequence for intracellular pigmentary changes is characteristic of each nucleus. Wahren's (1957) studies appear to provide some substance for this notion. He finds lipofuscin appearing in significant amounts in the pallidum only after the seventh or eighth decade. Pigment appears appreciably earlier (fifth to sixth decade) in the nucleus tuberomammilaris and even earlier in tuberolateralis. The contrast is even greater for cells of the olivary nucleus and nucleus dentatus which may show appreciable degrees of pigment storage by the sixth to tenth year of life (Höpker, 1951).

Although there have been a number of ideas as to the source—and significance—of lipochrome accumulations, recent histochemical and electron microscope studies have indicated that lysosomes are the most likely source (Sulkin, 1955; Essner and Novikoff, 1960; Hasan and Glees, 1973, etc.), although the degeneration of other organelles such as mitochondria (Duckett and White, 1974) has also been suggested. In any case, it seems reasonably clear from studies such as those of Hydén and Lindstrom (1950) and Morel and Wildi (1952) that ribonuclease is inactive in pigment-laden areas of neuronal cytoplasm and that total RNA content varies inversely with the total amount of pigment. On this basis it would appear that at least some cytoplasmic functions such as protein synthesis may be compromised as lipochrome deposits increase. In this regard, Murray and Stout (1947) noted a progressive loss of migratory capability in sympathetic ganglion cells maintained in tissue culture as pigment masses developed and darkened over a 2 to 3 week period.

Cell Loss

A general diminution in total numbers of neurons appears to be a regular concomitant of the aging process although it is frequently difficult to quantify the loss, and even more difficult to define a constant relationship between total cell loss with either the age of the subject or with the amount of intellectual deterioration. Brody's studies (1955) indicate a more or less constant pattern of loss of cortical neurons from age 20 to 90 which, depending on the cortical area involved, might make up as much as 30% of the total neuronal pool. Exclusive of the hippocampus which appears generally more reactive to the process of aging than any other telencephalic derivative, cell loss appears most prominent in prefrontal and superior temporal areas, especially among third-layer pyramids (Critchley, 1942). Larger pyramids also undergo progressive changes and become surrounded by large numbers of satellite glia (Andrew and Cardwell, 1940). Layer-4 granules may also diminish in number (Brody, 1973).

Equally dramatic cell loss has been reported by Harms (1944) in the cerebellum where up to 25% of the Purkinje neurons were lost in very old patients. As in cortex, certain portions of cerebellum appear more age-sensitive than others, the anterior lobe (Ellis, 1920) showing more extensive changes than the hemispheres. However, not all investigators are in agreement as to the existence of Purkinje cell loss. It is not clear whether neuroglia undergo significant changes in quantity or characteristics, although a progression from protoplasmic to fibrous astroglia has been reported (McMenemey, 1963).

Extracellular Space

Bondareff (1973) has recently reported on progressive changes in the nature and total volume of the extracellular compartment in aging brain. Most interesting was his conclusion that such space decreases by slightly over 50% in senile animals compared to young adults, and with this, an appropriate decrement in the spread of presumed synaptic mediator substances used as indicators. These observations indicate the interesting possibility that one general result of the shrinking extraneural space pool in the aging brain may be a generally decreased capacity for transport of ions and small molecules.

Granulovacuolar Changes

A number of changes are seen in neurons which are closely associated with the process of senescence, but are not found as regularly as lipofuscins, or in as diverse an array of brain areas. The granulovacuolar changes of Simchowitz (1911) represent a well-known change of cryptic origin which is largely limited to the pyramids of the hippocampus. It is characterized by the presence of small vacuoles in the neuronal cytoplasm or at the base of the dendrites in degenerating neurons (Fig. 1a). Each vacuole generally contains a small granule in its center. Electron micrographs of such structures in autopsy tissue from cases of Parkinson-dementia on Guam show a membrane-limited vacuole with a dense center (Hirano, Demlitzer, Kurland, and Zimmerman, 1968). The origin of these structural changes and the content of the vacuoles is still unknown. While these changes may be so extensive as to involve virtually all hippocampal pyramids in Alzheimer's disease or advanced senile dementia, they are rarely so disseminated in the nondemented aged. In the latter, Tomlinson (1972) found a maximum of 6% of cells in Sommer's sector (H_1) showing granulovacuolar changes.

Senile Plaques

Argyrophilic plaques or islets were first described in an epileptic brain by Blocq and Marinesco (1892) and later named "senile plaques" by Simchowicz (1910). They are found most densely throughout hippocampus and in many parts of neocortex in Alzheimer's disease, but are also frequent in senile dementias and in the brains of the nondemented aged. Although they are almost certainly related to degradative processes in the neuronal or glial milieu, their nature is still enigmatic, despite the powerful resolving power of the electron microscope. These structures range from 5 to 10 μm to as much as 100 μm or more in diameter and are best visualized with the light microscope through the use of reduced silver stains (Figs. 1b, c, d). Such stains suggest, and electron microscopy confirms, that they are generally composed of a central core of amyloid surrounded by masses of neural processes, apparently including both axons and dendrites showing varying degrees of degenerative changes. A corona of glia usually makes up the outer margin.

There is a wide range of speculation on the source of senile plaques, whether from neuron, glial cells, reticulum, axon, or dendrites. These points

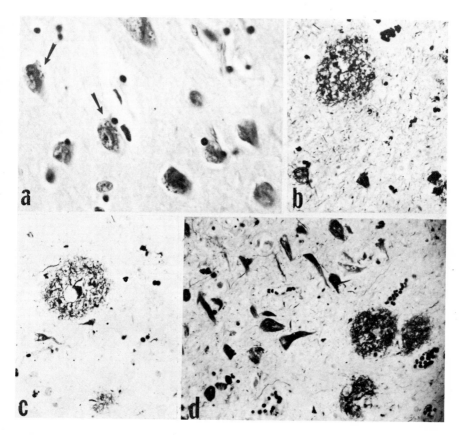

FIG. 1. Various structural changes found in aging brain tissue. **a:** Granulovacuolar changes in third-layer pyramids of superior temporal cortex, 70-year-old patient, H. and E. stain; **b** and **c:** senile plaques in neocortex of 64-year-old patient. The plaque in **c** has a characteristic "empty" center. Modified Bielschowsky stains. Combination of senile plaque cluster and a number of hippocampal neurons showing Alzheimer neurofibrillar changes are shown in **d.** Bielschowsky stain. Same patient as in **b** and **c.** Original magnifications: **a,** ×660; **b** and **d,** ×440; **c,** ×220. (Courtesy of Dr. U. Tomiyasu.)

of view are succintly reviewed in McMenemey's summary of the dementias (1963). Among the interesting properties of these enigmatic structures are metachromatic staining response to toluidine blue, double refractivity, and congophilia. They are thought to contain acid phosphatase (Morel and Wildi, 1952), and usually give a positive reaction to periodic acid-Schiff reagent (Schiffer, 1957).

Meticulous electron microscope studies by Terry and Wisniewski (1970) indicate that the earliest precursor of the plaque appears to be a very small group of enlarged neurites (axonal or dendritic processes) containing clusters of mitochondria and dense lamellar bodies of presumed lysosomal origin. Amyloid can usually be identified only after the nascent lesion contains at least five distended neurites. Plaque size then seems to grow and at a certain point, an inverse relationship is established between the amount of central amyloid and the number of peripheral neurites. The ultimate burnt-out plaque may appear to consist principally or entirely of amyloid, although ordinarily, at least some peripheral neural processes, rich in unusual intra-cellular inclusions, remain.

Whatever the pathophysiological significance of these structures, they are characteristic of the senescing process. However, the relationship is not ironclad, and they may appear absent in some cases of obvious senile de-mentia (Sjovall, 1932), or numerous in the brains of aged subjects con-sidered to be intellectually and emotionally intact. However, Roth and his colleagues have demonstrated an inverse correlation between plaque con-centrations and the subject's ability to perform well on psychological tests (Roth, Tomlinson, and Blessed, 1966).

Alzheimer's Neurofibrillary Changes

The neurofibrillary changes first described by Alzheimer (1907) in pre-senile dementia are now recognized as part of the pathological anatomy of senescence, especially with associated dementing changes, in Pick's dis-ease, the dementia complex found on Guam (Hirano, Malamud, Elizen, and Kurland, 1966) and postencephalitic parkinsonism (Greenfield and Bosan-quet, 1953). They may also be experimentally reproduced by the use of aluminum salts (Klatzo, Wisniewski, and Streicher, 1965) and by certain mitotic spindle inhibitors (Wisniewski, Karcezewski, and Wisniewska, 1967). As with most of the other histological changes already mentioned, neurofibrillary tangles are most obvious in the pyramidal cells of the hippo-campus and in third-layer pyramids of prefrontal and superior temporal neocortex (Figs. 1d, 2a-d). Tomlinson (1972) stresses that when they are present in the apparently intellectually intact aged, they are found almost exclusively in hippocampus. In any case, typical Alzheimer cells appear first in Ammon's Horn and only much later in neocortex (Morel and Wildi, 1952).

While the coarse dark neurofibrillar skeins are well visualized in classic reduced silver type stains, and even with aniline stains under certain condi-tions, electron microscopy has contributed powerfully to an understanding of the nature of the abnormal intracellular material. Neurofibrillary tangles consist of abnormally large numbers of intracytoplasmic tubules running as compact parallel bundles which eventually push the nucleus to one side as they progressively fill the cytoplasmic envelope. The tubules are abnormal in number and size, and bear regular constrictions along their length, sug-gestive of a twist approximately every 80 nm (Terry and Wisniewski, 1970) (Figs. 3, 4). Although little is known of their pathogenesis, or of the mecha-nism of their relation to mental deterioration, presenile or senile, they are

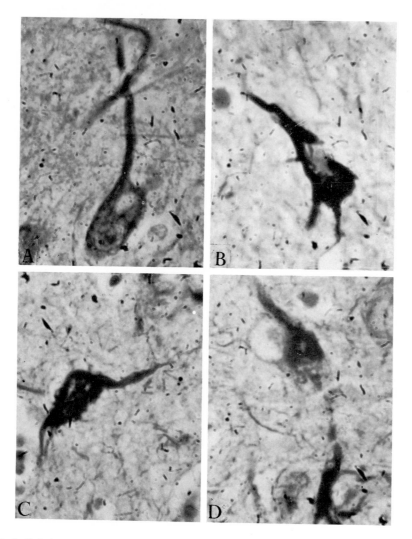

FIG. 2. Alzheimer neurofibrillary degeneration as seen in neocortical pyramids, **a** and **d**, and hippocampal pyramids, **b** and **c**. Seventy-nine-year-old patient, Bielschowsky stain. *Original magnification:* ×660.

thought to be the product of abnormal protein metabolism in the cell and may, when sufficiently numerous, obstruct the flow of cytoplasm and precursor substances from the cell body into axons and dendrites.

Figure 5, which is taken from Tomlinson (1972), shows in summary form the age incidence and developmental sequence of three of the commonest types of senile changes in 219 routine cases coming to autopsy in an acute general hospital. Note the appreciable incidence of neocortical senile plaques

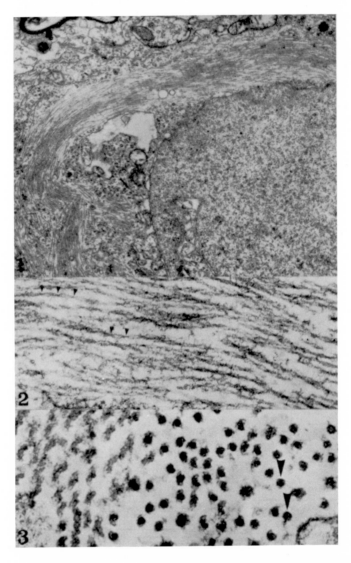

FIG. 3. Electron microscopic analysis of Alzheimer neurofibrillar changes at three different magnifications. (1) Neurofibrillar tangle in cortical cell displacing nucleus down and to the right, ×12,000. (2) Longitudinal section showing characteristic twisted tubules with periodic constrictions, ×77,000. (3) Cross section through twisted pathological tubules. Arrows point to central filaments, ×165,000. (From Terry and Wisniewski, 1970. With permission of the authors and publisher.)

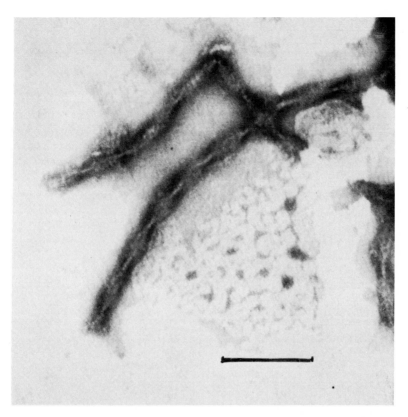

FIG. 4. Electron microphotograph of isolated twisted filaments from old formalin-fixed material from a case of Alzheimer's disease. One percent potassium phosphotungstate negative stain. The bar represents 100 nm. (From Kidd (1970): In: *Alzheimer's Disease and Related Conditions* (Ciba Symposium), edited by G. E. W. Wolstenholme and M. O'Connor, p. 203. J. and A. Churchill, London. With permission of the author and publisher.)

by the end of the third decade and the very high incidence of Alzheimer cellular changes in the hippocampus achieved during the seventh decade.

OBSERVATIONS BASED ON GOLGI IMPREGNATIONS

The use of Golgi impregnation methods can add substantially to our ability to visualize aging brain tissue. For many years, the classic methods employing aniline stains and reduced silver have been the mainstay for the neuropathologist using the light microscope, bolstered more recently by a growing array of histochemical, fluorescent, and radioautographic techniques. To this, the past two decades have added the greatly enhanced resolution of the electron microscope, bringing for the first time appreciation of the enormous complexity of intracellular machinery.

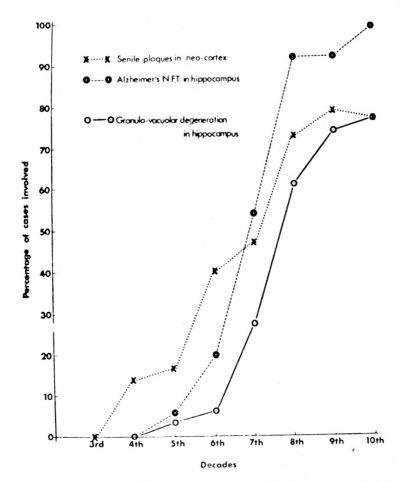

FIG. 5. Graph showing occurrence of senile plaques in the neocortex, and Alzheimer's neurofibrillary changes and granulovacuolar degeneration in the hippocampus in 219 unassessed cases coming to autopsy in a general hospital. (From Tomlinson, 1972, with the permission of the author and publisher.)

The unique power of the chrome-silver methods lies in their capacity to reveal at medium resolution and in panoramic scope the texture and character of the neuropil in which neurons are imbedded. Since it is ultimately this neuropil which provides the matrix within which information is received, processed, and acted upon, it is clearly of considerable importance to examine the status of this portion of the neural milieu.

Interestingly enough, the method seems to have been virtually unused in the study of senescing tissue, and we can only speculate on the reasons for this omission. In any case, the group of techniques deserves exploitation as long as its strengths and weaknesses are understood. The Golgi methods resemble the technique of electron microscopy in their sensitivity to post-mortem autolytic change and the consequent need for the freshest possible tissue. While there are obvious limitations in this regard, especially where human material is concerned, we have attempted to keep the interval between death and time of fixation to about 4 hr, and have established 8 hr as an upper working limit. However, we have been impressed, especially in the case of brain tissue receiving preliminary formalin immersion fixation, by the excellent state of preservation of the finer neural components in cortex, even in 8 to 12 hr-old material. This includes fine axonal plexuses, terminal dendritic branches, and, perhaps most significantly, dendrite spines. Obviously, the higher resolving power of the electron microscope is bound to pick up changes in neuronal and glial volume, loss of extraneuronal space, and early autolytic changes in nuclear and cytoplasmic organelles which are invisible to the light microscope.

On a number of occasions it has been possible to obtain "fresh" brain tissue at autopsy, and in these cases, satisfactory impregnations have been obtained using modifications of the classic Golgi osmic-dichromate fixation method. However, in the majority of cases, we have drawn on an archive of formalized brains fixed for 6 months or longer. In these cases, sensitive impregnations have been obtained through the use of a solution of mildly acidified chromates, a variant originally ascribed to Davenport (Report of the Stain Commission, 1960). As is characteristic of all Golgi-type impregnations, only 5 to 10% of neural elements are stained. However, the relative completeness of impregnation of these elements as visualized in tissue section 100 to 150 μm thick enables extensive assessment of the dendritic envelope, cell body, and axonal projection of individual elements. This kind of preparation is also amenable to quantitative studies of single neurons. Computer programs are presently being developed in our laboratory which should enable fuller description of neurons at various epochs in the process of senescence. For the present, our studies remain qualitative and descriptive and will attempt to relate neuronal morphology to the age and mental status of the small number of cases which have been examined.

The fine structure and organization of cerebral neocortex as revealed by Golgi impregnations is well known from the studies of Golgi (1886), Lorente de Nó (1949), Conel (1939 et seq.), Ramon y Cajal (1952), Poliakov (1972), and many others. Figures 6, 11a,c, 14, 15a emphasize some of the more familiar aspects of neocortical organization. Particular notice should be taken of the great masses of horizontally oriented dendrites consisting of basilar shafts derived from the broad end of the pyramidal cell bodies, and oblique branches growing from the apical shafts. In comparing these dendrite systems with their analogues in laboratory animals such as rodents, carnivores, and even small monkeys, it seems to us that they are very much more numerous in man, establishing veritable dendritic commissures at various depths throughout neocortex. A number of recent studies have

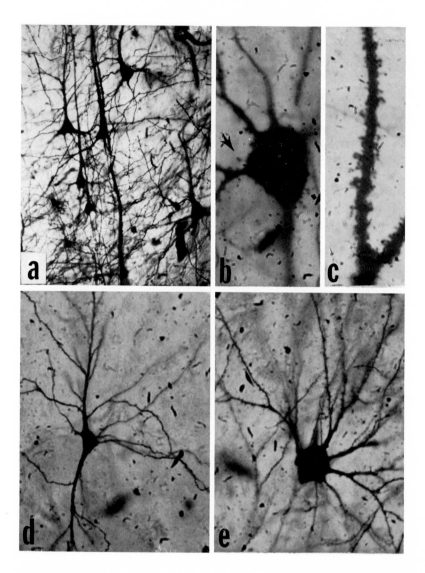

FIG. 6. Golgi impregnated neurons without obvious pathology from a 96-year-old patient. **a:** Layer-3 pyramids; **b:** large round cell, layer 4; **d:** bipolar (spindle) cell, layer 4; **e:** large stellate cell, layer 4. All cells from visual cortex. Spine-covered apical shaft in **c** is from layer 3 pyramid in motor cortex. Arrow in **b** points to spine on cell body. *Original magnifications:* **a,** ×75; **b** and **c,** ×440; **d** and **e,** ×220.

directed our attention to these horizontal components, both as preferential synaptic sites for intracortically derived axon systems (Globus and Scheibel, 1967) and as putative loci for the storage of central programs (Scheibel and Scheibel, 1973*b*, and Scheibel, Davies, Lindsay, and Scheibel, 1974). These are discussed below in appropriate context.

During the course of our study of brain tissue from patients whose age varied from 58 to 96 years, it rapidly became obvious that there was no direct correlation between the calendar age of the patient and the degree of obvious neuronal change. This is not necessarily to gainsay the results of several studies which have indicated an inexorable increase in concentration of senile plaques and fibrillar changes (Brody, 1955, 1973; Tomlinson, 1972) with intellectual deterioration (Fig. 5). The Golgi is not a quantitative method in the sense that most routine techniques which stain all neural components are quantitative. Hence, we can speak only on the basis of our overall impression of the ease with which age-related changes can be seen. Nonetheless, whatever the absolute number of changed elements in each brain specimen may be, a trend has been identified, suggesting the presence of a progressive, multistepped process affecting varying numbers of neurons in the aging brain. Limiting our data to neocortex for the time being, these changes have appeared most obvious among the pyramidal cells of layers 2 and 3 and will be described in relation to such elements. However, similar changes have been seen in stellate (local circuit) cells of layer 4, and to a lesser extent in large pyramids of layer 5.

The earliest change which we have identified in Golgi-stained preparations has been a loss of the smooth, slightly concave contour of the cortical pyramidal cell body. The cell silhouette begins to bulge (Fig. 7) symmetrically or asymmetrically and appears to become irregularly swollen. Shortly thereafter, local areas of swelling develop along the dendrite shafts, especially on the proximal portions of the apical and basilar branches while the latter appear to decrease in length and in numbers (Figs. 7–10). This increasing "lumpiness" of apical shaft and of the upper portion of the pyramidal cell body seems pathognomonic of early senescent changes in neurons. There is further diminution in the basilar dendrite apparatus either by shrivelling (Fig. 9a) or by complete disappearance of basilar shafts, first from one base angle of the soma (Figs. 8a, 11b) then the other (Figs. 8c,d, 9b,c,d). In the case of many of these unilaterally deprived neurons, there is an "amputated" look as if the basilar shafts had been cut off, guillotine fashion, or had abruptly lost capacity to accept impregnation. Although we have considered the possibility that this appearance might simply be an artifact due to vagaries of Golgi staining, we find this a very unlikely explanation. In the course of study of thousands of Golgi-stained sections of young and adult neocortex in rodent, cat, monkey, and man, we have almost never come across this type of Golgi staining variation. Ordinarily, if the soma stains, there will be some basilar dendritic representation at each base angle. Accordingly, it seems likely that this asymmetric appearance represents an intermediate stage in the process of senile deterioration of the neuron. We consider the pathogenesis of these changes and their possible correlation with the neurofibrillar changes of Alzheimer below.

As already indicated, with loss of basilar dendrites, there is also progressive diminution in the number of horizontal and oblique branches of the

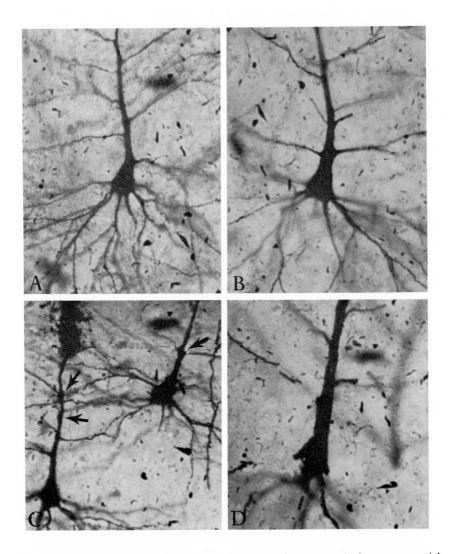

FIG. 7. Golgi impregnated neurons showing very early senescent changes. **a** and **b:** Pyramids from third and fifth layers, prefrontal cortex, in 83-year-old patients. Both are presumably within normal limits. **c:** Third layer pyramid from prefrontal cortex of 96-year-old patient showing early swelling of cell bodies and lumpiness developing in dendrite shafts (*arrows*). **d:** Third layer pyramid in prefrontal cortex of 83-year-old man showing swelling, especially of apical shaft and loss of most basilar dendrites. *Original magnifications:* ×220.

apical shafts (Figs. 7d, 8c,d, etc.). Unfortunately, our observations on the status of the apical arches have been unsatisfactory thus far due to problems with impregnation in the first cortical layer. What we have been able to see so far, however, suggests that there is progressive loss of the apical arches, with a "backing away" toward the original vertical, apical shaft.

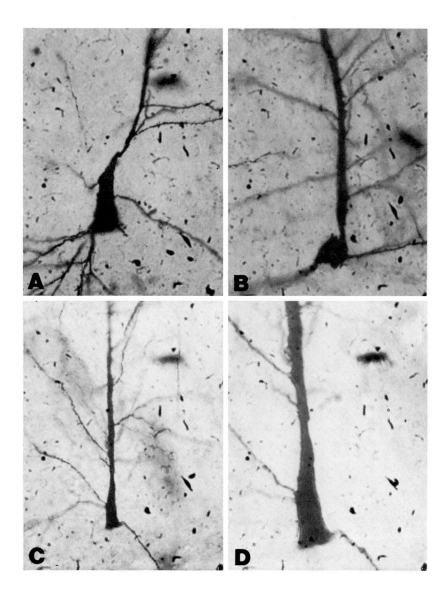

FIG. 8. Golgi impregnated neurons showing progressive senile changes in pyramids. **a:** Fifth layer pyramid, premotor cortex of 83-year-old man showing swelling of cell body and loss of basilar dendrites on one side. **b:** Upper fifth layer pyramid of motor cortex showing irregular swelling of cell body and apical shaft and partial loss of basilar dendrites, 83-year-old man. **c** and **d:** Fifth layer pyramid showing characteristic distortion of cell-dendrite outlines and loss of basilar branches, 83-year-old man. *Original magnifications:* **a, b,** and **d,** ×440; **c,** ×300.

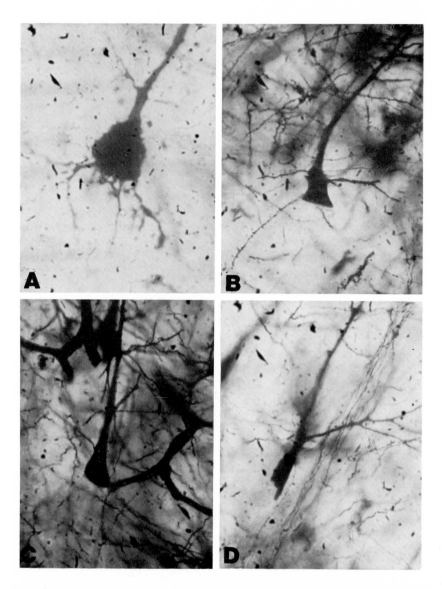

FIG. 9. Golgi impregnations showing advanced senile changes in pyramids. **a:** Small layer-3 pyramid in superior temporal gyrus of 58-year-old man showing swollen soma and shrivelled basilar dendrites. Irregularities in silhouette of apical shaft are also apparent. **b:** Fifth layer pyramid in superior temporal gyrus of 58-year-old man with loss of basilar shafts and characteristic bell-shaped outline of cell body. **c:** Fifth layer pyramid from middle temporal gyrus of same patient showing similar changes. **d:** Third layer pyramid from middle temporal gyrus of same patient showing essentially similar changes. Note that short initial segment of one basilar dendrite shaft can still be seen. *Original magnifications:* **a,** ×440; **b, c,** and **d,** ×300.

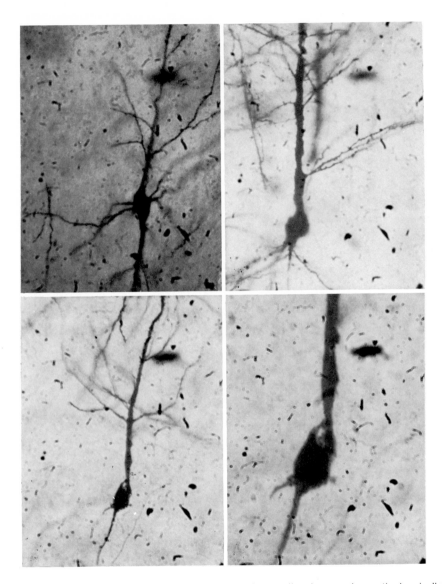

FIG. 10. Golgi impregnations showing progressive senile changes in cortical spindle cells. **a:** Fourth layer spindle from superior temporal gyrus, 89-year-old man. Cell appears normal. b:Spindle from area adjacent to that in **a,** showing irregular swelling of cell body and apical process with partial loss of deep process. **c** and **d:** Lower fourth layer spindle from superior temporal gyrus of 96-year-old man showing irregular swelling of soma and apical process and partial loss of horizontal branches. *Original magnifications:* **a, b,** and **c,** ×220; **d,** ×440.

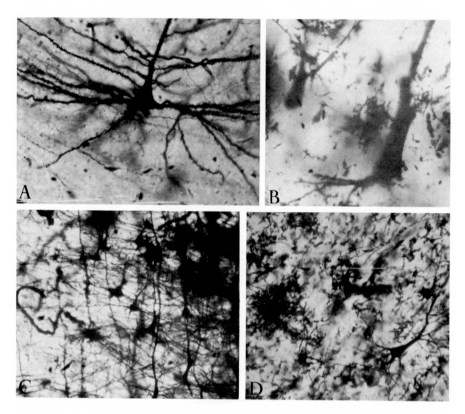

FIG. 11. Golgi impregnations comparing cortical zones of intellectually intact patients with those showing advanced senile behavioral changes. **a:** Superior temporal cortex, fifth layer pyramid from young adult accident victim; **b:** Fifth layer pyramid from superior temporal cortex from 60-year-old man with marked senile behavior. **c:** Third and fourth layers from superior temporal cortex of intellectually intact 54-year-old man. **d:** Third layer, superior temporal cortex from 72-year-old man with marked senile behavior. *Original magnifications:* **a, b,** ×440; **c, d,** ×120; *reduced magnifications:* **a, b,** ×343; **c, d,** ×94.

In many respects, the progression of senile changes in neurons retraces the path followed by the maturing cell during the perinatal phase of development (Scheibel and Scheibel, 1971b), but in reversed sequence. Figure 13 illustrates the appearance of neonatal kitten cortex, a stage which would correspond approximately to a 7 to 8 month human fetus. Apical shafts are developed and, for the most part, reach the first cortical layer where many have begun to develop initial bifurcations which will become apical arches. There is little or no indication of definitive oblique branches, although the shaft and soma bear many heteromorphic protospines which will later be resorbed (Scheibel and Scheibel, 1971b). There are still no definite basilar dendrites, although a cluster of short, hairy, extensions at each base angle of the soma represent precursors of basilar shafts.

From the point of view of Golgi impregnations, final stages of senile deterioration, as summarized in Fig. 12, show that the apical shaft becomes shorter and more tortuous, and may begin to break up as the soma enters final stages of distortion, pyknosis, and neuronopathy.

While lack of Golgi impregnation in itself does not necessarily mean that significant dropping out of neurons has occurred, when seen in conjunction with an apparent massive glial overgrowth, absence of neurons is probably meaningful. In some cases we have seen cortical fields heavily loaded with protoplasmic astrocytes and what appear to be fragments of such cells and (possibly) swollen microglia. Those neurons that are visible seem in many cases to be partially or completely devoid of their dendritic systems, especially the horizontally directed components. A good deal more work will be necessary to evaluate this type of picture but, at this point, we believe that this may represent the Golgi equivalent of those aniline stains which show massive loss of cortical neurons (Brody, 1955, 1973) and/or replacement gliosis (Fig. 11d).

We have previously summarized those histopathological changes which are now considered typical of the senile cortex. The picture revealed by

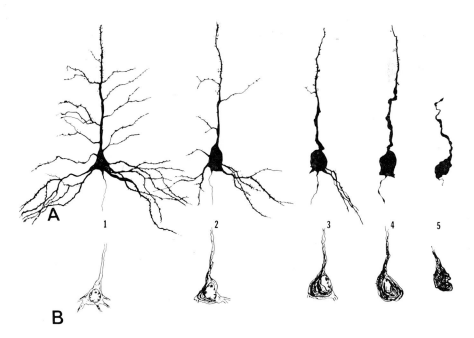

FIG. 12. Progression of senile changes in cortical pyramids as seen in Golgi impregnations, **A,** and in Bielschowsky stains, **B.** We suggest that the increasing swelling and distortion of the soma-dendrite silhouette, and progressive loss of dendrites, first horizontal, then vertical, are closely related to the increased choking of the cytoplasmic space with abnormal tubular material.

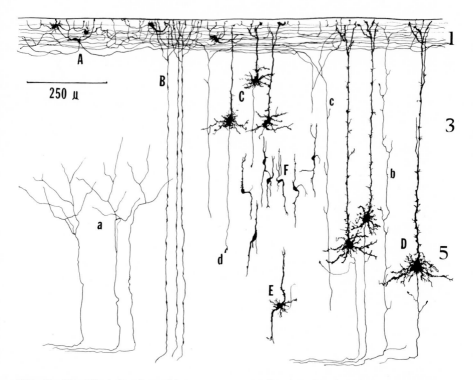

FIG. 13. Simplified drawing of immature cortex showing the almost complete lack of horizontal dendrite mass and the well-developed horizontal axon system in layer 1. **A:** Cajal-Retzius cells and horizontal fibers of layer 1. **B:** Fibers from ependymal glial cells. **C:** Developing third layer pyramids. **D:** Developing fifth layer pyramids. **E:** Immature bipolar spindle cell. **F:** Fourth layer granule cells at immature bipolar stage. Specific thalamocortical afferents (a); nonspecific thalamocortical afferents (b); ascending collateral of unknown origin (c); pyramidal cell axon with growth cone (d). See text for further explanation.

Golgi impregnations is, in many ways, quite different, and it has been difficult to establish the Golgi equivalent of the lipofuscin-loaded cell or the senile plaque. However, on the basis of position, incidence, and general appearance of involved cells, we believe that the pattern of neurofibrillar degeneration of Alzheimer develops in those neurons which Golgi impregnations reveal to be entering the sequence of degenerative changes described above, including swelling and lumpiness of silhouette, progressive loss of basilar dendrites and oblique branches of the apical system, followed by eventual loss of apical shaft and cell body. While the mechanisms underlying this massive dendritic loss are not known with any degree of certainty, several investigators such as Terry and Wisniewski (1970) have characterized the massive overdevelopment of pathological neurotubular protein as capable of cutting off transport of elements essential for membrane repair, protein synthesis, replacement of mediator substances, etc. In this

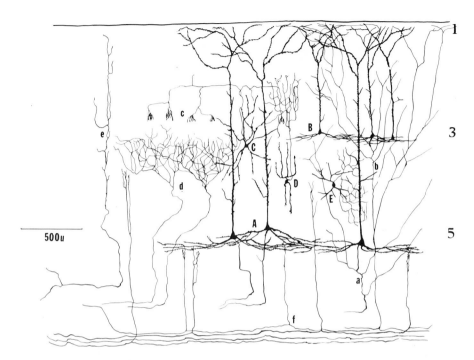

FIG. 14. Simplified drawing of mature cortex showing the marked development of horizontal dendritic mass and the loss of the horizontal fiber system in the first layer. **A:** Basilar shaft system of fifth layer pyramids. **B:** Basilar dendrites of third layer pyramids. **C:** Fourth layer stellate cell generating basket type terminals. **D:** Lower fourth layer stellate with ascending axon. **E:** Lower fourth layer stellate with very localized axon system. Pyramidal cell axon with recurrent collaterals (a); axon system of third layer pyramid (b); basket terminals of stellate cell (c); specific thalamocortical afferents (d); nonspecific thalamocortical afferent (e); ascending collaterals from association fibers in subcortical white matter (f). See text.

regard it is worth remembering that dendrites contain ribosomes and so can probably synthesize their own protein. But ribosomes must continually be replaced, as must messenger RNA and transfer RNA, all of which are manufactured in the nucleus.

Our own observations on reduced silver-stained material suggest that the coils or masses of abnormal neurofibrillar material have a much greater tendency to run long distances into the apical shafts than into side branches or basilar dendrites. In fact, in a considerable number of cases, the neurofibrillar masses loop entirely around the nucleus, appearing to block off entry into one or both sets of basilar dendrites. It is almost as if the basilar shafts die of strangulation. In the numerous instances where the pathological neurotubules develop asymmetrically, there may be persistence of one basilar system for some time afterward, as the Golgi indicates. In those situations where the tubular masses run parallel to the direction of transport (i.e., up the apical shaft), the movement of some substances along moderately intact channels probably continues for a period of time. This may account for the persistence of the apical shaft long after the basilar dendrites have disappeared.

The sequence of degenerative changes undergone by these neocortical pyramids traces in reverse order their development during the perinatal period. Figures 13 and 14 show in slightly schematic fashion the significant variance between late fetal and mature cerebral cortex. The most obvious differences are in the extent of horizontal dendritic systems, especially the basilar shafts, and in the presence of a horizontally running axonal system in the first layer which subsequently disappears (Ramon y Cajal, 1952). Both structural and functional data suggest that in the perinatal period, intra-cortical transmission, to the degree that it exists, is largely horizontal, based principally in this massive axonal system (Purpura, 1961; Scheibel and Scheibel, 1971b). It apparently establishes a number of synaptic contacts with the superficial tips of the apical shafts of pyramids which have developed little more than initial bifurcations at this time. The circuit arrangements are reminiscent of those established by the parallel fiber system of the cerebellum. Later in the postnatal period, this fiber system disappears and the first layer is virtually filled by widely spreading apical arches which cross and interlace, forming a dense dendritic continuum—almost a superficial commissure. Oblique branches of the apical shafts and the basilar dendrites all contribute to forming massive protoplasmic systems running more or less parallel to the pial surface, or else obliquely down into deeper cortical layers. The extent of these systems in human cortex is so impressive and the overlap, interlacing, and bundle formation (Scheibel et al., 1974) so intensive that it is difficult to escape the impression that these

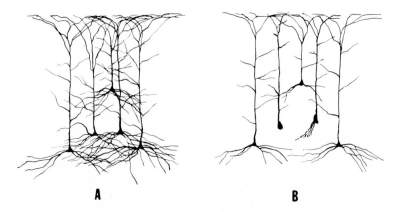

A　　　　　　　　**B**

FIG. 15. Simplified drawing showing the loss of horizontal dendrite mass in senile cortex, **B,** compared with younger adult cortex, **A.** This change is believed to bear a significant causal relation to the development of senile behavior.

dendritic systems may serve functions other than those of postsynaptic receptive sites.

DISCUSSION

As part of an extended interest in the role of dendrites in information processing and storage, we have recently described the development of dendrite bundles in a number of portions of the central nervous system, and indicated how their appearance appears time-locked with the inception of output programs peculiar to those areas (Scheibel and Scheibel, 1970, 1971a,b, 1972, 1973a,b; Scheibel et al., 1974). In the mammalian neocortex, we have described one such example of dendritic interrelations in the bundles formed by the basilar dendrites of giant pyramidal cells of Betz (Scheibel et al., 1974). Reasoning from available neurophysiological data, we showed how it was possible to conceive of these bundles as reservoirs harboring central programs necessary to the inception of motion in the anti-gravity (weight-bearing) muscles of the lower extremity and back. Specifically in this case, the early-developing phasic bursts of activity peculiar to these cells (Evarts, 1965) could be understood to initiate lysis of tone in the extensor muscle mass (Preston, Shende, and Uemura, 1967; Hore and Porter, 1972). This was followed in turn by definitive motor activity undoubtedly generated from other program sources.

In a broader frame, it is possible that all of the extremely complex horizontal dendrite systems throughout the entire depth of cortex serve coupling or programming functions, constituting, in a sense, program libraries responsible for a significant fraction of cortical output. A second and more obvious role for the dendrite systems is to provide recipient postsynaptic surfaces for the enormous concentrations of presynaptic terminals throughout cortex. On the basis of a series of studies carried out in our laboratory (Globus and Scheibel, 1967), it would appear that vertically oriented cortical (pyramidal) dendrite systems preferentially receive extracortically originating fibers, while horizontally oriented dendrites such as basilar, oblique, and apical arch branches develop synaptic relationships primarily with intracortically derived fibers.

On the basis of these data, some tentative conclusions may be drawn regarding functional consequences of senescing changes in cortex. First, selective loss of horizontal dendritic components as demonstrated above must interrupt progressively greater numbers of strictly intracortical circuits. These connections are the latest to develop, phylogenetically and ontogenetically, and consist principally of the projections of stellate (Golgi 2, local circuit, class 2) cells, and the recurrent branches of pyramidal axons. These are also the systems which are generally believed to add the more subtle, modulating, probably inhibitory components to cortical activity. Because of the enormous circuit redundancy which characterizes primate and human cortex, it is obvious that considerable loss may occur without noticeable clinical results. Eventually, however, the sheer weight of loss must make itself apparent in the blurring of cortical output patterns, increasingly ineffective or imprecise cut-off points on pyramidal cell output sequences, etc.

A second putative consequence of deterioration of horizontal dendritic mass may be the loss of output programs stored or coded in the bundling and interlacing of dendrite shafts. Again, such a loss would not initially be obvious due to the enormous redundancy of the systems involved. Eventually, the total amount of loss would begin to manifest itself in evidence of impoverishment of output such as decreasing motor strength, lack of dexterity and agility, failing cognitive performance, problems in association, retrieval, recall, etc. *Obviously, the severity of symptoms is not only a function of the total number of lost cells but also — and perhaps more significantly — of the number of neurons that have reached an intermediate phase of senescence marked by horizontal dendrite loss.* On the basis of the two factors we have just mentioned, selective loss of local circuit connections and loss of central program storage area, senile symptoms can be considered a function of quality of neuropil as well as total cell loss.

It is undoubtedly gratuitous to add that the process of aging in the central nervous system is an especially complex one. The changes in neural substrate which we have described are relatively gross in nature compared to those of membrane, molecule, and ion, which are only beginning to be appreciated. Our suggestions regarding the functional significance of dendrite loss must be considered hypothetic in the present frame. Even if our suppositions have substance, the mechanisms responsible for triggering neural senescence remain obscure. Dayan has summarized and discussed five frequently cited etiologic factors including: somatic mutation, accumulation of molecular errors, free radical affects, cross-linking of macromolecules, and immunological changes (Dayan, 1972). However, an "explanation" advanced by the Vogts almost 30 years ago to account for neuronal deterioration still has the dignity and satisfying qualities that uncluttered ideas often provide. They reason that when cells divide, they are temporarily lost to the function they ordinarily subserve. Frequent mitotic activity in the brain might produce an organ whose capacity to process information would vary continuously. Additionally, reestablishment of connections and splitting of axons as much as 1 meter in length were both seen as impossibly formidable neurobiologic problems. "We may therefore interpret the cessation of nerve cell division during embryonic development as a biological progress (sic!) useful for selection but achieved at the price of (ultimate) individual cell death" (Vogt and Vogt, 1946).

SUMMARY

The methods of Golgi have been used in the histological evaluation of brain tissue from aged patients with and without evidences of senility. It was difficult to correlate the picture revealed by the Golgi method with those known from classic histologic methods employing aniline dyes, reduced silver, etc. However, a sequence of changes were identified, particularly in third-layer pyramids in prefrontal and superior temporal cortex which were seen with variable frequency in all aged brains. This sequence involved increasing swelling and lumpiness in the outline of the soma and proximal dendrites, progressive loss of horizontally oriented dendrite systems, especially the basilar shafts, and eventual loss of the apical shafts with cell death. Special significance was attached to the loss of horizontal dendrite masses for two reasons: (1) they have been shown to receive, selectively, synaptic terminals from intracortical loops and (2) their densely intertwined and bundled configurations have been proposed as storage sites for central programs. Preferential loss of this dendrite system would appear likely to remove, progressively, the more subtle, modulatory (probably inhibitory) aspects of cortical activity along with a number of essential output programs coded along their surfaces. Deterioration of psychomotor performance with aging may accordingly be conceived in significant degree as a function of the quality of neuropil, rather than solely of the total number of neurons that have been lost or senile plaques that have appeared.

ACKNOWLEDGMENTS

This study was supported by U.S. Public Health Service Grant 10567 N.I.N.D.B. We thank Dr. U. Tomiyasu, Veterans Administration Hospital, West Los Angeles, for making the brain tissue available to us, and Mr. Abe Green for preparing the histological material.

REFERENCES

Alzheimer, A. (1907): Ueber eine eigenartige Erkrankung der Hirnrinde. *Cbl. Nervenheilk Psychiat.*, 18:177–179. *Cited in:* Torack, R. (1971): In: *Dementia*, edited by C. Wells. F. A. Davis Co., Philadelphia.

Andrew, W., and Cardwell, E. (1940): Neuronophagia in the human cerebral cortex in senility and in pathologic conditions. *Arch. Pathol.*, 29:400–414.

Blocq, P., and Marinesco, G. (1892): Sur les lésions et la pathologie de l'epilepsie dite essentiale. *Semin. Med. Paris*, 12:445–446.

Bondareff, W. (1973): Age changes in the neuronal microenvironment. In: *Development and Aging in the Nervous System*, edited by M. Rockstein, pp. 1–17. Academic Press, New York.

Brody, H. (1955): Organization of the cerebral cortex. III. A study of aging in the human cerebral cortex. *J. Comp. Neurol.*, 102:511–556.

Brody, H. (1973): Aging of the vertebrate brain. In: *Development and Aging in the Nervous System*, edited by M. Rockstein, pp. 121–133. Academic Press, New York.

Conel, J. L. (1939): *The Postnatal Development of the Human Cerebral Cortex, Vols. 1–7.* Harvard University Press, Cambridge, Massachusetts.

Critchley, M. (1942): Aging of the nervous system. In: *Problems of Aging* (2nd ed.), edited by E. V. Cowdrey, Chapter 19. Williams and Wilkins Co., Baltimore.

Davenport, H., and Combs, M. (1960): Staining method *as quoted in: Staining Procedures* (rev. ed.), Biological Stain Commission, University of Rochester Medical Center, New York, p. 102. Williams and Wilkins Co., Baltimore.

Dayan, A. D. (1972): The brain and theories of aging. In: *Aging of the Central Nervous Sys-

tem, edited by H. M. Van Praag and A. K. Kalverboer, pp. 58–75. De Erven F. Bohn, New York.

Duckett, S., and White, R. (1974): Cerebral lipofuscinosis induced with tellurium electron dispersive X-ray spectrophotometry analysis. *Brain Res.,* 73:205–214.

Ellis, R. S. (1920): Norms for some structural changes in the human cerebellum from birth to old age. *J. Comp. Neurol.,* 32:1–34.

Esquirol, E. (1838): *Des Maladies Mentalis,* Paris, 2:44. *Quoted from:* McMenemey, W. H. (1963): The dementias and progressive diseases of the basal ganglia. In: *Greenfield's Neuropathology* (2nd ed.), pp. 520–576. Williams and Wilkins Co., Baltimore.

Essner, E., and Novikoff, A. B. (1960): Human hepatocellular pigments and lysosomes. *J. Ultrastruct. Res.,* 3:374–391.

Evarts, E. (1965): Relation of discharge frequency to conduction velocity in pyramidal tract neurons. *J. Neurophysiol.,* 28:216–228.

Globus, A., and Scheibel, A. B. (1967): Pattern and field in cortical structure: The rabbit. *J. Comp. Neurol.,* 131:155–172.

Golgi, C. (1886): Sulla fina Anatomia degli organi centrali del sistema nervosa, Pavia.

Greenfield, J. G., and Bosanquet, F. D. (1953): The brainstem lesions in parkinsonism. *J. Neurol. Neurosurg. Psychiatry,* 16:213–226.

Grinker, R. P., and Bucy, P. C. (1949): *Neurology* (4th ed.). Charles C Thomas, Springfield, Illinois.

Harms, J. W. (1944): Altern und Somatod der Zellverbandstiere. *Z. Alternsforsch.,* 5:73–126.

Hasan, M., and Glees, P. (1972): Genesis and possible dissolution of neuronal lipofuscin. *Gerontologia,* 18:217–236.

Hasan, M., and Glees, P. (1973): Lipofuscin in monkey "lateral geniculate body." An electron microscope study. *Acta Anat.* 84:85–95.

Hirano, A., Demlitzer, H. M., Kurland, L. T., and Zimmerman, H. M. (1968): The fine structure of some intraganglionic alterations. Neurofibrillary tangles, granulo-vacuolar bodies and "rod-like" structures as seen in Guam amyotrophic lateral sclerosis and Parkinson-dementia complex. *J. Neuropathol. Exp. Neurol.,* 27:167–182.

Hirano, A., Malamud, N., Elizen, T. S., and Kurland, L. T. (1966): Amyotrophic lateral sclerosis and Parkinson-dementia complex on Guam. *Arch. Neurol.,* 15:35–51.

Höpker, W. (1951): Das Altern des Nucleus dentatus. *Z. Alternsforsch.,* 5:256–277.

Hore, J., and Porter, R. (1972): Pyramidal and extrapyramidal influences on some hindlimb motoneuron populations of the arboreal brush-tailed possum, Trichosurus vulpecula. *J. Neurophysiol.,* 35:112–121.

Hydén, H., and Lindstrom, B. (1950): *Discuss. Faraday Soc.,* 9:436.

Klatzo, I., Wisniewski, H., and Streicher, E. (1965): Experimental production of neurofibrillary degeneration. I. Light microscopic observations. *J. Neuropathol. Exp. Neurol.,* 24:187–210.

Lorente de Nó, R. (1949): Cerebral cortex: Architecture, intracortical connections, motor projections. In: *Physiology of the Nervous System* (3rd ed.), edited by J. F. Fulton, pp. 288–330. Oxford University Press, London.

McMenemey, W. H. (1963): The dementias and progressive diseases of the basal ganglia. In: *Greenfield's Neuropathology* (2nd ed.), pp. 520–576. Williams and Wilkins Co., Baltimore.

Morel, F., and Wildi, E. (1952): Clinice pathologique génerale et cellulaire des altérations seniles et preseniles du cerveau. Proceedings of the First International Congress on Neuropathology, Rome. 2:237.

Murray, M. R., and Stout, A. P. (1947): Adult human sympathetic ganglion cells cultivated *in vitro. Am. J. Anat.,* 80:225–273.

Poliakov, G. I. (1972): *Neuron Structure of the Brain,* p. 122. Harvard University Press, Cambridge, Massachusetts.

Preston, J. B., Shende, M. C., and Uemura, K. (1967): The motor cortex-pyramidal system: Patterns of facilitation and inhibition on motoneurons innervating limb musculature of cat and baboon and their possible adaptive significance. In: *Neurophysiological Basis of Normal and Abnormal Motor Activities,* edited by M. D. Yahr and D. P. Purpura, pp. 61–72. Raven Press, New York.

Purpura, P. D. (1961): Morphophysiological basis of elementary evoked response patterns in the neocortex of the newborn cat. *Ann. N.Y. Acad. Sci.,* 92:840–859.

Ramon y Cajal, S. (1952): Histologie du Systeme Nerveux de l'Homme et des Vertebres. Vol. II. Trans. L. Azoulay. Institute Ramon y Cajal, Madrid.

Roth, M., Tomlinson, B. E., and Blessed, G. (1966): Correlation between score for dementia and counts of senile plaques in cerebral grey matter of elderly subjects. *Nature (Lond.)*, 209:106.

Scheibel, M. E., Davies, T. L., Lindsay, R. D., and Scheibel, A. B. (1974): Basilar dendrite bundles of giant pyramidal cells. *Exp. Neurol.*, 42:307–319.

Scheibel, M. E., and Scheibel, A. B. (1970): Organization of spinal motoneuron dendrites in bundles. *Exp. Neurol.*, 28:106–112.

Scheibel, M. E., and Scheibel, A. B. (1971a): Developmental relationship between spinal motoneuron dendrite bundles and patterned activity in the forelimb of cats. *Exp. Neurol.*, 30:367–373.

Scheibel, M. E., and Scheibel, A. B. (1971b): Selected structural-functional correlations in postnatal brain. In: *Brain Development and Behavior*, edited by M. B. Sterman, D. J. McGinty, and A. M. Adinolfi, pp. 1–21. Academic Press, New York.

Scheibel, M. E., and Scheibel, A. B. (1972): Specialized organizational patterns within the nucleus reticularis thalami of the cat. *Exp. Neurol.*, 34:316–322.

Scheibel, M. E., and Scheibel, A. B. (1973a): Dendrite bundles in the ventral commissure of cat spinal cord. *Exp. Neurol.*, 39:482–488.

Scheibel, M. E., and Scheibel, A. B. (1973b): Dendrite bundles as sites for central programs: An hypothesis. *Int. J. Neurosci.* 6:195–202.

Schieffer, D. (1957): Mucopolisaccaridi nel sistema nervosa di individui senili. *Acta Neuroveg.*, 15:25–42.

Simchowitz, T. (1911): Histologische Studien ueber die Senildemenz. *Nissl-Alzheimer Arbeiten*, 3:268.

Sjovall, E. (1932): Aldersforandringarna i centralnervosystemet och deras betydelse. *Nord. Med. Tidskr.*, 4:1011–1014.

Sulkin, N. M. (1955): The properties and distribution of PAS positive substances in the nervous system of the senile dog. *J. Gerontol.*, 10:135–144.

Terry, R. D., and Wisniewski, H. (1970): The ultrastructure of the neurofibrillary tangle and the senile plaque. In: *Alzheimer's Disease and Related Conditions*, edited by G. E. W. Wolstenholme and M. O'Connor, pp. 145–165. J. and A. Churchill, London.

Tomlinson, B. E. (1972): Morphological brain changes in non-demented old people. In: *Aging of the Central Nervous System*, edited by H. M. Van Praag and A. K. Kalverboer, pp. 38–57. De Ervon F. Bohn, New York.

Vogt, C., and Vogt, O. (1946): Aging of nerve cells. *Nature (Lond.)*, 158:304.

Wahren, W. (1957): Neurohistologischer Beitrag zu Fragen des Alterns. *Z. Alternsforsch.*, 10:343–357.

Wisniewski, H., Karczezewski, W., and Wisniewska, K. (1967): Experimental colchicine encephalopathy. I. Induction neurofibrillary degenerator. *Lab. Invest.*, 17:577–587.

Aging. Volume 1, edited by H. Brody, D. Harman, and J. M. Ordy. Raven Press, New York © 1975.

Accumulation and Distribution of Lipofuscin, Amyloid, and Senile Plaques in the Aging Nervous System

***Kenneth R. Brizzee, †James C. Harkin, *J. Mark Ordy, and *Bernice Kaack

*Delta Regional Primate Research Center, Tulane University, Covington, Louisiana 70433, and Departments of **Anatomy and †Pathology, Tulane University School of Medicine, New Orleans, Louisiana 70112

As part of aging in the nervous system and in certain disease conditions, a number of distinct cellular and tissue morphological alterations occur in man and other mammalian species. Among the more universal and consistently observable alterations with age and with increasing incidence of neuropathology in senescence are the accumulation of lipofuscin, amyloid, and senile plaques. Although there is no evidence concerning a common origin or direct relation concerning the accumulation of these substances in the nervous system in aging, this question is discussed more fully in this chapter as part of the normal process of aging or in the context of their increasing frequency of occurrence in certain neurological disorders with advancing age.

LIPOFUSCIN

Historical Notes

The occurrence and distribution of lipid pigment in the human brain has been described by numerous investigators over a period of many years. Among the more notable of the early descriptions were those of Hannover (1842), Koneff (1886), Hodge (1894), Obersteiner (1903), Wolf and Pappenheimer (1945), and Riese (1946). The term "lipofuscin" was first applied to such pigments by Borst (1922). It is derived from the Greek term *lipo* meaning "fat" and from the Latin term *fuscus* meaning "dark" or "dusky." The term "ceroid" was first used by Lillie, Daft, and Sebrell (1941) to describe a yellow-to-brown pigment, closely resembling lipofuscin, observed in cases of nutritional cirrhosis in rats. Considerable difference of opinion has existed, since the first descriptions of lipofuscin and ceroid, as to the similarities and the distinguishing structural and chemical characteristics between the two substances. Many of the uncertainties regarding the chemi-

cal differences between these two types of substances have been clarified
in recent ultrastructural and chemical investigations (Siakotos, Watanabe,
Saito, and Fleischer, 1970), which are described later in this chapter.

One of the first investigators to consider the question of the possible
physiological significance of lipofuscin was Schäfer (1893) who postulated
an enhancement of cell functional activity with the accumulation of the
pigment. An opposing view was expressed by Dolley and Guthrie (1918)
who suggested that pigment accumulation indicated a functional depression
of cells. This question is discussed more fully in this chapter.

Morphological and Histochemical Characteristics

Light Microscopy

At light microscopic magnifications, intracellular lipofuscin appears
in the cell cytoplasm neurons throughout the nervous system as clumped
masses or fine granules, 1 to 3 μm in diameter. It is clearly visualized in
sections stained in Nile blue A or S (Fig. 1B), periodic acid Schiff (PAS)
(Fig. 1A), Sudan black, and Ziehl-Neelsen. However, it appears that

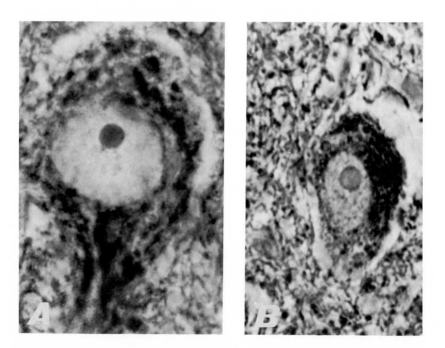

FIG. 1. A: Neuron in dorsal nucleus of lateral cell column of oculomotor nucleus in old
rhesus monkey. PAS stain. ×1950. **B:** Neuron in dorsal nucleus of lateral cell column of
oculomotor nucleus in old rhesus monkey. Nile blue stain. ×1650.

fluorescence microscopy may offer a more sensitive method for visualizing the early appearance of the pigment than do staining or histochemical techniques (Brizzee, Ordy, and Kaack, 1974).

The distribution of the pigment within the cell perikaryon varies greatly from region to region and appears to differ somewhat in specific structures in different species. For example, in the pyramidal neurons of the motor cortex in the rat, and pyramidal layer of the hippocampus in the rat and monkey, the pigment tends to congregate in a polar pattern deep to the base of the apical dendrites (Brizzee, Cancilla, Sherwood, and Timiras, 1969; Brizzee and Johnson, 1970; Brizzee et al., 1974). In pyramidal neurons of the motor cortex of the monkey, the pigment appears to be distributed in a random fashion in the perikaryon. In most other types of neurons, the distribution of the pigment is variable and appears quite randomly distributed within the perikaryon. Some workers (e.g., Nandy, 1971) have described the earliest formed pigment in the rat as having a perinuclear location. However, in preparations from rhesus monkeys, the early pigment formed in juvenile animals appeared in a random distribution in the perikaryon in all types of neurons.

Histochemical studies (Samorajski, Keefe, and Ordy, 1964) have revealed acid phosphatase, cathepsin type-C esterase, and acid deoxyribonuclease II activity at the same sites in which lipofuscin was identified by fluorescence methods. As summarized by Strehler (1964), lipofuscin exhibited moderate to strong reactions to histochemical tests for protein, lipids, phospholipids, plasmalogen, acid-fast groups, vicinal poly-OH groups, acid phosphatase, and esterase. Weak reactions were observed for tyrosine, trytophan, SH groups — S-S groups, unsaturated lipids, and reducing groups. The tests for succinoxidase, diphosphopyridine nucleotide diaphorase, lactic dehydrogenase, leucine amino peptidase, β-glucuronidase, cholesterol, and acid mucopolysaccharides were negative.

In young mice (Nandy, 1971), the pigment stained more selectively with the PAS method than with Nile blue A. In older animals, the reverse was true with the pigment in old neurons exhibiting a high affinity for Nile blue A and being less selectively stained with PAS.

In blue-light fluorescence with appropriate filters (Brizzee et al., 1969; Nandy, 1971) the pigment appeared a bright yellow-orange in adult and aged animals (Fig. 2B), in contrast to a lighter yellow-white color observable in neurons of juvenile animals (Fig. 2A — Nandy, 1971; Brizzee et al., 1974). Nandy (1971) suggested that these differential staining and fluorescence characteristics between young and old animals might be indicative of two different types of lipofuscin or that they may reflect merely the manifestation of early and late stages in the formation of the pigment. Based on differences in form and composition of the lipofuscin granules, Braak (1971) also described two types of pigment in the nucleus dentatus and olivary nucleus in the human brain. Altschul (1938) differentiated a

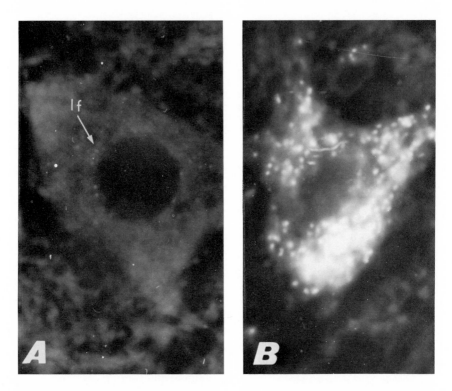

FIG. 2. A: Scattered lipofuscin (lf) granules in oculomotor nucleus (lateral nucleus of dorsal column) in an 80-day-old rhesus monkey, near-ultraviolet fluorescent light. ×1950. **B:** Compact masses and scattered lipofuscin granules in oculomotor nucleus (lateral nucleus of dorsal column) of old rhesus monkey, near-ultraviolet fluorescent light. ×1950.

fatty component from a pigment component in lipofuscin bodies. The former was relatively more prominent early, whereas the pigmented component was relatively more evident later. These structural and histochemical comparisons have suggested possible chemical differences in the pigment bodies from their early appearance to old age.

Electron Microscopy

Ultrastructural studies have shown the lipofuscin bodies to be composed essentially of a granular electron-dense component and a vesicular, probably lipid-containing, electron-lucent component with the entire structure ensheathed in a single limiting membrane (Fig. 3).

Based on the relative preponderance of granular and lamellar or linear configurations and vesicular components in the pigment granules, Siakotos et al. (1970) have classified the lipofuscin bodies as granular, granulolinear,

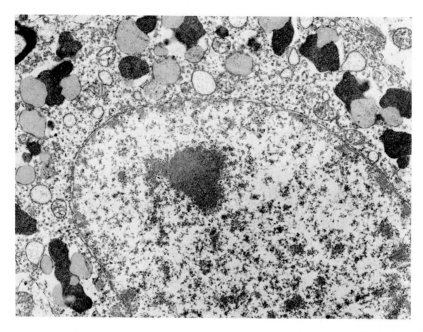

FIG. 3. Electron micrograph of lipofuscin bodies forming polar cap in perikaryon at base of apical dendrite in pyramidal cell neuron of human frontal cerebral cortex. Lipofuscin bodies show electron-lucent and electron-dense components. ×12,000.

macrogranular, and amorphous globules. Miyagishi, Takahata, and Iizuka (1967) proposed a somewhat similar classification based on essentially the same criteria.

Ceroid pigment, which has been observed and isolated only in pathological conditions (e.g., neuronal ceroid-lipofuscinosis, Siakotos et al., 1970), was classed as granular or light ceroid, heavy ceroid, curvilinear ceroid, and lamellar ceroid. Light ceroid was described as exhibiting a finer granularity than the granular type of lipofuscin. In heavy ceroid, extremely dense spherical areas were found in a less dense material, resulting in an appearance resembling neuromelanin. Curvilinear ceroid showed curvilinear bodies with a marked lamellar pattern seen at high magnification. A fourth type of ceroid, isolated from the brain of a dog, exhibited an extreme lamellar form. A comparison of the chemical characteristics of ceroid and lipofuscin is given in a subsequent section of this chapter.

In the present ultrastructural studies of lipofuscin, it has been observed that the lipofuscin bodies in neurons of human cerebral cortex (Fig. 3) have essentially the same ultrastructural characteristics as in the rat cortex (Brizzee et al., 1969; Brizzee and Johnson, 1970). In these studies, the electron-lucent (vesicular) bodies appeared to be occupied by a pale, homogeneous substance surrounded by a single-layered membrane, which also invested the granular component. The latter was composed of relatively small electron-dense granules of varying size and density, and occasionally lamellar figures were seen. The lamellar figures, which have been described as relatively prominent structures by some investigators (Samorajski, Ordy, and Keefe, 1965; Samorajski, Ordy, and Rady-Reimer, 1968), formed only a minor component of the lipofuscin bodies in these studies (Brizzee et al., 1960; Brizzee and Johnson, 1970).

Chemical Composition of Lipofuscin and Ceroid

According to earlier studies (Bjorkerud, 1964), 50% of lipofuscin in cardiac muscle was lipid, 30% was protein, and 10% was made up of a hydrolysis-resistant material. Of the lipid fraction, 75% was phospholipid. The highest specific fluorescence was found in the nonlipid fraction (Hendley, Mildvan, Reporter, and Strehler, 1963), and the principle lipids present were cholesterol esters, triglycerides, cholesterol, cephalins, lecithin, and sphingomyelin. The nonphosphatide/phosphatide ratio was 1:3.

In normal human brain tissue, as well as heart and liver, Siakotos, Pennington, and McInnes (1971) and Siakotos, Watanabe, Pennington, and Whitfield (1973) found that the density of lipofuscin varied from 1.00 to 1.03, whereas the major ceroid species obtained from brains of subjects with ceroid-lipofuscinosis had an average density of 1.29. Studies of fluorescence spectra revealed a lipofuscin excitation maximum of 360 nm and emission peak at 450 nm. For ceroid, the excitation maximum was 350 nm and the emission maximum was 435 nm. After treatment of lipofuscin with salt, the characteristic density was decreased, but it was not sensitive to chelating agents. Ceroid, on the other hand, was not sensitive to treatment with salt but dissolved in the presence of chelating agents. Other contrasting chemical differences between these two classes of lipopigment were a high concentration of iron and calcium in ceroid and a high concentration of zinc in lipofuscin.

Genesis and Possible Extrusion or Disposition of Pigment

According to Artiukhina (1968), the lipofuscin pigment granules of neurons are formed in lysosomes and Golgi vesicles. This conclusion was largely based on the similar acid phosphatase reaction in lysosomes, and in Golgi and pigment bodies. The inference of a lysosomal origin of lipofuscin also received support from studies of Samorajski et al. (1964) who observed a similarity of fine structural characteristics between lysosomes and lipofuscin and noted that sites of enzymatically deposited lead sulfide were concurrently identified with lysosomes and lipofuscin pigment. Observations by other workers supporting the lysosomal origin of the pigment included Essner and Novikoff (1960), Koenig (1962), Gonatas, Korey, and Terry

(1964), Pilgrim (1964), Alexandrowskaja (1966), Bergener and Gerhard (1966), Goldfischer, Villaverde, and Forschirm (1966), Miyagishi et al. (1967), Novikoff (1967), Sekhon, Andrew, and Maxwell (1969), and Hirsch (1970).

Evidence in favor of a mitochondrial origin, based on the presence of lipofuscin in or adjacent to mitochondria, or correlations of changes in mitochondria with pigmentation, was furnished by Payne (1952), Hess (1955), Duncan, Nall, and Morales (1960), Ghosh, Bern, Ghosh, and Nishioka (1962), Lampert, Blumberg, and Pentschew (1964), Roisin (1964), Takahashi, Philpott, and Miquel (1970), and Miquel (1971). Very recent studies by Gopinath and Glees (1974) showed that areas of pigment accumulation in neurons of the mesencephalic nucleus of the trigeminal nerve in the rat were characterized by a high mitochondrial content. They considered this increased abundance or clumping of mitochondria as an early sign of mitochondrial degeneration, and the primary event in the formation of lipofuscin. Following such clumping of mitochondria, there was a gradual disappearance of mitochondrial membranes followed by disruption of their cristae and the appearance of vacuoles. These investigators were of the opinion that the degeneration of mitochondria must result in a disturbance of normal metabolic pathways leading to an accumulation of insoluble fatty acids which presumably would be directly involved in the genesis of the lipofuscin pigment bodies.

Studies proposing the origin of lipofuscin from the Golgi apparatus have based their support largely on a tendency of the Golgi material to fragment with age, and on the sudanophilic and osmiophilic characteristics of both the Golgi apparatus and lipofuscin (Gatenby and Moussa, 1950; Gatenby, 1951; Heidenreich and Siebert, 1955; Dalton and Felix, 1956; Dalton, 1957; Bondareff, 1957). Other workers, including Issidorides and Shanklin (1961) and Strehler (1964), believed lipofuscin originated from endoplasmic reticulum. Evidence in support of this origin included a positive reaction for RNA in lipofuscin and the location of the pigment in relation to striations in cardiac muscle. Despite the large number of investigations, convincing evidence supporting the origin of lipofuscin from any single organelle is lacking. It seems possible that lipofuscin pigment may be formed through auto-oxidative alterations in structural lipids of cytomembranes from a number of different types of cellular organelles.

The interesting question of the possible disposition by extrusion of the pigment from neurons has been studied in the frog by Srebro and Scislawski (1966). These authors observed lipofuscin-containing glial cells which penetrated the ependymal layer and appeared to "extrude" the pigment into the brain ventricles. The "lipofuscin-containing" cells then appeared to disintegrate while the pigment was observed adjacent to the plexus epithelium. Such cells could also be observed in perivascular spaces of the brain.

From observations on reptiles and rats, Singh (1969) and Singh and

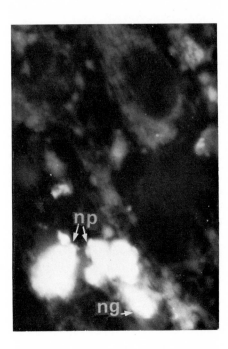

FIG. 4. Fluorescence microscope preparation of medial nucleus of superior olive in rhesus monkey showing neuron with no evident lipofuscin adjacent to two glial cells with relatively large autofluorescent lipofuscin bodies. Np = neuropil; ng = neuroglia. ×1,950.

Mukherjee (1972) postulated a continuous turnover of lipofuscin with a constant elimination from the tissue into the bloodstream. They proposed that lipofuscin granules might be extruded from neurons and traverse the neuropil to reach the capillaries and be discharged as neurohumors into the blood.

In more recent studies (Brizzee et al., 1974), it has been observed that neurons of some CNS structures exhibit very little lipofuscin even in very old subjects. An example is the medial nucleus of the superior olive (Fig. 4). Within the confines of this nucleus in the CNS of the rhesus monkey, lipofuscin accumulated with age in considerable quantities in glial cells (Fig. 4, ng), perivascular spaces, and the neuropil. In view of the very small amount of the pigment in the neurons, the question arises as to whether these neurons may be particularly efficient in extrusion and elimination of the pigment, which may then be taken up by neuroglial cells. Is it possible that the neurons which exhibit the greatest amount of pigment with age in other CNS structures are those whose mechanisms for eliminating the pigment becomes less efficient as the cell ages? The answer to this intriguing question concerning neuron-glia relationships in lipofuscin formation and disposition must await additional experimentation.

Early Appearance

Although lipofuscin has been generally regarded as a "wear-and-tear" or "aging" pigment, its presence in nerve cells has been reported in the spinal cord of human fetuses (Humphrey, 1944). Obersteiner (1903) and Chu (1954) also observed lipofuscin pigment in motor neurons of the lumbar spinal cord in children. Brody (1960) observed no pigment in neurons of the newborn but did observe lipofuscin in inferior olive in children 3 months of age (Brody, 1974, *personal communication*). However, other workers (e.g., Pallis, Duckett, and Pearse, 1967) found no lipofuscin in brains from normal children under 10 years of age.

In the dog and hog, the pigment was observed as early as 5 and 6 months of age in neurons of the spinal cord and spinal and autonomic ganglia, respectively, and at 1 year of age in the hypoglossal and red nucleus (Whiteford and Getty, 1966; Few and Getty, 1967). In the hog, Nanda and Getty (1971) identified lipofuscin at 1 year 2 months in inferior olivary nucleus; 1 year 6 months in hypoglossal nucleus; 2 years in dorsal motor nucleus of vagus; 2 years 9 months in nucleus cuneatus and the accessory cuneate nucleus; 1 year 5 months in vestibular nuclei (specific nuclei not identified); 2 years 11 months in cochlear nuclei; 2 years in Purkinje neurons of cerebellum, red nucleus, and oculomotor nucleus; 2 years 5 months in the thalamus (nucleus ventralis caudalis and ventralis rostralis); 3 years 9 months in the parahippocampal gyrus; and 1 year 11 months in the precentral cerebral cortex (lamina V).

Wilcox (1959) reported that the pigment first appeared in the mesencephalic nucleus of the trigeminal nerve in the guinea pig at 650 days of age, and in the vestibular nuclei and motor nuclei of cranial nerves 3, 4, 5, 6, 7, and 12 at 3 years of age. The pigment appeared in the nucleus of the trigemino-spinal tract, the main sensory nucleus of the trigeminal nerve, and the nucleus of the solitary tract at 5 years of age. The cells of the cochlear nuclei, even in the oldest animals, did not exhibit pigment at any age.

In recent studies (Brizzee et al., 1974), the early appearance and regional accumulation of lipofuscin was examined in the rhesus monkey brain in two cortical laminae, one hippocampal and two cerebellar areas, and 11 subcortical nuclei. The earliest appearance of lipofuscin in that initial investigation occurred at 3 months of age in the inferior olive, with the hypoglossal nucleus and main sensory nucleus of nerve 5 exhibiting the pigment by 6 months of age. All the structures studied, with the exception of the medial nucleus of the superior olive, revealed pigment granules by 10 months of age. More recently, finely scattered autofluorescent pigment granules were observed in the hypoglossal nucleus and oculomotor nucleus (Fig. 2A) in an 80-day-old rhesus monkey and in the mesencephalic nucleus of the trigeminal nerve in a 1-month-old squirrel monkey. From the above reports it is clear that wide species differences exist as to the time of earliest appearance of lipofuscin in various CNS structures. It is also apparent that there is considerable regional variation as to time of origin of the pigment in different CNS structures within a given species.

It seems likely that the variable early appearance of lipofuscin may be closely correlated with differences in the oxidative metabolic properties of different cell populations. These neurons which are most active in early developmental stages, such as the neurons of the mesencephalic nucleus of the trigeminal nerve (Gopinath and Glees, 1974), might be expected to exhibit the pigment at an earlier age than less active neurons. The early appearance of lipofuscin in neuroglia cells and neuropil has received little attention thus far, and further studies are needed on intra- and extracellular accumulation of the pigment and on the functional implications of this varied accumulation.

Accumulation and Regional Distribution

In their studies on lipofuscin accumulation in the nervous system of the dog and hog, Whiteford and Getty (1966) and Few and Getty (1967) grouped the structures into three categories with reference to the relative rate of accumulation of the pigment throughout the life-span. Those with the highest rate of accumulation were the inferior olive, the cochlear, and red nuclei. The lowest rate was observed in the cerebellar cortex, parahippocampal gyrus, and thalamus, while a number of other CNS structures constituting a third group were intermediate between the first two.

Dayan (1971) has also emphasized the variability in lipofuscin accumulation in different regions of the nervous system with age. Friede (1962) has classified various CNS structures as lipophil or lipophob according to the amount of lipofuscin demonstrated in the neurons. Braak (1971) suggested the term "pigment architectonic" to characterize the various arrangements of the pigment relative to specific nervous system structures.

In studies on rhesus monkeys (Brizzee et al., 1974), aggregation of dispersed pigment granules into a congregated pattern with an increasingly brighter yellow-orange fluorescence, occurred progressively from young adulthood to old age. Marked regional variations in the amount and pattern of distribution of lipofuscin were observed in these studies. Before reviewing the tabulated results of counts of neurons exhibiting lipofuscin bodies in a congregated pattern, a few illustrations will serve to indicate this regional variability in the primate brain. The nucleus with the highest pigment content was the inferior olive (Fig. 5A), followed closely by the hypoglossal nucleus (Fig. 5B), main sensory (Fig. 5C) and mesencephalic nuclei (Fig. 5D) of the trigeminal nerve. In marked contrast to these nuclei, the neurons of the medial nucleus of the superior olive exhibited only very fine, widely scattered lipofuscin granules (Fig. 4), even in the oldest rhesus monkeys. The neurons of the dentate nucleus of the cerebellum (Fig. 5E) and cerebral cortex (Fig. 5F,G) also exhibited relatively little neuronal pigment although a greater amount than in the superior olive. Nuclei such as the oculomotor (Fig. 2B), lateral vestibular (Fig. 5H), and dorsal motor nucleus of the vagus nerve (Fig. 5I) exhibited moderate amounts of pigment.

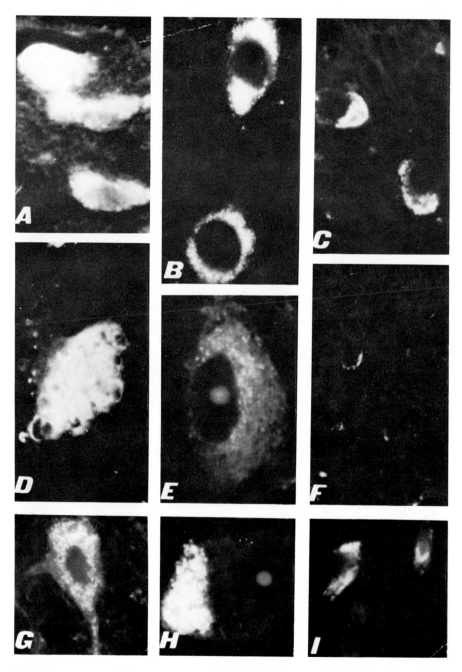

FIG. 5. Fluorescence microscope preparations showing relative amount of autofluorescent lipofuscin pigment accumulation in neurons of CNS structures of old rhesus monkey. ×1462. **A:** inferior olive; **B:** hypoglossal nucleus; **C:** main sensory nucleus of trigeminal nerve; **D:** mesencephalic nucleus of trigeminal nerve; **E:** dentate nucleus of cerebellum; **F:** lamina II, area 4 of cerebral cortex; **G:** abducens nucleus; **H:** Lateral vestibular nucleus; **I:** dorsal motor nucleus of vagus nerve.

An overall ($3 \times 6 \times 4$—ages $\times$ regions $\times$ subjects) statistical analysis of variance (ANOVA) of the tabulated data indicated significant age differences (F, 16.17; df, 219, $p < 0.001$) as well as significant differences among regions (F, 34.20; df, 5/45, $p < 0.001$). The rank order for lipofuscin pigment, from the lowest to the highest regional means, according to the multiple range test (MRT) for homogeneous subsets of means, from lowest to highest was (1) cerebellum, (2) neocortex, (3) pons, (4) midbrain, (5) hippocampus, and (6) medulla. The rank order of these regional means across four age levels is illustrated in a three-dimensional array in Fig. 6.

Statistical evaluations were also made of the differential pattern of congregated intraneuronal lipofuscin accumulation among all 17 brain areas across three age levels. According to an overall ($3 \times 17 \times 4$, ages $\times$ lamina-nuclei $\times$ subjects) ANOVA, both the age (F, 79.20; df, 2/9; $p < 0.001$) and lamina-nuclei (F, 22.59; df, 16/144; $p < 0.001$) main effects differed significantly. Differential lipofuscin accumulation among the specific nuclei and cortical laminae, according to the MRT across the three ages, increased significantly from the mean age of 4.0 years, where there were five different homogeneous subsets, to seven subsets at 9.5, and 10 subsets at 19.5 years. The rank order of intraneuronal lipofuscin accumulation in six regions combined across three ages and the differential pattern of lipofuscin among all

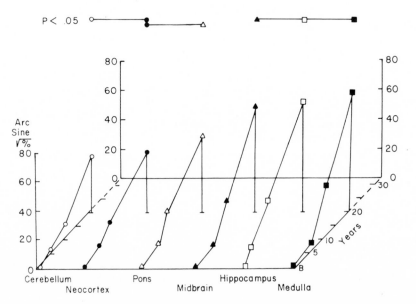

FIG. 6. A three-dimensional array with the rank order of regional differences in lipofuscin accumulation across four age levels, from lowest to highest means: (1) cerebellum, (2) neocortex, (3) pons, (4) midbrain, (5) hippocampus, and (6) medulla. (Reprinted with the permission of the *Journal of Gerontology*, Brizzee et al., 1974.)

17 areas of the brain at each of the three age levels separately are illustrated schematically in Fig. 7.

An analysis of the differential accumulation of intraneuronal lipofuscin among specific sensory, relay, and motor nuclei in a specific major division of the brainstem, namely the pons, was also carried out (Brizzee et al., 1974). This was done in order to ascertain whether significant differences in lipofuscin accumulation might occur over four age levels in such functionally specific structures in a single major division of the brainstem. The rank order of lipofuscin accumulation from low to high nuclear means, according to the MRT was (1) medial nucleus of the superior olive, (2) abducens nu-

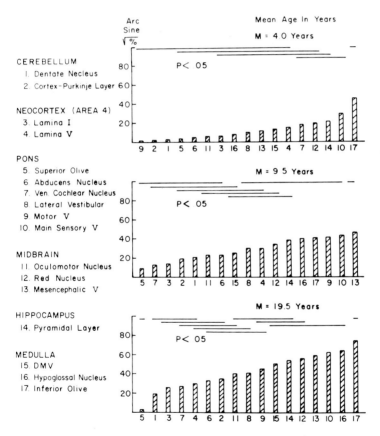

FIG. 7. Differential pattern of intraneuronal lipofuscin accumulation among two neocortical lamina, one hippocampal and two cerebellar sites, and 11 subcortical nuclei at three age levels. The figure illustrates schematically the rank order of intraneuronal lipofuscin accumulation in six regions combined across three age levels in the left column. The differential pattern of lipofuscin among the 17 areas in the brain are shown at each of the three age levels separately, from top to bottom on the right side. (Reprinted with the permission of the *Journal of Gerontology*, Brizzee et al., 1974.)

cleus, (3) ventral cochlear nucleus, (4) lateral vestibular nucleus, (5) motor nucleus, of the trigeminal nerve, and (6) main sensory nucleus of the trigeminal nerve. The differential rank order of the intraneuronal lipofuscin accumulation among these functionally specific structures is illustrated in a three-dimensional array in Fig. 8.

The increase in the number of subsets of related data from the young adult to older stages indicated that the various structures accumulated lipofuscin at different rates. If lipofuscin accumulation is considered to be one major morphological index of aging in the brain, it would appear that the neurons of the various CNS regions tended to be aging at different rates.

The neurons of the mesencephalic nucleus of the trigeminal nerve, in addition to exhibiting a very large quantity of normal appearing lipofuscin, also revealed vacuolar changes of the pigment material with a pronounced reddish-brown discoloration of the pigment bodies in fluorescence preparations. This was commonly observed in mature monkeys, but was also observed in some young adults. In old animals, this type of alteration in the pigment was very marked as viewed with the fluorescence microscope, but appeared only as vacuolar alterations in black-and-white prints (Fig. 5D). In ultrastructural preparations of the neurons of this nucleus, the vacuolar component of lipofuscin bodies commonly were as large as or larger than the electron-dense component and exhibited an array of smaller "subvacuoles"

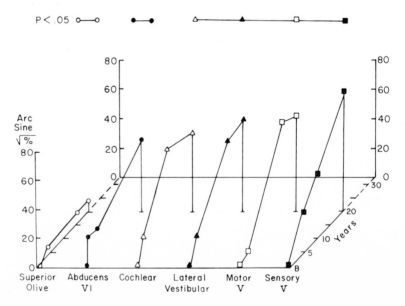

FIG. 8. Differential pattern of intraneuronal lipofuscin accumulation in the pons. The figure illustrates in a three-dimensional array the differential rank order of intraneuronal lipofuscin accumulation among specific sensory, relay, and motor nuclei of the pons across four age levels. (Reprinted with the permission of the *Journal of Gerontology*, Brizzee et al., 1974.)

of varying dimensions (Fig. 9). Whether these modified electron-lucent components account for the reddish-brown discoloration of lipofuscin observed in fluorescence preparations remains to be determined. Gopinath and Glees (1974) have described multivacuolated round-to-oval structures surrounded by lipofuscin pigment in the neurons of this nucleus. The vacuoles had a single limiting membrane and were frequently observed to coalesce to form large vacuoles. Some of these multivacuolated structures were seen to be completely engulfed.

In sensory ganglia (nodose, semilunar, dorsal spinal) the distribution of the pigment in the perikaryon was variable. As in the neurons of the mesencephalic nucleus of the trigeminal nerve, some of the lipofuscin bodies in the perikarya exhibited a vacuolated appearance characterized by a marked reddish-brown discoloration with fluorescence microscopy. In black-and-white photomicrographs, vacuolar changes were seen which were identical to those in the neurons of the mesencephalic nucleus of the trigeminal nerve (Fig. 10). Ultrastructural evaluations of neurons in sensory ganglia are now in progress.

In sympathetic ganglia (stellate and paravertebral trunk ganglia), the neurons showed variable amounts of pigment in the form of large clumps of relatively fine granules, distributed randomly in the perikaryon (Fig. 10A).

Distinct age and regional differences in lipofuscin accumulation also occurred in glia and neuropil. In neuroglia of the rhesus monkey brain (Brizzee et al., 1974) the pigment was most prominent in the medial nucleus of the superior olive (Fig. 4), but large amounts of the pigment were also observed in neuroglia in the dentate nucleus and Purkinje cell layer of the cerebellum (Fig. 11A,B). The pigment appeared to be present in all three of the major types of glial cells in all these structures. It was also prominent in the Fānanas cells of the Purkinje layer of the cerebellum. In all the other CNS structures, lipofuscin was invariably present in glial cells. It occurred in lesser amounts than in those structures noted above, with no distinct regional variations.

The results of this study clearly revealed that lipofuscin appeared early in life and exhibited a gradual but dramatic age-dependent and differential-regional accumulation in the brain of the nonhuman primate. As already noted, Friede (1962) classified a large number of brainstem nuclei and other components of the brain in terms of subjective estimates of the relative amounts of lipofuscin to four categories: (1) strongly lipophobe, (2) lipophobe, (3) intermediary, and (4) lipophil. The rank-order evaluation of the relative amounts of pigment in 17 structures in the CNS observed in the monkey (Brizzee et al., 1974; Fig. 7), based on actual comparative counts of neurons exhibiting lipofuscin in a congregated pattern at five different age levels, appeared to be in general agreement with the proposal of Friede (1962).

Species differences in the amount and distribution of lipofuscin are clearly

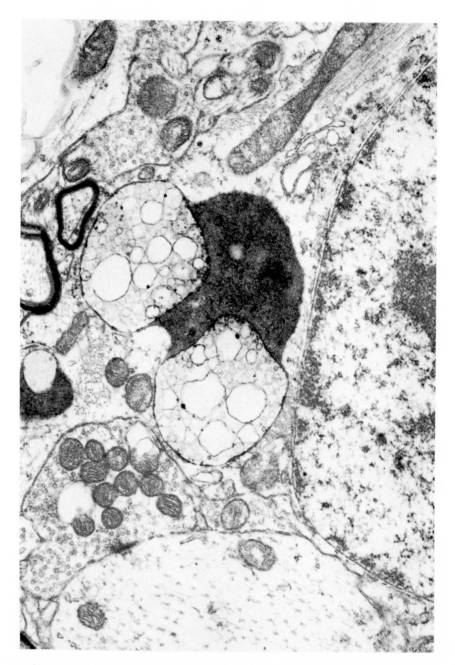

FIG. 9. Electron micrograph of lipofuscin body in neuron of mesencephalic nucleus of the trigeminal nerve in old squirrel monkey showing large electron—lucent components with multidimensional subvacuoles. ×28,000.

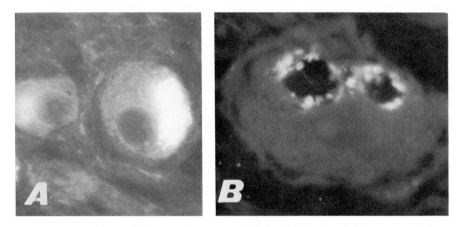

FIG. 10. Fluorescence microscope preparations showing lipofuscin pigment in neurons of sympathetic and sensory ganglia of old rhesus monkey. ×1950. **A:** stellate ganglion; **B:** gasserian ganglion.

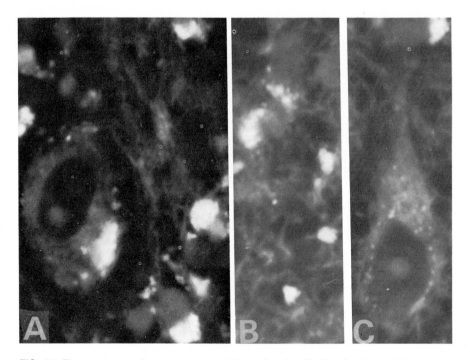

FIG. 11. Fluorescence microscope preparations showing lipofuscin pigment in neurons and neuroglia of cerebellum of old rhesus monkey. ×1950. **A:** Purkinje cell layer; **B:** dentate nucleus, neuroglia; **C:** dentate nucleus, neuron.

evidenced in comparing the observations of Whiteford and Getty in the dog and hog with observations in the monkey. In the latter (Brizzee et al., 1974) autofluorescent pigment granules were observed in a congregated pattern in about 50% of the neurons of the dorsal motor nucleus of the vagus nerve in aged monkeys. Whiteford and Getty (1966), on the other hand, observed no pigment in this nucleus at any age in the dog and hog. The observations of Vogt and Vogt (1946), Buttlar-Brentano (1954), and Reichel, Hollander, Clark, and Strehler (1968) further support regional specificity with reference to amount and distribution of lipofuscin in the mammalian nervous system.

Experimental Modifiability

Under normal conditions, the accumulation of lipofuscin in nervous tissues is presumably progressive and irreversible. Under laboratory conditions, however, it has been reported that the rate of accumulation of the pigment may be inhibited and that lipofuscin deposits can also be depleted. In one series of investigations, Nandy and Bourne (1966) and Nandy (1968) injected the drug meclofenoxate (Lucidril®, Centrophenoxine®) intraperitoneally or intramuscularly (80 mg/kg) into old guinea pigs daily for 4 to 12 weeks. At the completion of the series of injections, it was observed that the amount of lipofuscin in neurons of the brainstem reticular formation decreased markedly. The drug also reduced the activity of succinic and lactic dehydrogenases and cytochrome oxidase and enhanced that of glucose-6-phosphate dehydrogenase. The authors suggested that meclofenoxate may help to eliminate the old-age pigments by a possible diversion of the glucose metabolism via the pentose cycle. An observed reduction in simple esterase and acid phosphatase was believed to be due to the effect of the drug on lysosomes, which the majority of investigators believe are intimately related to the genesis of the pigments. In another study, daily administration of meclofenoxate (80 mg/kg) to rats of various ages (Meier and Glees, 1971) resulted in a decrease in the amount of pigment present in neurons of spinal ganglia after 8 or more weeks of treatment. Electron micrographs revealed vacuolization of pigment granules in satellite cells after only 4 weeks of treatment, and after 8 weeks similar changes could be seen in many neurons, including a disintegration of a large accumulation of pigment in the perikaryon of large neurons. Chemnitius, Machnik, Low, Arnrich, and Urban (1970) also showed a decrease in the amount of lipofuscin in neurons of the nucleus gigantocellularis following administration of meclofenoxate. In a very recent study, the reduction of lipofuscin by the same drug in the rat was supported by the application of morphometric techniques (Riga and Riga, 1974).

In rats raised on vitamin E-deficient diets (Einarson and Telford, 1960; Sulkin and Srivanij, 1960) and in adult mice, guinea pigs, rabbits, and monkeys maintained for prolonged periods on such diets (Einarson and

Telford, 1960) "lipid products" were deposited in neurons throughout the CNS. The appearance and distribution of such lipid products in stained and fluorescence microscope preparations provide evidence that the pigment material observed in those studies was lipofuscin.

In a study of modifiability of age pigments (Kerenyi, Haranghy, and Hüttner, 1968), rats were subjected to repeated modification of the alimentary and defense reflexes for a period of 6 months. Following repeated "cross conditions" (neurotraumatization), lysosomes, elementary pigment "clots," and aggregates were seen to accumulate near the nucleus of Purkinje cell neurons in the vicinity of the Golgi apparatus. The pigment ultrastructure resembled that of lipofuscin pigment masses observed in the course of normal senescence. Following the first reflex impact, increased acid phosphatase and nonspecific esterase activity were observed to develop in the Purkinje cells, but after repeated impacts these effects almost ceased. After a 6 week rest period the lysosome enzyme activity in the Purkinje neurons revived, but the pigment masses remained. The authors were of the opinion that the lipofuscin pigment masses were irreversibly injured lysosomes which developed under the influence of a specific stress on the nervous system.

Varkonyi, Domokos, Maurer, Zoltan, Csillik, and Földi (1970) have reported that both magnesium orotate and kavain will prevent the intracellular deposition of lipofuscin.

Clinical Significance

A number of pathological conditions in the brain are characterized by large accumulations of lipofuscin pigment in neurons. Among the most prominent of these are Kuf's disease (generalized lipofuscinosis — Kornfeld, 1972) and neuronal ceroid-lipofuscinosis (Batten's disease — Zeman and Dyken, 1969). Lipofuscin deposits in hippocampal neurons in patients with progeria have also been noted recently (Reichel and Garcia-Bunuel, 1970).

In a patient with Kuf's disease (26-year-old white female) Kornfeld (1972) reported that cytoplasmic constituents of some neurons in cerebral cortex were in part replaced by lipofuscin bodies, and numerous lysosome-like bodies were scattered throughout the cytoplasm with a tendency to aggregate around the lipofuscin particles. Lipofuscin bodies were also present in axons and in astrocytes. In the thalamus, the lipofuscin appeared more in the form of amorphous masses than granular components. In the cerebellum the cytoplasm of granule cells was heavily loaded with lipofuscin.

In Batten's disease (Zeman and Dyken, 1969) the predominant characteristic was a severe loss of neuronal perikarya in the retina, cerebral and cerebellar cortex, and subcortical nuclei. The remaining neuronal perikarya were enlarged with rounded contours and contained cytoplasmic granules of yellowish color which gave a positive reaction with all stains for lipofuscin.

Diffuse lipofuscinosis may also occur in dyssynergia cerebellaris myo-clonica. In a 49-year-old patient with this disease, Pallis, Duckett, and Pearse (1967) observed a widespread distribution and excessive amount of lipofuscin. Kristensson and Sourander (1966) observed a much greater than normal amount of lipofuscin in the dentate nucleus in infants with meta-chromatic leukodystrophy, and in the cerebral cortex, inferior olive, and dentate nucleus in a child with Tay-Sachs disease.

In cases of the infantile type of so-called ceroid-lipofuscinosis (Haltia, Rapola, and Santavuori, 1973), the pigment material was sudanophilic and resistant to lipid solvents. Ultrastructurally the granules consisted of membrane-bound conglomerations of spherical globules 0.2 to 0.5 μm in diameter, with homogeneous, finely granular internal structure. The authors proposed that the infantile type of neuronal ceroid-lipofuscinosis should be considered a separate nosological entity.

While lipofuscin is a "normal" constituent of neurons in brains of aged subjects, its presence in large amounts in young or even middle-aged sub-jects may be considered abnormal. The significance of this increased amount of the pigment in relation to the disease process itself is unknown. How-ever, until this relationship can be clarified through additional findings, currently, lipofuscin cannot be characterized as a harmless by-product of lipid metabolism.

Possible Functional Significance

As noted in the introductory statements above, Schäfer (1893) suggested that the presence of pigment in nerve cells was indicative of increased func-tional activity rather than age decline. On the other hand, Dolley and Guthrie (1918) believed that the pigment can be associated with a func-tional depression of the cell.

Altschul (1938) suggested that lipofuscin may be a useful material not sufficiently utilized by the cell as a result of decreased cellular activity. Wilcox (1959) favored the view that cells which are inactive tend to become pigmented to a greater extent than active cells. On the other hand, Friede (1962) concluded, from correlative data on enzyme activity in nerve cells and relative amount of lipofuscin present, that the more active the oxidative metabolism, the greater the likelihood of lipofuscin accumulation.

On the basis of the observations that the pigment (1) occurs in young subjects, (2) is affected by diet and chemical agents and by radiation, (3) occurs in pathologic states, and (4) is present in large concentration in the brain and heart, Hasan and Glees (1972) concluded that the pigment may have a compensatory storage function without adverse effect on cellular metabolism. Evidence against this view includes the observation of Sand-ritter, Bierfreund, Parmen, and Adler (1972) to the effect that a positive correlation exists between the lipofuscin content in heart muscle and the degree of cardiac hypertrophy (increased fiber width and nuclear size). These authors also noted a direct relationship between increased lipofuscin content and increased functional output of the hypertrophied heart.

A new hypothesis relative to the possible functional significance of lipofuscin has recently been set forth by Karnaukhov (1973) and Karnaukhov, Tataryunas, and Petrunyaka (1973). These authors proposed that lipofuscin granules contain carotenoids, myoglobin, and respiratory enzymes, form the "intracellular oxygen stock," and provide the energy requirements of cells under conditions of low rate of oxygen penetration into tissues. The significance of the very great accumulation of lipofuscin in neurons of certain CNS structures in relation to such postulated functions is not clear.

Zeman (1974) has suggested that the pigments in disease conditions (e.g., neuronal ceroid-lipofuscinosis) form at the expense of the cytoplasm and that the inert pigment material could conceivably damage the cell by distorting and disturbing the cellular geometry, changing diffusion pathways, and crowding out subcellular organelles. Such cells would become metabolically less efficient, and the rate of biosynthetic molecular replacement would be decreased leading to a negative biosynthetic balance. One of the more significant effects of such alterations might be an interference with axon transport. This, together with the other intracellular changes, might lead to loss of dendritic spines (Feldman, 1974) or loss of dendrites as demonstrated in aging cerebral cortex (Scheibel and Scheibel, *this volume*).

A contrasting view to those given above is that of Hyden and Lindström (1950). These workers noted that the decrease in motor function accompanying increasing age is not proportional to the considerable "chemical reconstruction" of the nerve cell with age. According to their view, a large part of this chemical reconstruction was due to replacement of pentose nucleic acids by lipofuscin. They concluded that their results did not favor the concept that lipofuscin was a "slag product" detrimental to cell function, without commenting on a possible beneficial role for the pigment. Other authors (e.g., Ranson and Clark, 1959; Bloom and Fawcett, 1962; Nandy, 1968; Kormendy and Bender, 1971) have suggested that lipofuscin may be a harmless product of normal cell metabolism.

Summary

Lipofuscin accumulates in a progressive manner in most neurons in the mammalian nervous system, though the rate of increase varies greatly in various structures. The amount of pigment appears to be amenable to modification through various treatment regimens, including administration of meclophenoxate, a vitamin E-deficient diet, magnesium orotate, and kavain.

Lipofuscin is commonly observed in neuroglial cells throughout the mammalian nervous system, but in aged rhesus monkeys has been observed to occur in greater amounts in glial cells in structures in which the constituent neurons exhibit relatively little pigment (e.g., medial nucleus of superior olive; dentate nucleus of cerebellum) than in most other sites in the nervous system. The pigment occurs in abnormally large amounts in certain disease conditions, including Kuf's disease, Batten's disease, and dyssynergia myoclonica cerebellaris, and has been observed in large amounts in neurons in some cases of Tay-Sachs disease and progeria.

The effects of lipofuscin on cell function are unknown, but there is some evidence favoring the view that cells having a high oxidative metabolic rate invariably accumulate larger amounts of lipofuscin over a time-span than do cells having a less active oxidative metabolism.

From a review of the rather extensive literature on lipofuscin accumulation as a possible fundamental characterization of aging in the nervous system, it can be concluded that evidence from phylogenetic, regional, single unit electrical, and microchemical studies should provide the essential evidence as to whether lipofuscin accumulation enhances cell function, has no effect, or is clearly detrimental not only to cellular but also regional functions and the entire nervous system.

AMYLOID AND SENILE PLAQUES

There is no specific evidence concerning a common origin or direct relationship between lipofuscin and amyloid accumulation in the nervous system with age. The presence of amyloid in the nervous system during aging has generally been described in relation to the three commonly recognized types of amyloidoses, namely, primary, secondary, or familial forms. However, it has recently been pointed out that cerebral amyloid degeneration, amyloid infiltration of the pancreatic islets, and cardiovascular deposition of amyloid "form a characteristic patho-anatomic triad of senile deterioration" (Schwartz, 1968). Walford and Sjaarda (1964) have also noted that senile amyloidosis is "a major accompaniment of aging in humans."

While many clinical investigators consider amyloid disease as of no more than casual clinical importance, there is a growing awareness of its potential significance in gerontology, especially in relation to neuron loss and the aging process in the brain. The possible roles of amyloid accumulation in altering glial cell populations and glia-neuron relationships have also not received appropriate attention as important features of aging in the nervous system. Whereas amyloid, senile plaques, and neurofibrillary tangles have been considered in a context of age-related neuropathological lesions, the possibility that they may develop to some degree in everyone past 80 to 90 would make them of considerable importance in any review of aging in the nervous system.

With recent advances in biochemical methodology for solubilization and isolation of amyloid, it has been possible to characterize the major proteins of several types of amyloid and to identify certain chemically and immunologically related serum and urine proteins. It seems possible that these new techniques may permit a biochemical classification of the various forms of amyloid observed in different disease conditions. This biochemical approach may also offer, for the first time, some prospect of gaining insights into the pathogenesis of amyloidosis and its relation to "normal" aging in the nervous system. It seems worthwhile, therefore, to give greater attention to the problem of amyloid accumulation in relation to aging than has been done previously. The aims of this review were to examine amyloid as a clinical entity in the context of its increasing frequency of occurrence with advancing age in certain neurological disorders. This included a brief examination of the history of amyloid as a clinical entity, its chemical classification, the morphological and histochemical characterization, its regional distribution, and its possible role in decreasing cell and organ function, including cell loss, in relation to a similar role frequently proposed or implied for lipofuscin.

Historical Notes

Virchow (1855, 1857) applied the term "amyloid" to a hyaline substance, observed in nervous tissues obtained at autopsy from aged patients, on the basis of its starch-like appearance when treated with iodine. At the same time, however, he noted certain differences from the typical staining properties of starch, but some similarities to the staining characteristics of cellulose. Friedreich and Kekule (1859) found by chemical analysis that amyloid contained proteins, but neither starch nor cellulose.

From observations on argyrophilic plaque-like structures in brains of elderly epileptic patients, Blocq and Marinesco (1892) coined the term "plaque sclerotique neuroglie," believing them to be nodules of glial sclerosis. A few years later Alzheimer (1907), Perusini (1910), and Simchowicz (1911) identified similar structures in patients with senile dementia. Simchowicz (1911) labeled these structures "senile plaques," implying a relationship to the aging process. The presence of amyloid-like material in the central core of senile plaques was clearly shown by Bielschowsky in 1911 and this has been observed by many workers since that time.

Alzheimer (1907) was the first to note peculiar fibrillar alterations of nerve cells in patients with dementia. Kraepelin (1910) confirmed the observation and termed the condition "Alzheimer's disease." Other authors (Corten and Ostertag, 1930; Gellerstedt, 1938) noted that such lesions were not necessarily related to disturbances in cognitive functions. The existence of amyloid-like material within the walls of cerebral blood vessels was described by Scholz (1938), Morel and Wildi (1952), and Pantelakis (1954).

General Classification and Patterns of Distribution of Amyloidoses

Whereas it is now commonly recognized that present classifications of amyloid disease will probably be altered as new biochemical data become available, the categories of amyloid disease which are most frequently recognized at present are as follows.

Primary (Idiopathic)

This form tends to be widespread in the body but it is mainly localized in the gastrointestinal and cardiovascular organs. Generally, it occurs in the absence of an associated disease process, other than multiple myeloma. Amyloid fibrils of immunoglobulin origin are most commonly demonstrated in patients with this type of amyloidosis.

Secondary

This type is generalized throughout the body, but it is most characteristically located in the reticulo-endothelial system, tending to be more prevalent in certain viscera such as liver and spleen. It is generally associated with a chronic suppurative disease condition. It has been observed in such diseases as tuberculosis, ulcerative colitis, bronchiectasis, rheumatoid arthritis, and juvenile rheumatoid arthritis. Amyloid fibrils of immunoglobulin origin have not been demonstrated in this form of amyloidosis.

Hereditofamilial Variants

These genetic variants generally tend to be confined to one organ and commonly occur in the absence of associated diseases.

In all types of generalized amyloidosis, the same tissues tend to be effected. The difference in classification or diagnoses lies in the relative preponderance of amyloid in a particular group of organs. Many clinical investigators are of the opinion that all varieties of amyloidosis are related manifestations of one fundamental disturbance which includes the fibrillar deposition of antiparallel β-pleated sheet protein as a result of proteolytic cleavage or other physicochemical modifications of the protein of origin.

Chemical Classes of Amyloid Substances

Type A

On the basis of chemical studies of amyloid obtained from visceral structures, mainly liver, this type of amyloid is reported to be composed of amyloid protein A as a major constituent. It was found in the "secondary" type of amyloidosis (Benditt and Eriksen, 1973). It has a higher affinity for Congo red than type B, at the proper pH, and loses its affinity for Congo red at a lower pH than the substance derived from type B. Type A has a high concentration of glycine and alanine, an absence of cystine, and low combined percentages of threonine and serine. The major constituent is an undescribed protein (MW8000) whose amino acid sequence appears to have no homology to any immunoglobulin or other previously sequenced protein. It is believed that protein A may be derived from a larger protein by proteolytic digestion. Thus far, it has not been demonstrated chemically in cases in which the major fibril protein was of immunoglobulin origin. The type of protein of origin for this class of amyloid fibril is as yet unknown.

Type B

The A-protein is lacking in this amyloid substance (Benditt and Eriksen, 1973). It is composed of heterogeneous constituents, including light chain immunoglobulin-like proteins (8,000–25,000 molecular weight). It has a uniform complement of amino acids characterized by a relatively high concentration of serine, glutamine, aspartic acid, and threonine, low concentrations of methionine and cystine, and a relatively low combined concentration of tyrosine, phenylalanine, and tryptophane. It is generally found as a major constituent in "primary" and "myeloma-associated" amyloidosis.

According to Glenner and Terry (1974), the major protein of the amyloid fibril of immunoglobulin origin is a homogeneous light polypeptide chain (L) or its amino-terminal variable (V_L) fragment, or both. The capacity to form β-pleated sheet fibrils when the V_L region was cleaved from the intact light chain was believed to be inherent in the structure of the V_L region. These amyloid fibril proteins, according to amino acid-sequence analysis (Glenner, Terry, Harada, Iseraky, and Page, 1971; Kimura, Guyer, Terry, and Glenner, 1972; Terry, Page, and Kimura, 1973) and immunochemical investigations (Isersky, Ein, Page, Harada, and Glenner, 1972) have been shown to be either kappa or lamda type, based on their chemical homology and/or sharing of their antigenic determinants with kappa or lambda Bence-Jones proteins. The lamda type was more frequently shown to be the source of amyloid fibril proteins than the kappa type.

These workers have proposed that amyloid fibrils may be formed following endocytosis of light polypeptide chains by phagocytic cells and subsequent intralysosomal proteolysis to provide V_L fragment aggregates. Ensuing exocytosis would presumably deposit these aggregates extracellularly as amyloid fibrils. It was further postulated by these workers that only certain light chain variable regions on the immunoglobulin molecule possess an amyloidogenic structure, and this structure was believed to be more prevalent in light than in heavy chains.

Possible C-Proteins

According to Hobbs (1973) preliminary studies indicate that thyroid medullary carcinomatous amyloid is distinct from the known A- and B-proteins. Amyloid associated with tumor formation, in general, appears to be formed locally with no clear evidence for a circulating precursor. Localized accumulations of amyloid are also found in tumors of the Islets of Langerhans, in brain tissue from senile human patients, in certain areas of the heart, and in large arteries where nerve elements are located.

It is important to note that such amyloid deposits in nervous tissue have not been fully characterized, and their relationships to A-, B-, or C-type amyloid remains to be determined. Hobbs (1973) has suggested that the amyloid in such areas may be connected with amine-metabolizing cells of neurogenic origin. He postulated further that, in splitting off such protein moieties as the C-peptide of insulin, such cells might eventually accumulate amyloid.

General

Gammaglobulin is a constant, although minor, constituent of the amyloid complex, but it does not seem to be part of the amyloid fibril. In centrifuged material, "doughnut"-shaped particles are seen in electron micrographs, which are believed to be identical with or related to α-2 globulin of normal plasma. Amyloid, in general, has a high nitrogen content but there is no hydroxylysine, desmosine, isodesinosine, or lipinorlysine. Neutral sugars are present in small amounts.

Morphological and Histochemical Characteristics of Amyloid

As pointed out in the historical notes above, the earliest histochemical identification of amyloid was based on the iodine reaction (Alzheimer, 1907). It was shown shortly thereafter that the substance exhibited marked crystal violet metachromasia. The latter technique for many years was the most common method for histological identification of amyloid in tissues. More recently, Congo red, green birefringence, and dichrosim in polarized light and thioflavin-S fluorescence staining (Schwartz, Kurucz, and Kurucz, 1965) have provided more accurate and specific means for histological identification of amyloid. The typical appearance of amyloid as seen in a senile plaque from the human cerebral cortex at light microscope magnification is shown in Fig. 12.

The fine structure of amyloid has been studied by a number of investigators (Terry, Gonatas, and Weiss, 1964; Luse and Smith, 1964; Kidd, 1964; Krigman, Feldman, and Bensch, 1965; Bladen, Nylen, and Glenner,

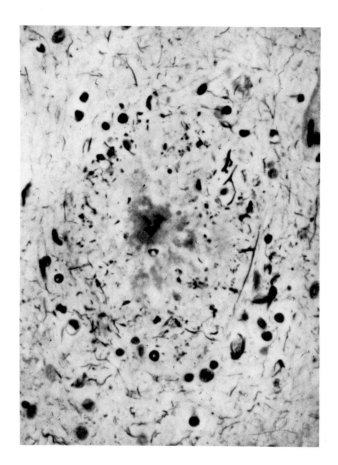

FIG. 12. Photomicrograph of senile plaque showing amyloid substance in central core in human cerebral cortex. Bodian and Congo red stains. ×800.

1966; Shirahama and Cohen, 1967). Ultrastructurally, the primary component of amyloid is seen to be made up of fibrils 300 to 100,000 Å long and 70 to 100 Å in diameter with a parallel or slightly oblique arrangement. The filaments often seem to disperse into several longitudinal rows. This component stains with Congo red.

Shirahama and Cohen (1967) have suggested that the protofibrils consist of two or three subunit strands helically arranged with a 35 to 70 Å repetition or, less likely, that they are composed of globular subunits aggregated end-to-end. Protofibrillar strands have been estimated to be approximately 10 to 15 Å in diameter.

A second and minor component (pentagonal unit or plasma component) is 90 Å in diameter. This may aggregate face-to-face to form rods with a different periodicity from amyloid fibrils. This component does not stain with Congo red or show crystal violet metachromasia. It is more readily soluble than the fibril and does not contain antigens in common with it. This element exhibits an irregular beaded structure with the beads spaced at 35 to 50 Å. The typical ultrastructural configuration of amyloid fibrils at a relatively low magnification is shown in Fig. 13A.

Tissue extracts of amyloid contain doughnut-shaped particles 80 to 100 Å in diameter. These are composed of five small structures, each 20 to 25 Å in diameter, clustered around a central zone.

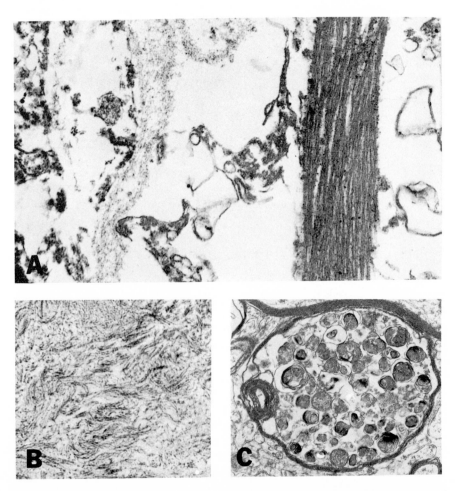

FIG. 13. A: Electron micrograph showing amyloid fibers in human dentate nucleus of cerebellum. ×48,000. **B:** Electron micrograph showing typical nonaligned distribution of amyloid fibrils in human kidney. ×25,000. **C:** Electron micrograph of a dystrophic axonal neurite in human cerebral cortex as commonly found in senile plaques. ×13,000.

Regional Distribution in the Nervous System

Peripheral Nervous System

In peripheral nerves, amyloid is distributed as stellate plaques and homogeneous perivascular clumps (DeNavasquez and Treble, 1938; Divry, 1942; Kernohan and Woltman, 1942; Fisher and Preuss, 1951; Sullivan, Twitschell, Gherardi, and van der Laan, 1955; Lampert, 1968). These plaques and clumps commonly result in compression and displacement of nerve fibers, demyelination, axon degeneration, destruction of internal elastic lamina, and occlusion of blood vessels. In the perineurium and epineurium, amyloid is most frequently observed in the walls of arteries and veins. Deposition of amyloid in endoneurium and perineurium is commonly observed in "primary" amyloidosis and very often is associated with clinical symptoms. Deposition in the epineurium is often seen in "secondary" amyloidosis. In dorsal root ganglia and sympathetic ganglia amyloid occurs in perivascular aggregates and tends to surround and compress ganglion cells.

CNS

In the CNS, amyloid commonly occurs in relation to senile plaques, although this is not the only pattern of distribution. Three types of plaques are now generally recognized (Wisniewski and Terry, 1973a). The first type, described as the "primitive" plaque, is characterized by a small cluster of a few dystrophic neurites, small wisps of amyloid, and a few microglial cells. A second type of plaque, which appears to be formed from the primitive form, is termed the "classical" type. This is characterized by many dystrophic neurites, generally found in a peripherial position and characterized by degenerative mitochondria, abnormal synaptic complexes, and dense bodies. There are many reactive nonneural cells and, most characteristically, a central relatively large amyloid core. This type of plaque is illustrated in Fig. 12. A third type of plaque is referred to as the "burned-out" form. This is made up mainly of amyloid with a few microglia, macrophages, and astrocytic processes but very few or no dystrophic neurites. Senile plaques are primarily located in the frontal, temporal, and occipital cortex and hippocampus. They have been observed predominantly in human subjects but have also been noted in monkeys and dogs (Wisniewski and Terry, 1973a).

Amyloid deposits, other than in plaques, are commonly found in the blood vessels of meninges and brain and in the pituitary gland. Vascular amyloid deposits in the frontal cerebral cortex are generally brilliantly metachromatic with the crystal violet method (Wright, Calkins, Breen, Stolte, and Schultz, 1969). In the meninges, amyloid is distributed irregularly within the adventitia and outer media in arteriolar vessels. In small intracerebral vessels, amyloid commonly involves the entire wall thickness and sometimes extends into the adjacent cerebral cortex. In this position, the amyloid appears to form the nucleus of perivascular senile plaques.

Amyloid deposits have also been observed in blood vessels of choroid plexus, infundibulum, area postrema, and subpial zone of the pons, medulla, spinal cord, and cerebral hemispheres. In the subpial zone, amyloid deposits are seen as nodular patches extending into fiber tracts and the molecular layer of the cortex. Such deposits are usually bordered by a row of microglial cells or an astrocytic reaction. In the subependymal zone, amyloid deposits are commonly seen in the septum pellucidum in small nodules which extend between ependymal cells (Lampert, 1968).

A greater incidence of cerebral, aortic, and cardiac amyloid (Wright, et al., 1969) was seen in patients over 70 years of age than in a group from 30 to 70 years old ($p < 0.001$). However, there was no difference in the incidence of pancreatic amyloidosis between the two groups. The tendency for multiple-organ involvement was significantly greater in the older group (Wright et al., 1969).

In the condition known as angiopathie congophile (Pantelakis, 1954), amyloid was confined to the media of arterioles and small arteries. The cerebral and cerebellar cortical vessels were also commonly involved. The same changes were described by Braünmuhl (1957) in senile dogs. Scholz (1938) described a type of amyloid angiopathie which affected cortical arterioles more than meninges. The Congophilic material was deposited as brush-like or stellate patches in the adventitia or perivascular space. Vessels, mainly arterioles, exhibiting such amyloid degeneration were seen in cerebral and cerebellar cortex, and occasionally in the striatum. These seemed to be abundant in, or limited to, cerebral cortical area 17 (Morel and Wildi, 1952). Vessels which appeared normal in the subarachnoid space commonly exhibited an affinity for Congo red when they entered the molecular layer. Characteristically, the media was broadened, but the elastic lamina and intima were normal. The adventitial deposits were comparable in structure to stellate senile plaques or stellate amyloid foci in peripheral nerves.

Neurofibrillary Tangles

The fibrillar tangles first noted by Alzheimer (1907) in neurons of patients with dementia have been the subject of a number of intensive studies over a period of many years. According to one hypothesis (Braünmuhl, 1957), the Alzheimer fibrils result from an inhibition phenomenon of the precursors of the endofibers, a process presumed to be related to aging of colloids and resulting in thickening of fibers. Another hypothesis proposed that the fibrillary material was of amyloid nature (Braünmuhl, 1932, 1957; Divry, 1952). More recent comprehensive studies on this problem (Terry and Wisniewski, 1970; Wisniewski and Terry, 1970, 1973*b,c;* Wisniewski, Terry, and Hirano, 1970; Wisniewski, Ghetti, and Terry, 1973; Tellez-Nagel and Wisniewski, 1973) have indicated that neither of the above proposed hypotheses were correct. Results of these investigations indicated that the affected neurons did not show degeneration of the preexisting filaments or tubules and did not accumulate filaments of the amyloid type. Rather they formed a new type of fibrillary substance. These "abnormal" tubules measured 200 to 220 Å in width, varying from 180 to 350 Å, and displayed periodic constrictions of 100 to 150 Å about every 800 Å. In cross section, they exhibited an electron-lucent center in which a small dense core was frequently seen. The "constrictions" were later determined to be due to a spiral "twisting" of the fibers, and have been designated as twisted fibrils.

The twisted fibrils were PAS negative or weakly positive, in contrast to amyloid which is strongly positive. They were slightly Congo red positive and birefringent, especially after treatment with thioflavin-S. They were also strongly argentophilic, but their ultrastructural characteristics differed markedly from those of amyloid fibrils. While normal neurotubules were not well preserved, or disappeared after osmic acid fixation, the abnormal twisted tubules, like normal neurofilaments, were well preserved. It should be emphasized that, while twisted tubules are commonly found in neuron perikarya in Alzheimer's disease, there is no apparent direct relationship between such tubules and amyloid.

The areas of the nervous system in which neurofibrillary tangles are most commonly observed are the frontotemporal cerebral cortex, various hypothalamic nuclei, substantia nigra, locus caeruleus, the reticular formation of the brainstem, and the hippocampus. The areas in which neurons do not ordinarily exhibit altered fibrils are the mesencephalic nucleus of the trigeminal nerve, sensory ganglia, and Purkinje cells of the cerebellum (Hirano and Zimmerman, 1962; McMenemey, 1963).

Neurofibrillary alterations have been observed in aged human brains in the absence of dementia (Matsuyama, Namiki, and Watanabe, 1966; Tomlinson, Blessed, and Roth, 1968; Dayan, 1970).

Summary

A review of the literature suggests that the accumulation of amyloid with age is a consistent phenomenon in certain tissues and organs of human subjects. Some findings have indicated a similar accumulation in the rhesus monkey and the dog. The chemical composition of amyloid is not fully known, but available data suggest that it is composed of two types, designated as A and B. Type A is believed to be composed of type A protein and to be present in the "secondary" type of amyloidoses. It has a molecular weight of about 8,000, it has no homology to any immunoglobulin, and it is characterized by a high concentration of glycine and alanine. Type B possesses more heterogenous constituents, including immunoglobulin-like proteins with molecular weights varying from about 8,000 to 25,000. It is a major constituent of "primary" and "myeloma-associated" amyloidoses. Amyloid exhibits crystal violet metachromasia, a positive staining reaction to Congo red dye, Congo-red green birefringence, and dichroisin in polarized light, and a positive reaction to thioflavin-T and -S. Ultrastructurally, amyloid is composed of fibrils 300 to 100,000 Å long and 70 to 100 Å in diameter, each composed of two or more subunits (protofibrils) 35 Å in diameter.

In generalized amyloidosis, amyloid is observed in the peripheral nervous system where it tends to compress nerve fibers and sensory and sympathetic ganglion cells, resulting in demyelination, axon degeneration, and occlusion of blood vessels. In the CNS, amyloid is commonly seen in senile plaques, predominantly in the frontal, temporal, and occipital regions of the cortex. Amyloid deposits are also seen in meninges, blood vessels of the brain, choroid plexus, infundibulum, pituitary gland, the subpial zone of the pons, medulla, spinal cord, cerebral hemispheres, and in subependymal locations.

General Discussion—Lipofuscin and Amyloid in the Aging Nervous System

Although they do not have a common origin or direct relation in their accumulation, there are some noteworthy similarities and differences between lipofuscin and amyloid as two of the more prominent manifestations of aging in the nervous system. Major points of comparison can best include similarities and differences in morphology, histochemistry, chemical composition, time of appearance, phylogenetic occurrence, and functional significance in normal and clinical conditions. Lipofuscin has been shown to accumulate with age in a progressive manner in most neurons of the mammalian nervous system. A significant body of literature suggests that the accumulation of amyloid is a common phenomenon in nervous tissues primarily during senescence. The two substances stand in marked contrast, however, in that lipofuscin accumulates in cell somata or processes while amyloid is deposited in extracellular locations.

Ultrastructurally, lipofuscin is composed of granular, lamellar, and vesicular components of variable dimensions, while amyloid is constituted almost entirely of fibrils and subunits identified as protofibrils.

Histochemical techniques have revealed considerable hydrolytic enzyme activity and lipid moieties in lipofuscin, while amyloid exhibits no enzyme activity or lipid components. Amyloid is stained selectively with Congo red and is revealed by fluorescence microscopy after treatment with thioflavins T and S. Lipofuscin cannot be visualized by such methods but is selectively stained with Nile blue, Carbol fuchsin, and the Sudan stains, and, unlike amyloid, exhibits strong autofluorescence in ultraviolet light. Both substances are stained with the PAS method but the reaction is much more specific with lipofuscin than with amyloid.

Chemically, lipofuscin has been shown to be composed of lipids (50%), proteins (30%), and nonhydrolyzable residues. Studies on amyloid derived from visceral structures have shown that it is composed of one of two, or possibly three, types of protein. These have been designated as amyloid proteins, A and B with a possible C-type remaining to be more fully characterized. Types A and B each have their own characteristic uniform complement of amino acids. Type A is derived from immunoglobulin proteins, while type B appears to have no relation to such proteins. No information as to the amino acid complements of lipofuscin is available.

Considerable data are now available on the early appearance and progressive accumulation of lipofuscin with age, but little attention has been given to this question in the case of amyloid. On the other hand, the presence of amyloid and its regional distribution in aged subjects and in patients with pathological disease conditions is well documented. The characteristic meningeal, vascular, subpial, cortical, and subependymal distributions of amyloid in cases of generalized amyloidosis appear to have nothing in common with the regional distribution patterns of lipofuscin. In one situation, however, the two substances do consistently appear in a close topographic relationship. This condition occurs in the senile plaques in cerebral cortex characterized by a central amyloid core, surrounded by dystrophic neurites and cells containing considerable amounts of lipofuscin. The significance of this rather constant relationship is unknown.

Lipofuscin is believed by nearly all investigators to be formed from degradative processes involving cell organelles, although there is considerable difference of opinion as to which organelles (e.g., lysosomes, mitochondria, Golgi apparatus) are involved. The majority of investigators at the present time support the concept of a lysosomal origin of lipofuscin. Some of the most prominent investigators in the field of amyloidosis and amyloid chemistry (Glenner and Terry, 1974) have suggested that amyloid fibrils may be formed following endocytosis of light polypeptide chains by phagocytic cells. Subsequent intralysosomal proteolysis would presumably provide V_L fragment aggregates, and ensuing exocytosis would deposit these aggregates extracellularly as amyloid fibrils.

It is of particular interest to note from the above comparisons, that the majority of investigators who have considered the problem of the origin of lipofuscin or amyloid have held the opinion that lysosomes may be directly involved in the genesis of each of these substances. In the case of lipofuscin, the process would presumably involve autoxidation of the lipids and lytic changes in protein components of fragments of cytomembranes, with the resulting product remaining in an intracellular location. In the nervous system, neurons, glia, and vascular elements would all form the substance in this manner. In the case of amyloid, presumably only phagocytic cells would be involved and would be responsible for the deposition of the amyloid fibrils in its characteristic extracellular locations in the nervous system.

It has been reported by several investigators that the accumulation and amount of lipofuscin in neurons can be experimentally altered. Animals which are maintained on vitamin E-deficient diets, subjected to acetaldyhyde injections or to stress, exhibit greater amounts of lipofuscin than controls. Conversely, in animals which receive daily injections of meclophenoxate over a period of several weeks, the amount of lipofuscin in CNS neurons has been reported to decrease.

It has also been shown that the amount of amyloid in various nonnervous tissues can be modified clinically. Increased amounts have been demonstrated in certain tissues in animals maintained for relatively long periods on high casein diets. Conversely, it has also been shown that the accumulation of amyloid may be inhibited through immunosuppressive techniques for periods up to 21 months, and in Persian children with Still's disease, reversals from positive to negative renal biopsies have been observed. In nervous tissues, there is no evidence that the accumulation of amyloid has been altered or that the amount has been reduced.

The relationship of amyloid to clinical syndromes has been more fully explored than has the clinical significance of lipofuscin. Only in recent years has the possible clinical importance of lipofuscin been seriously considered. Amyloid, on the other hand, has been associated with clinical disease for many years, and the various classifications of amyloidoses have been based largely on its regional distribution and relationships to clinical syndromes.

Although it is generally accepted that cell and tissue destruction occur as a result of infiltration of nervous tissues and visceral organs with amyloid, there is still uncertainty concerning the importance of lipofuscin in regard to cell loss in either nervous or visceral structures.

Although amyloid has been assumed to damage nervous tissues through infiltration and compression of both vascular and parenchymal elements in these tissues, the problem of cell loss in the brain relating to either amyloid or lipofuscin requires particular attention. This is due to the fact that the brain is uniquely characterized by tissue interdependence, organizational complexity, and variable redundancy in sensory-inter and motor neuronal networks, all of which may be differentially vulnerable through modification of the cellular environment by substances such as lipofuscin or amyloid.

REFERENCES

Alexandrowskaja, M. M. (1966): Altersbesonderheiten des gehirns und damit verbundene erkrankungen. Proceedings of the Seventh International Congress of Gerontology, Vol. 3, pp. 39–41.

Altschul, R. (1938): Über das sogenannte "alterspigment" der Nervenzellen. *Virchows Arch. Pathol. Anat.*, 301:273–286.

Alzheimer, A. (1907): Uber eine eigenartige erkrankung der hirnrinde. *Zentralbl. Nerv. Psychol.*, 30:177–179.

Artiukhina, N. I. (1968): Electron microscope study of the intracellular pigment in the rat brain cortex. *J. Cytol. Acad. Sci. USSR*, 10:26–35.

Benditt, E. P., and Eriksen, N. (1973): The chemical classes of amyloid substance in men, monkeys and ducks. *Protides Biol. Fluids*, 20:81–85.

Bergener, M., and Gerhard, L. (1966): Altersgebundene Veränderungen an pigmentieren Nervenzellen des Gehirns unter besonderer Berücksichtigung der submikroskopischen Morphologie. Proceedings of the Seventh International Congress of Gerontology, Vol. 3, pp. 42–53. Weiner Medizinische Akademie, Vienna.

Bielschowsky, M. (1911): Zur Kenntnis der Alzheimerschen Krankheit (präesemlen Demenz mit Herdsymptomen). *J. Psychol. Neurol.*, 18:273–292.

Bjorkerud, S. (1964): Studies on lipofuscin granules of human cardiac muscle. II. Chemical analysis of the isolated granules. *Exp. Mol. Pathol.*, 3:377–389.

Bladen, H. A., Nylen, M. U., and Glenner, G. G. (1966): The ultrastructure of human amyloid as revealed by the negative staining technique. *J. Ultrastruct. Res.*, 14:449–459.

Blocq, P., and Marinesco, G. (1892): Sur les lésions et la pathogénie de l'epilepsie dite essentialle. *Semin. Med.*, 12:445–446.

Bloom, W., and Fawcett, D. W. (1962): *Textbook of Histology* (8th ed.), p. 216. W. B. Saunders Co., Philadelphia.

Bondareff, W. (1957): Genesis of intracellular pigment in the spinal ganglia of senile rats. An electron microscope study. *J. Gerontol.*, 12:364–369.

Borst, M., editor (1922): *Pathologische Histologie*. Vogel, Leipzig.

Braak, H. (1971): Über das Neurolipofuscin in der unteren Olive und dem Nucleus dentatus cerebelli im Gehirm des Menschen. *Z. Zellforsch. Mikrosk. Anat.*, 121:573–592.

Braunmühl, A. von (1932): Kolloidchemische Betrachtungsweise seniler und präseniler Gewebsveränderungen. Das hysteretische Syndrom als cerebrale Reaktionsform. *Z. Neurol. Psychiat.*, 142:1–54.

Braunmühl, A. von (1957): Alterserkrankungen des Zentralnervensystems. Senile Involution. Senile Demenz. Alzheimersche Krankheit. In: *Hanbuch der Speziellen Pathologischen Anatomie und Histologie, Vol. 13* (Pt. 1, Sect. A: Erkrankungen des zentralen Nervensystems), edited by O. Lubarsch, F. Henke, and R. Rössle, pp. 335–539. Springer-Verlag, Berlin.

Brizzee, K. R., Cancilla, P. A., Sherwood, N., and Timiras, P. S. (1969): The amount of distribution of pigments in neurons and glia of the cerebral cortex. *J. Gerontol.*, 24:127–135.

Brizzee, K. R., and Johnson, F. A. (1970): Depth distribution of lipofuscin pigment in cerebral cortex of rat. *Acta Neuropathol.*, 16:205–219.

Brizzee, K. R., Ordy, J. M., and Kaack, B. (1974): Early appearance and regional differences in intraneuronal and extraneuronal lipofuscin accumulation with age in the brain of a nonhuman primate (*Macaca mulatta*). *J. Gerontol.*, 29:366–381.

Brody, H. (1960): The deposition of aging pigment in the human cerebral cortex. *J. Gerontol.*, 15:258–261.

Buttlar-Brentano, K. von (1954): Zur Ledensgeschicte des Nucleus basalis, tuberomannilaris, supraopticus and paraventricularis unter normalen und pathogen Bedingungen. *J. Hirnforsch.*, 1:337–419.

Chemnitius, K.-H. von, Machnik, G., Low, O., Arnrich, M., and Urban, J. (1970): Versuche zur medikamentösen Beeinflussung altersbedingter Veränderungen. *Exp. Pathol.*, 4:163–167.

Chu, L. (1954): A cytological study of anterior horn cells isolated from human spinal cord. *J. Comp. Neurol.*, 100:381–413.

Corten, M. H., and Ostertag, B. (1930): Ueber die senilen Drusen und ihre Beziehungen zum Hyalin und Amyloid. *Verh. Dtsch. Ges. Pathol.*, 25:175–180.

Dalton, A. J. (1957): Mitochondria and other cytoplasmic inclusion. *Symp. Soc. Exp. Biol.*, 10:148.

Dalton, A. J., and Felix, M. D. (1956): A comparative study of the Golgi complex. *J. Biophys. Biochem. Cytol.*, 2:79–84.

Dayan, A. D. (1970): Quantitative histological studies on the aged human brain. I. Senile plaques and neurofibrillary tangles in "normal" patients. *Acta Neuropathol.*, 16:85–94.

Dayan, A. D. (1971): Comparative neuropathology of ageing. Studies on the brains of 47 species of vertebrates. *Brain,* 94:31–42.

DeNavasquez, S., and Treble, H. A. (1938): A case of primary generalized amyloid disease with involvement of the nerves. *Brain,* 61:116–128.

Divry, P. (1942): Del'amyloidose vasculaire cerebrale et meningee (meningopathie amyloide) dans la demence senile. *J. Belge Neurol. Psychiat.,* 42:141–158.

Divry, P. (1952): La pathochimie générale et cellulaire des processus séniles et préséniles. Proceedings of the First International Congress of Neuropathology, Vol. 2, pp. 312–345.

Dolley, D. H., and Guthrie, F. V. (1918): The pigmentation of nerve cells. *J. Med. Res.,* 34:123–142.

Duncan, D., Nall, D., and Morales, R. (1960): Observations on the fine structure of old age pigment. *J. Gerontol.,* 15:366–372.

Einarson, L., and Telford, I. R. (1960): Effect of vitamin-E deficiency on the central nervous system in various laboratory animals. *Biol. Skr. Dan. Vid. Selsk.,* 11:1–81.

Essner, E., and Novikoff, A. B. (1960): Human hepatocellular pigments and liposomes. *J. Ultrustruct. Res.,* 3:374–391.

Feldman, M. L. (1974): Degenerative changes in aging dendrites. *Gerontologist,* 14:36.

Few, A., and Getty, R. (1967): Occurrence of lipofuscin as related to aging in the canine and porcine nervous system. *J. Gerontol.,* 22:357–368.

Fisher, H., and Preuss, F. S. (1951): Primary systemic amyloidosis with involvement of the nervous system. *Am. J. Clin. Pathol.,* 21:758–763.

Friede, R. L. (1962): The relation of formation of lipofuscin to the distribution of oxidative enzymes in the human brain. *Acta Neuropathol.,* 2:113–125.

Friedreich, N., and Kekule, A. (1859): Zur amyloidfrage. *Arch. Pathol. Anat.,* 16:50–65.

Gatenby, J. B. (1951): The neurone of the human autonomic system and the so-called senility pigment. *J. Physiol. (Lond.),* 114:252–254.

Gatenby, J. B., and Moussa, T. A. A. (1950): The sympathetic ganglion cell, with Sudan black and the Zernicke microscope. *J. Roy. Microsc. Soc.,* 70:342–364.

Gellerstedt, N. (1938): Die elektive, insulaere (Para) Amyloidose der Banch-speicheldruese. Zugleich ein Betrag zur Kenntnis der "senilen Amyloidose." *Beitr. Pathol. Anat.,* 101:1–13.

Ghosh, A., Bern, H. A., Ghosh, J., and Nishioka, R. S. (1962): Nature of inclusions in the lumbosacral neurons of birds. *Anat. Rec.,* 143:195–218.

Glenner, G. G., and Terry, W. D. (1974): Characterization of amyloid. *Annu. Rev. Med.,* 25:131–135.

Glenner, G. G., Terry, W., Harada, M., Iserky, C., and Page, D. (1971): Amyloid fibril proteins: Proof of homology with immunoglobulin light chains by sequence analyses. *Science,* 172:1150–1151.

Goldfischer, S., Villaverde, H., and Forschirm, R. (1966): The demonstration of acid hydrolase, thermostable reduced diphosphopyridine nucleotide tetrazolium reductase and peroxidase activities in human lipofuscin pigment granules. *J. Histochem. Cytochem.,* 14:641–652.

Gonatas, N. K. Korey, S., and Terry, P. D. (1964): A case of juvenile lipoidosis. Electron microscopic and biochemical observations of a cerebral biopsy. *J. Neuropathol. Exp. Neurol.,* 23:185–187.

Gopinath, G., and Glees, P. (1974): Mitochondrial genesis of lipofuscin in the mesencephalic nucleus of the V nerve of aged rats. *Acta Anat.,* 89:14–20.

Haltia, M., Rapola, J., and Santavuori, P. (1973): Infantile type of so-called neuronal ceroid-lipofuscinosis. *Acta Neuropathol.,* 26:157–170.

Hannover, A. (1842): Mikroskopiske Undersögelser af Nervesystemet. In: *Danske Videnskabernes Selskab, Copenhagen. 2. Naturvidenskapsselsk. Og Mathe. Matisk. Afdeling.,* Ser. 4, Vol. 10., pp. 1–112.

Hasan, M., and Glees, P. (1972): Genesis and possible dissolution of neuronal lipofuscin. *Gerontologia,* 18:217–236.

Heidenreich, O., and Siebert, G. (1955): Untersuchungen an isoliertem lipofuscin. *Virchows Arch. Pathol. Anat.,* 327:112–126.

Hendley, D., Mildvan, A., Reporter, M., and Strehler, B. (1963): The properties of isolated human cardiac age pigment. II. Chemical and enzymatic properties. *J. Gerontol.,* 18:250–259.

Hess, A. (1955): The fine structure of young and old spinal ganglia. *Anat. Rec.,* 123:399–423.

Hirano, A., and Zimmerman, H. M. (1962): Alzheimer's neurofibrillary changes. A topographic study. *Arch. Neurol.,* 7:227–242.

Hirsch, H. E. (1970): Enzymic levels of individual neurons in relation to lipofuscin content. *J. Histochem. Cytochem.,* 18:268–270.

Hobbs, J. R. (1973): An ABC of amyloid. *Proc. R. Soc. Med.,* 66:705–710.

Hodge, C. F. (1894): Changes in ganglion cells from birth to senile death. Observations on man and honey-bee. *J. Physiol. (Lond.),* 17:129–134.

Humphrey, T. (1944): Primitive neurons in the embryonic human central nervous system. *J. Comp. Neurol.,* 81:1–45.

Hyden, H., and Lindström, B. (1950): Microspectrographic studies on the yellow pigment in nerve cells. *Farady Soc. Discuss.,* 9:436–441.

Isersky, C., Ein, D., Page, D. L., Harada, M., and Glenner, G. G. (1972): Immunochemical cross-reactions of human amyloid proteins with immunoglobulin light polypeptide chains. *J. Immunol.,* 108:486.

Issidorides, M., and Shanklin, W. (1961): Histochemical reactions of cellular inclusions in the human neurone. *J. Anat.,* 95:151–159.

Karnaukhov, V. N. (1973): The role of carotenoids in the formation of lipofuscin and the adaptation of animal cells to oxygen insufficiency. *Tsitologiia,* 15:538–542.

Karnaukhov, V. N., Tataryunas, T. B., and Petrunyaka, V. V. (1973): Accumulation of carotenoids in brain and heart of animals of aging: The role of carotenoids in lipofuscin formation. *Mech. Ageing Dev.,* 2:201–210.

Kerenyi, T., Haranghy, L., and Hüttner, I. (1968): Investigations on experimentally produced age-pigment in the nervous system. *Exp. Gerontol.,* 3:155–158.

Kernohan, J. W., and Woltman, H. W. (1942): Amyloid neuritis. *Arch. Neurol. Psychiatry,* 47:132–140.

Kidd, M. (1964): Alzheimer's disease—An electron microscope study. *Brain,* 87:307–364.

Kimura, S., Guyer, R., Terry, W. D., and Glenner, G. G. (1972): Chemical evidence for lambdatype amyloid proteins. *J. Immunol.,* 109:891.

Koenig, H. (1962): Histochemical distributions of brain gangliosides. Lysosomes as glycolipoprotein granules. *Nature (Lond.),* 195:782–784.

Koneff, H. (1886): Beiträge zur Kentniss der Nervenzellen in den peripheren Ganglien. *Mitt. Naturforsch. Ges. Bern.,* 44:13–44.

Kormendy, C. G., and Bender, A. D. (1971): Chemical interference with aging. *Gerontolgia,* 17:52–64.

Kornfeld, M. (1972): Generalized lipofuscinosis. (Generalized Kufs' Disease). *J. Neuropathol. Exp. Neurol.,* 31:668–682.

Kraepelin, E. (1910): Psychiatrie. *Leipzig,* 2:624. Cited in: McMenemey, W. H. (1963): Alzheimer's disease: Problems concerning its concept and nature. *Acta Neurol. Scand.,* 39:369.

Krigman, M. R., Feldman, R. G., and Bensch, K. (1965): Alzheimer's presenile dementia. A histochemical and electron microscopic study. *Lab. Invest.,* 14:381–396.

Kristensson, K., and Sourander, P. (1966): Occurrence of lipofuscin in inherited metabolic disorders affecting the nervous system. *J. Neurol. Neurosurg. Psychiatry,* 29:113–118.

Lampert, P. (1968): Amyloid and amyloid-like deposits. In: *Pathology of the Nervous System, Vol. 1,* edited by J. Minckler, pp. 1113–1121. McGraw-Hill, New York.

Lampert, P., Blumberg, J. M., and Pentschew, A. (1964): An electron microscopic study of dystrophic axons in the gracile and cuneate nuclei of vitamin E deficient rats. *J. Neuropathol. Exp. Neurol.,* 23:60–77.

Lillie, R. D., Daft, F. S., and Sebrell, W. H. (1941): Cirrhosis of the liver in rats on a deficient diet and the effects of alcohol. *Public Health Rep. (Wash.),* 56:1255.

Luse, S., and Smith, K. R. (1964): The ultrastructure of senile plaques. *Am. J. Pathol.,* 44:553–563.

Matsuyama, H., Namiki, H., and Watanabe, I. (1966): Senile changes in the brain in the Japanese. Incidence of Alzheimer's neurofibrillary change and senile plaques. In: *Fifth International Congress of Neuropathology Proceedings,* edited by F. Luthy and A. Bischoff, pp. 979–980. Excerpta Medica Foundation, Amsterdam.

McMenemey, W. H. (1963): The dementias and progressive diseases of the basal ganglia. In: *Greenfield's Neuropathology,* edited by W. Blackwood, W. H. McMenemey, A. Meyer, R. M. Norman, and D. S. Russell, pp. 525–546. Williams and Wilkins, Baltimore, Md.

Meier, C., and Glees, P. (1971): Der Einfluss des Centrophenoxins auf das alterspigment in Sattellitenzellen und Neuronen der Spinalganglien seniler Ratten. *Acta Neuropathol.,* 17:310–320.

Miquel, J. (1971): Aging of male *Drosophila melanogaster.* Histological, histochemical and ultrastructural observations. *Adv. Gerontol. Res.,* 3:39–70.

Miyagishi, T., Takahata, N., and Iizuka, R. (1967): Electron microscopic studies on the lipopigments in the cerebral cortex nerve cells of senile and vitamin E deficient rats. *Acta Neuropathol.,* 9:7–17.

Morel, F., and Wildi, E. (1952): General and cellular pathochemistry of senile and presenile alterations of the brain. Proceedings of the First International Congress of Neuropathology, Vol. 2, pp. 347–374.

Nanda, B. S., and Getty, R. (1971): Lipofuscin pigment in the nervous system of aging pig. *Exp. Gerontol.,* 6:447–452.

Nandy, K. (1968): Further studies on the effects of centrophenoxine on the lipofuscin pigment in the neurons of senile guinea pigs. *J. Gerontol.,* 23:82–92.

Nandy, K. (1971): Properties of neuronal lipofuscin pigment in mice. *Acta Neuropathol.,* 19:25–32.

Nandy, K., and Bourne, G. H. (1966): Effect of centrophenoxine on the lipofuscin pigments in the neurons of senile guinea pigs. *Nature (Lond.),* 210:313–314.

Novikoff, A. B. (1967): Lysosomes in nerve cells. In: *The Neuron,* edited by H. Hyden, pp. 319–377. Elsevier, Amsterdam.

Obersteiner, H. (1903): Über das hellgelbe Pigment in den Nervenzellen und das Vorkommen weiterer fettähnlicher Körper im Centralnervensystem. *Arb. Neurol. Inst. Wien Univ.,* 10:245–274.

Pallis, C. A., Duckett, S., and Pearse, A. G. E. (1967): Diffuse lipofuscinosis of the central nervous system. *Neurology (Minneap.),* 17:381–394.

Pantelakis, S. (1954): Un type particulier d'angiopathie senile du systeme nerveux central: L'angiopathie congophile; topographie et frequence. *Moschr. Psychiat. Neurol.,* 128:219.

Payne, F. (1952). Cytological changes in the cells of pituitary, thyroids, adrenals and sex glands of ageing fowl. In: *Problems of Ageing* (3rd ed.), edited by A. I. Lansing, pp. 381–402. Williams and Wilkins, Baltimore.

Perusini, G. (1910): Ueber klinische und histologisch eigenartige psychische Erkrankungen des spateren Lebensalters. *Histol. Histopathol. Arb. Grosshirnrinde,* 3:297–358.

Pilgrim, C. (1964): Altersbedingte anhaufung von lysosomen residualkorpern in neurosekretorischen zellfortsatzen. *Z. Zellforsch. Mikrosk. Anat.,* 109:573–582.

Ranson, S. W., and Clark, S. L. (1959): *The Anatomy of the Nervous System* (10th ed.), p. 622. W. B. Saunders Co., Philadelphia.

Reichel, W., and Garcia-Bunuel, R. (1970): Pathologic findings in progeria: Myocardial fibrosis and lipofuscin pigment. *Am. J. Clin. Pathol.,* 53:243–253.

Reichel, W., Hollander, J., Clark, J. H., and Strehler, B. L. (1968): Lipofuscin pigment accumulation as a function of age and distribution in the rodent brain. *J. Gerontol.,* 23:71–78.

Riese, W. (1946): The cerebral cortex in the very old human brain. *J. Neuropathol. Exp. Neurol.,* 5:160–164.

Riga, S., and Riga, D. (1974): Effects of centrophenoxine on the lipofuscin pigments in the nervous system of old rats. *Brain Res.,* 72:265–275.

Roizin, L. (1964): Some basic principles of "molecular pathology." 3. Ultrastructural organelles as structural metabolic and pathogenetic gradients. *J. Neuropathol. Exp. Neurol.,* 23:209–252.

Samorajski, T., Keefe, J. R., and Ordy, J. M. (1964): Intracellular localization of lipofuscin age pigments in the nervous system. *J. Gerontol.,* 19:262–276.

Samorajski, T., Ordy, J. M., and Keefe, J. R. (1965): The fine structure of lipofuscin age pigment in the nervous system of aged mice. *J. Cell Biol.,* 26:779–795.

Samorajski, T., Ordy, J. M., and Rady-Reimer, P. (1968): Lipofuscin pigment accumulation in the nervous system of aging mice. *Anat. Rec.,* 160:555–574.

Sandritter, W., Bierfreund, B., Parmen, F., and Adler, C. P. (1972): Lipofuscin in cardiac hypertrophy. *Beitr. Pathol.,* 147:280–292.

Schäfer, A. E. (1893): The nerve cell considered as the basis of neurology. *Brain,* 16:134–169.

Scholz, W. (1938): Studien zur Pathologie der Hirngefässe. II. Die drusige Entartung der

Hirnarterien und Kapillaren (eine Form seniler Gefässerkrankung). *Z. Ges. Neurol. Psychiat.*, 162:693.

Schwartz, P. (1968): New patho-anatomic observations on amyloidosis in the aged. Fluorescence microscopic investigations. In: *Amyloidosis*, edited by E. Mandema, L. Ruinen, F. H. Sholten, and A. S. Cohen, pp. 400–415. Excerpta Medica Foundation, Amsterdam.

Schwartz, P., Kurucz, J., and Kurucz, A. (1965): Fluorescence microscopy demonstration of cerebrovascular and pancreatic insular amyloid in presenile and senile states. *J. Am. Geriatr. Soc.*, 13:718–722.

Sekhon, S. S., Andrew, J. M., and Maxwell, D. S. (1969): Accumulation and development of lipofuscin pigment in the aging central nervous system of the mouse. *J. Cell Biol.*, 43:127A.

Shirahama, T., and Cohen, A. S. (1967): High resolution electron microscopy of amyloid. *J. Cell Biol.*, 33:679–708.

Siakotos, A. N., Pennington, K., and McInnes, A. (1971): New loading system for preparing density gradients for swinging-bucket rotors using programmed gradient pumps. *Anal. Biochem.*, 43:32–41.

Siakotos, A. N., Watanabe, I., Pennington, K., and Whitfield, M. (1973): Procedures for the mass isolation of pure lipofuscins from normal human heart and liver. *Biochem. Med.*, 7:25–38.

Siakotos, A. N., Watanabe, I., Saito, A., and Fleischer, S. (1970): Procedures for the isolation of two distinct lipopigments from human brain: Lipofuscin and ceroid. *Biochem. Med.*, 4:361–375.

Simchowicz, T. (1911): Histologische Studien uber die senile Demenz. *Histol. Histopathol. Arb. Grosshirnrinde*, 4:267–244.

Singh, R. (1969): Some points of consideration about metabolic and physiologic aspects of neuronal age pigment-lipofuscin. *Indian J. Gerontol.*, 1:99–103.

Singh, R., and Mukherjee, B. (1972): Some observations on the lipofuscin of the avian brain with a review of some rarely considered findings concerning the metabolic and physiologic significance of lipofuscin. *Acta Anat.*, 83:302–320.

Srebro, Z., and Scislawski, A. (1966): Fuscin pigment in the brain of frogs. *Folia Biol. (Krakow)*, 14:265–272.

Strehler, B. L. (1964): On the histochemistry and ultrastructure of age pigment. In: *Advances in Gerontological Research, Vol. 1*, edited by B. L. Strehler, pp. 343–384. Academic Press, New York.

Sulkin, N. M., and Srivanij, P. (1960): The experimental production of senile pigment in nerve cells of young rats. *J. Gerontol.*, 15:1–9.

Sullivan, J. F., Twitschell, T. E., Gherardi, G. J., and van der Laan, W. P. (1955): Amyloid polyneuropathy. *Neurology (Minneap.)*, 5:847–865.

Takahashi, A., Philpott, D. E., and Miquel, J. (1970): Electron microscope studies on aging *Drosophila melanogaster*. I. Dense bodies. *J. Gerontol.*, 25:210–217.

Tellez-Nagel, I., and Wisniewski, H. M. (1973): Ultrastructure of neurofibrillary tangles in Steele-Richardson-Olszewski syndrome. *Arch. Neurol.*, 29:324–327.

Terry, R. D., Gonatas, N. K., and Weiss, M. (1964): Ultrastructural studies in Alzheimer's presenile dementia. *Am. J. Pathol.*, 44:269–297.

Terry, R. D., and Wisniewski, H. (1970): The ultrastructure of the neurofibrillary tangle and the senile plaque. In: *Ciba Foundation Symposium on Alzheimer's Disease and Related Conditions*, edited by G. E. W. Wolstenholm and M. O'Connor, pp. 145–168. J. and A. Churchill, London.

Terry, W., Page, D. L., and Kimura, S. (1973): Structural identity of Bence Jones and amyloid fibril proteins in a patient with plasma cell dyscrasia and amyloidosis. *J. Clin. Invest.*, 52:1276–1281.

Tomlinson, B. E., Blessed, G., and Roth, M. (1968): Observations on the brain of non-demented old people. *J. Neurol. Sci.*, 7:331–356.

Varkonyi, T., Domokos, H., Maurer, M., Zoltan, O. T., Csillik, B., and Földi, M. (1970): Die Wirkung von D,L-Kavain und Magnesium-Orotat auf die feinstrukturellen neuropathologischen Veränderungen der experimentellen lymphogenen Enzephalopathie. II. Mitteilung. *Z. Gerontol.*, 3:254–260.

Virchow, R. (1855): Uber den Gang der amyloiden degeneration. *Virchows Arch. Pathol. Anat.*, 8:364–368.

Virchow, R. (1857): Neue Beobachtu gen über amyloide degeneration. *Virchows Arch. Pathol. Anat.,* 11:188–189.

Vogt, C., and Vogt, O. (1946): Aging of nerve cell. *Nature (Lond.),* 158:304.

Walford, R. L., and Sjaarda, J. R. (1964): Increase in thioflavine-T-staining material (amyloid) in human tissues with age. *J. Gerontol.,* 19:57–61.

Whiteford, R., and Getty, R. (1966): Distribution of lipofuscin in the canine and porcine brain as related to aging. *J. Gerontol.,* 21:31–44.

Wilcox, H. H. (1959): Structural changes in the nervous system related to the process of aging. In: *The Process of Aging in the Nervous System,* edited by J. E. Birren, H. A. Imus, and W. F. Windle, pp. 16–39. Charles C Thomas, Springfield, Illinois.

Wisniewski, H. M., Ghetti, B., and Terry, R. D. (1973): Neuritic (senile) plaques and filamentous changes in aged rhesus monkeys. *J. Neuropathol. Exp. Neurol.,* 32:566–584.

Wisniewski, H. M., and Terry, R. D. (1970): An experimental approach to the morphogenesis of neurofibrillary degeneration and the argyrophilic plaque. In: *Ciba Foundation Symposium on Alzheimer's Disease and Related Conditions,* edited by G. E. W. Wolstenholme and M. O'Conner, pp. 223–248. J. and A. Churchill, London.

Wisniewski, H. M., and Terry, R. D. (1973a): Reexamination of the pathogenesis of the senile plaque. In: *Progress in Neuropathology, Vol. 2,* edited by H. M. Zimmerman, pp. 1–26. Grune and Stratton, New York.

Wisniewski, H. M., and Terry, R. D. (1973b): Morphology of the aging brain, human and animal. In: *Progress in Brain Research, Vol. 40: Neurobiological Aspects of Maturation and Aging,* edited by D. H. Ford, pp. 167–186. Elsevier, Amsterdam.

Wisniewski, H. M., and Terry, R. D. (1973c): Reexamination of the pathogenesis of the senile plaque. In: *Progress in Neuropathology, Vol. 2,* edited by H. M. Zimmerman, pp. 1–26. Grune and Stratton, New York.

Wisniewski, H., Terry, R. D., and Hirano, A. (1970): Neurofibrillary pathology. *J. Neuropathol. Exp. Neurol.,* 29:163–176.

Wolf, A., and Pappenheimer, A. M. (1945): Occurrence and distribution of acid-fast pigment in the central nervous system. *J. Neuropathol.,* 4:402–406.

Wright, J. R., Calkins, E., Breen, W. J., Stolte, G., and Schultz, R. T. (1969): Relationship of amyloid to aging. Review of the literature and systematic study of 83 patients derived from a general hospital population. *Medicine,* 48:39–60.

Zeman, W. (1974): Studies in the neuronal ceroid-lipofuscinoses. *J. Neuropathol. Exp. Neurol.,* 33:1–12.

Zeman, W., and Dyken, P. (1969): Neuronal ceroid-lipofuscinosis (Batten's disease): Relationship to amaurotic family idiocy? *Pediatrics,* 44:570–583.

Aging. Volume 1, edited by H. Brody,
D. Harman, and J. M. Ordy. Raven
Press, New York © 1975.

The Histochemical Relationships and the Nature of Neuromelanin

Herbert Barden

Department of Neurotoxicology, New York State Psychiatric Institute, New York, New York 10032

Progress toward elucidating the nature of neuromelanin has produced few areas of investigation in which the accumulated information has been thoroughly enough detailed for the making of definitive judgments. Fortunately, and essentially, from the viewpoint of the theme of these chapters, aging in the central nervous system, adequate information and a unanimity of opinion exists that establishes that neuromelanin accumulation is an age-correlated process. Beyond this limited area of agreement, one encounters inconclusive or contradictory evidence pertaining to neuromelanin in relation to several broad categories of interest including its functional and structural identity, chemical composition, biogenesis, and evolutionary significance. Nevertheless, despite these unresolved matters, the existing evidence now seems sufficient enough to permit an evaluation and generalized description of this intraneuronal pigment.

ONTOGENETIC CHANGES IN NEUROMELANIN CONTENT

Individual neuromelanin granules in neurons of pigmented nuclei in humans and other neuromelanin-bearing mammalian species are smallest in size (Adler, 1939; Moses, Ganote, Beaver, and Schuffman, 1966; Barden, 1970) and least in amount (Mann and Yates, 1974) at the youngest age of detection. An age-correlated increase in the size of individual neuromelanin granules of humans has been demonstrated in the substantia nigra and locus ceruleus by an electron microscopic comparison of the granules in young and old individuals (Moses et al., 1966). Other studies in humans have revealed that, on the average, neuromelanin appears slightly earlier in the locus ceruleus than in the substantia nigra, although these findings are in dispute (Fenichel and Bazelon, 1968). Neuromelanin pigmentation in the locus ceruleus has been stated to occur variously, at 5 months gestation (Foley and Baxter, 1958), at birth (Mann and Yates, 1974), and postnatally at about 1 year of age (Pilcz, 1895; Calligaris, 1908; Fenichel and Bazelon, 1968). Neuromelanin in the substantia nigra has been reported to occur during gestation at midterm (Cooper, 1946), and postnatally at 5 weeks (Fenichel and Bazelon, 1968), 18 months (Foley and Baxter, 1958; Mann

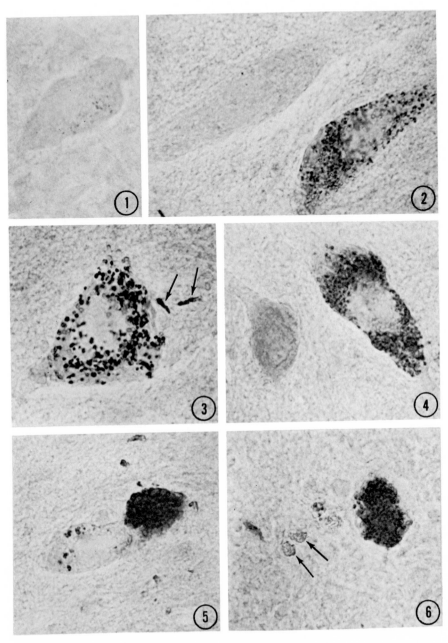

FIGS. 1–6. The cupric ion uptake reaction for neuromelanin in 10 μm, formol-calcium, postfixed cryostat sections of rhesus monkey (*Macaca mulatta*) substantia nigra visualizes the pigment with DMABR. ×1079. Age of aging monkey in Figs. 2–6 was estimated partly by weight and partly by the presence of well-worn and missing teeth, in addition to a ruddy and scaly facial skin.

FIG. 1. Section from the brain of an immature, recently weaned 3.5-lb rhesus monkey. Neuromelanin granules in the perikaryon are small, sparce, and lightly tinted.

FIG. 2. These neurons from an aging 22-lb rhesus monkey demonstrate wide variation in their neuromelanin content with the neuron above manifesting one or possibly two clearly defined, small neuromelanin granules and with the neuron below manifesting numerous, large granules that occupy most of its perikaryon.

FIG. 3. This neuron from an aging 22-lb rhesus monkey manifests numerous, scattered, large neuromelanin granules in its perikaryon. Two, elongated masses of neuromelanin (*arrows*) are situated in the neural parenchyma.

FIG. 4. Two neurons from an aging 22-lb rhesus monkey. The neuron on the right contains numerous, closely aggregated neuromelanin granules that occupy nearly its entire perikaryon. The neuron on the left is filled with lipofuscin, which is only vaguely stained by the cupric ion uptake reaction.

FIG. 5. This unusually formed bipolar neuron from an aging 22-lb rhesus monkey is apparently in the process of degeneration with only a few large neuromelanin granules toward one pole and a large aggregate of granules seen swelling the opposite pole. Several individually situated neuromelanin granules are scattered in the nearby neural parenchyma.

FIG. 6. In this section from an aging 22-lb rhesus monkey, a large mass of neuromelanin seems to lie free in the neural parenchyma in which two unstained ferric iron-containing granules (*arrows*) are also seen.

and Yates, 1974), 2 years (Calligaris, 1908), 3 years (Pilcz, 1895), and 4
years of age (Adler, 1939; Nieto, Nieto, and Briones, 1967). The pigment
was observed by Fenichel and Bazelon (1968) in the dorsal motor nucleus
of the vagus in a fetus of 34 weeks gestation and, in other individuals, from
birth onwards. These authors included 44 deceased children ranging in age
from the one just noted at 34 weeks gestation to a maximum of 16 years of
age; these individuals having been grouped into four consecutive chronological age categories in which neuromelanin pigmentation in the substantia
nigra, locus ceruleus, and dorsal motor nulceus of the vagus was semi-
quantitatively estimated. When Fenichel and Bazelon (1968) utilized as their
criterion for the presence of pigmentation, at the very least, the mere detection of neuromelanin, an increasing proportion of pigmented nuclei was
recorded in each of the three neuroanatomic nuclei with each advance in
age. Mann and Yates (1974) more thoroughly quantitated the proportion
of pigmented neurons in the substantia nigra and locus ceruleus and found
that the proportion continued to increase in linear progression up to 60
years of age after which time they observed a decline in the proportion of
neurons containing neuromelanin. Mann and Yates suggested that the decline of neuromelanin-bearing neurons may have been due to the atrophy
and loss of those neurons that were most highly pigmented. In several less
detailed studies, increasing neuromelanin pigmentation correlated with
increasing age was shown to occur in the substantia nigra of the chimpanzee,
orangutan (Scherer, 1939), and rhesus monkey (*Macaca mulatta*) (Barden,
1970) (Figs. 1 to 6), and in both the substantia nigra (Brown, 1943) and
hypothalamus (Gutner, 1954; Barden and Barrett, 1973) of dog.

Although differences in the time of detection of neuromelanin may have
been due to the limitation of the age range of the particular sample and to
natural variation, they may also have been due to differences in the specificity and interpretation of the staining methods utilized. Both Foley and
Baxter (1958) and Nieto et al. (1967) were critical of Cooper (1946) who
may have mistaken Nissl-stained structures in fetal substantia nigra cells
for neuromelanin granules. The Nissl and silver stains utilized by Foley
and Baxter (1958) to demonstrate neuromelanin granules in their fetal
material were then questioned by Fenichel and Bazelon (1968) as having
the capability to demonstrate those granules adequately. There seems little
reason to doubt, however, that neuromelanin was correctly identified in the
more recent reports in which the diamine silver (Fenichel and Bazelon,
1968) and Schmorl (Mann and Yates, 1974) methods were utilized. Sensitive staining methods that distinguish neuromelanin from lipofuscin have
not been available until recently (Lillie, 1957a; Barden, 1969), and their
utilization would be especially helpful for the detection and identification of
neuromelanin at the time of its appearance when the intraneuronal pigment
granules are smallest in size and least in number. The cupric ion uptake
method for the demonstration of neuromelanin can be undertaken with
little difficulty according to the following procedure.

CUPRIC ION UPTAKE METHOD FOR THE DEMONSTRATION OF NEUROMELANIN (BARDEN, 1969)

Deparaffinized sections cut from blocks fixed in Formalin, acetone, alcohol, etc., or similarly fixed, perfused, frozen, or cryostat sections can be utilized:

1. Immerse sections in 0.09 M $CuSO_4$ (3.6 g/250 ml H_2O) for 1 hr at room temperature.
2. Rinse sections in five changes of distilled water, 4 min each change.
3. Stain paraffin sections with rubeanic acid and stain frozen or cryostat sections with either rubeanic acid or dimethylaminobenzilidine rhodanine (DMABR) according to the following:
   (A) Rubeanic acid (dithio-oxamide) (Uzman, 1956)
      (a) Dissolve 100 mg rubeanic acid in 70 ml absolute ethanol prior to raising the volume to 100 ml with water.
      (b) Incubate sections in solution overnight at 37°C.
      (c) Rinse in several changes of water; counterstain with eosin if desired.
      (d) Dehydrate and mount in balsam, histoclad, or other nonaqueous medium.
   (B) DMABR (Howell, 1959)
      (a) Mix 3 ml of a saturated absolute ethanolic solution of DMABR with 100 ml of distilled water.
      (b) Incubate sections in solution overnight at 37°C in a sealed staining dish containing no more than 2 to 3 sections per 50 ml solution.
      (c) Rinse in several changes of water; counterstain with hematoxylin if desired.
      (d) Mount in glycerol jelly.

NEUROMELANOGENESIS AND ENZYME ACTIVITIES

Several enzyme activities that have been proposed as mediators of melanogenesis in neurons are tyrosinase, lysosomal hydrolases, monoamine oxidase, peroxidase, and the peroxidatic activity of catalase.

Tyrosinase

Tyrosinase activity, which historically has received wide acceptance as the biochemical basis for melanin production in skin, pia, eye, and melanoma is separable into two components, a monophenolase which hydroxylates tyrosine to DOPA, and a diphenolase which oxidizes DOPA to DOPA quinone (Fitzpatrick, Miyamoto, and Ishikawa, 1967). Melanin forms when DOPA quinone proceeds through a series of spontaneous and rapid nonenzymatically directed molecular rearrangements. In sections of substantia nigra of adult rhesus monkey and cat containing potential neuromelanin-accumulating neurons, Marsden applied the DOPA reaction, this histochemical procedure being regarded as valid for the demonstration of tyrosinase activity, and observed a melanizing of substantia nigra neurons which he believed to be the combined effect of the monophenolase (Marsden, 1961*b*) and diphenolase (Marsden, 1961*a*) components of tyrosinase activity. In a subsequent study, autoradiographs of labeled L-tyrosine were maximally positive in substantia nigra neurons of kittens 2 months after birth while the earliest appearance of neuromelanin in these neurons was not before 5 postnatal months (Marsden, 1965*a*). Although Marsden regarded the autoradiographs of labeled tyrosine in substantia nigra neurons to represent tyrosinase activity, the 3 month hiatus between maximal tyrosine labeling and the first appearance of neuromelanin was believed to indicate that tyrosinase was principally associated with a metabolic process other than neuromelanogenesis. Other workers, however, were unable to obtain a positive DOPA reaction in substantia nigra neurons (Foley and Baxter, 1958; Lillie, 1965; Sansone, 1967; Barden, 1969). Moreover, in basal epidermal melanocytes characteristically reactive as DOPA reaction positive, Riley (1966) was unable to demonstrate, by histochemical means, those typical monophenolase properties reported by Marsden to be demonstrable in substantia nigra neurons. Autoradiographic results with substantia nigra neurons were interpreted differently by Ishii and Friede (1968) and by Marsden. Ishii and Friede interpreted their autoradiographic images of substantia nigra neurons to be indicative of norepinephrine binding sites while similar images with tyrosine were interpreted by Marsden to be sites of enzyme activity. Nevertheless, the discrepancy between Marsden's observations and those of others may have been more a matter of emphasis in interpretation than an actual difference in results, as Marsden reported but did not stress the potential significance of his additional observation of an absence of specificity in the distribution of DOPA reaction-stained neurons and autoradiographic silver deposition in both the substantia nigra and adjacent midbrain regions in rhesus monkey and cat.

The absence of tyrosinase activity in brain would currently be anticipated, as tyrosine metabolism in brain is now known to proceed by way of the catecholamine pathway toward dopamine production (Hornykiewicz, 1966) through tyrosine hydroxylase (Nagatsu, Levitt, and Udenfriend, 1964) and DOPA decarboxylase (Lovenberg, Weissbach, and Udenfriend, 1962). Côté and Fahn (1969) were able to biochemically reveal the presence of the activities of tyrosine hydroxylase and DOPA decarboxylase as well as the absence of tyrosinase activity in the substantia nigra of adult rhesus monkey. The existence of this catecholamine pathway in brain is emphasized by the condition in human albinism in which there is a genetically determined inhibition or absence of tyrosinase activity and a concomitant reduction of melanin pigment in skin, pia, and eye (Fitzpatrick and Quevedo, 1966) but not in the substantia nigra, which remains normally pigmented (Foley and Baxter, 1958). There is the converse of this in idiopathic Parkinson's disease, in which there is a loss of neuromelanin, particularly from the substantia nigra, but in which a reduction of cutaneous pigmentation does not occur (Parkes, Vollum, Marsden, and Branfoot, 1972).

Lysosomal Hydrolases

In contrast to the absence of tyrosinase activity in neuromelanin-accumulating neurons, several studies have clearly demonstrated an association of lysosomal hydrolase activities with this intraneuronal pigment. Intraneuronal acid phosphatase activity was initially demonstrated by light microscopy to be in close proximity to neuromelanin by use of an azo dye technique incorporating hexazonium pararosanilin and α-naphthol or α-naphthyl phosphates as substrate (Anderson and Song, 1962) and subsequently as a direct stain of neuromelanin granules with a modified Gomori lead-capture method incorporating β-glycerophosphate as substrate and sodium rhodizonate for visualization of the lead phosphate reaction product (Barden, 1969; 1970; 1971a). By light microscopy, nonspecific esterase activity, another of the lysosomal hydrolase activities, was also demonstrated in neuromelanin by use of the above azo dye method but with α-naphthyl acetate as substrate (Barden, 1969; 1971a). Moreover, electron microscopic evidence of acid phosphatase activity in neuromelanin has been presented, but the histochemical method utilized was not specified (Hirosawa, 1968).

Monoamine Oxidase

The possibility of an enzymatic reaction serving as a basis for the formation of neuromelanin was first made evident by Friede (1953) who experimentally darkened neuromelanin-bearing neurons in tissue slices of substantia nigra of human by spraying epinephrine on the surface of the slice. Friede (1953) pointed out that the reaction could not be the effect of tyrosinase activity, as this enzyme lacked the capacity to oxidize epinephrine. That catecholamines might serve as substrates for neuromelanogenesis was also discussed by Fellman (1958). An enzymatic formation of melanin from dopamine was observed biochemically in homogenates of rat brain (Vanderwende and Spoerlein, 1963; Vanderwende, 1964), a species whose brain, nonetheless, does not produce neuromelanin (Hanaway, McConnell, and Netsky, 1970). On the other hand, in the substantia nigra of a neuromelanin-bearing species, the rhesus monkey, Côté (cited in Marsden, 1969) biochemically detected an apparently similar melanin-forming enzyme activity which he identified as monoamine oxidase by use of two selective inhibitors of this enzyme activity, iproniazid and tranylcypromine.

Monoamine oxidase activity in brain of rhesus monkey was estimated by
Côté and Fahn (1969) to have a relatively even distribution, whether or not
the estimation was from a neuromelanin-containing area. The possibility
of a relationship between monoamine oxidase and neuromelanin has been
suggested by the histochemical demonstration of strong staining for monoamine oxidase in the dorsal motor nucleus of the vagus and locus ceruleus
of cat (Friede, 1966) which, if these nuclei are not neuromelanin-bearing
in this species, do contain neuromelanin in some primates. In a very general
manner, the distribution of monoamine oxidase activity in the brain of the
anurans, *Bufo vulgaris japonicus* and *Rana nigromaculata* paralleled, in
part, the distribution of melanin granules in those brains (Kusunoki, Ishibashi, and Masai, 1967). Further discussion of monoamine oxidase activity
and neuromelanogenesis (Hirosawa, 1968) is given in a subsequent section,
Genesis of Neuromelanin.

Peroxidatic Activities

It is known that peroxidase activity is capable of oxidizing DOPA,
5,6-dihydroxyindole, and other catechol derivatives to melanin (Saunders,
Holmes-Seidle, and Stark, 1964; Van Der Ploeg and Van Duijn, 1964*a*,
1964*b;* MacMillan and Brandt, 1966; Marsden, 1966). More recently, it
has been reported that peroxidase activity, rather than tyrosinase activity,
is present in mammalian cells and that this enzyme manifests the capacity
to oxidize tyrosine to DOPA (Patel, Okun, Edelstein, and Epstein, 1971;
Okun, Donnellan, Patel, and Edelstein, 1973). That peroxidase may have
a role in neuromelanogenesis had been suggested by Okun, Donnellan,
Lever, Edelstein, and Or (1971*a*) following their histochemical observation
of a positive benzidine reaction in neurons and intraneuronal organelles
suggestive of lysosomes in guinea pig frontal lobe. These staining results
were interpreted as peroxidase activity but are difficult to evaluate by the
usual histochemical criteria, as the stained neurons were stated to be found
most often in those portions of sections damaged by tears. Similar results
in damaged portions of sections were also observed in this study following
application of the DOPA reaction, the tyrosine-DOPA reaction, and following radioautography of L-tyrosine and DL-DOPA. In order to give added
support to their peroxidase hypothesis, Okun, Patel, Donnellan, Lever,
Edelstein, and Epstein (1971*b*) demonstrated melanogenesis in guinea
pig frontal lobe neurons with a modified DOPA reaction containing tyrosine
supplemented with dihydroxyfumarate as the cofactor, as the latter cannot
itself be oxidized to melanin while serving as a substitute for the melanogenic
cofactor, DOPA, in this melanin-forming reaction. The relevancy of these
studies to neuromelanogenesis seems problematical, nonetheless, as guinea
pig brain does not contain neuromelanin (Marsden, 1961*c*) and frontal
lobe—localized neuromelanin does not occur in any species.

Less problematical and suggestive of a causal relationship to neuromelanin were biochemical determinations of peroxidase activity in human brain that revealed the highest activity level in the substantia nigra and the lowest in the temporal cortex (Van Woert and Ambani, 1974). Detailed examination of Van Woert and Ambani's peroxidase determinations for various brain regions, however, do not strengthen this observation, as wide standard errors of variation demonstrate an overlap between activities in the substantia nigra and pigment-free regions of brain including hypothalamus and vermis. Furthermore, the locus ceruleus, which in human brain contains substantial quantities of neuromelanin (Russell, 1955; Olszewski and Baxter, 1959) and would also be expected to manifest a high level of peroxidase activity if peroxidase were associated with neuromelanogenesis, was found by Van Woert and Ambani (1974) to have statistically significant less peroxidase activity than the pigmented substantia nigra. Barden (1969) could not histochemically detect peroxidase activity in rhesus monkey substantia nigra neuromelanin-bearing neurons, with diamino-benzidine, DOPA, or dopamine as substrates, although peroxidatic activity in neuromelanin was observed as a pseudoperoxidase in which a metal-catalyzed polymerization of diaminobenzidine occurred in the presence of hydrogen peroxide. Subsequently, even pseudoperoxidase activity was considered to be no longer tenable as a postulated neuromelanogenic mechanism as the pseudoperoxidative reaction of neuromelanin was found to have been an effect of the binding of traces of copper when this metallic cation was encountered as a contaminant in the formaldehyde solution serving as fixative (Barden, 1971*a*). In still another instance of questioned validity, peroxidase activity in periventricular glia of adult mice and rats was reported to be present in cystine and/or cystine-rich cytoplasmic granulations on which staining was seen with diaminobenzidine in the presence of hydrogen peroxide (Srebro and Cichocki, 1971). The basis of this doubt rests on the fact that these authors reported no attempt to define the peroxidase activity by use of specific enzyme activity inhibitors (Marsden, 1966; Citkowitz and Holtzman, 1973) or to distinguish between heat-labile peroxidase activity and heat-stabile pseudoperoxidase activity, the latter resulting from the presence of metal (Goldfischer, Villaverde, and Forschirm, 1966; Barden, 1969, 1971*a*). Indeed, in the periventricular area of rat, such metal has already been identified in structures displaying a generally similar appearance and distribution akin to Srebro and Cichocki's (1971) peroxisome-like organelles (Kaneta, 1966).

If peroxidase activity were present in neural elements of brain, and if the enzyme activity and its localization in brain cells were consistent with the activity and its localization in other tissues, one would expect to identify this activity as catalase localized to peroxisomes, to microperoxisomes, or to both (DeDuve, 1973; Novikoff and Novikoff, 1973). Nevertheless, in this context, catalase as peroxidase activity has not been found in brain but rather in the spinal cord and peripheral nervous system histochemically localized to peroxisomes, both in satellite cells encapsulating dorsal root neurons and in Schwann cells of rat (Citkowitz and Holtzman, 1973), in mouse glia, in embryonic chick symathetic ganglia (Holtzman, Teichberg, Abrahams, Citkowitz, Crain, Kawai, and Peterson, 1973), and in guinea pig dorsal root ganglia (Hruban, Vigil, Slesers, and Hopkins, 1972). Biochemical studies by Gaunt (cited in DeDuve, 1973), have shown that D-amino acid oxidase, a universal component of catalase containing peroxisomes, occurs plentifully in rat cerebellum in the near absence of catalase and in the form of particles that sediment by centrifugal fractionation to a very great extent differently from that of the small amount of catalase found to be present. It seems apparent that, as of the present time, our level of knowledge of peroxidase activity in brain is insufficient to attribute to it any function in neuromelanogenesis.

ELECTRON MICROSCOPIC MORPHOLOGY OF NEUROMELANIN GRANULES IN RELATION TO LIPOFUSCIN GRANULES AND LYSOSOMES

In a manner analogous to those earlier light microscopic reports, which presently have undergone reinterpretation but in which it had been originally observed that tyrosinase activity occurred either in association with neuromelanin or in association with substantia nigra neurons prior to the formation of neuromelanin, the earliest electron microscopic study of the structure of neuromelanin granules (D'Agostino and Luse, 1964) found them to be characterized by a linearly arranged or striated substructure which was not seen in lipofuscin but which, as these authors noted in their discussion, was known to be characteristic of melanosomes from skin, hair, and melanoma. These observations were not confirmed by any of several subsequent investigations of neuromelanin ultrastructure reporting a dissimilarity between neuromelanin granules and melanosomes and/or a close similarity between neuromelanin granules and lipofuscin granules. Duffy and Tennyson (1965) observed that human substantia nigra neuromelanin granules manifested a lobulated configuration and a tripartite substructure consisting of protruding vacuolar bodies partially included in a linear or granular matrix on which a very dense particulate material was irregularly distributed. They further observed that lipofuscin granules in human pontine nuclei, in comparison to neuromelanin granules, were lacking the very dense, irregularly distributed particulate material but were otherwise similar and suggested that the neuromelanin granule might be a lipofuscin granule upon which a very dense melanin was deposited. The observations of Duffy and Tennyson (1965) were confirmed by Forno and Alvord (1974) for normal human neuromelanin and extended by Moses et al. (1966) who, in addition to having observed substructural configurations similar to those of Duffy and Tennyson in neuromelanin granules of human and rhesus monkey substantia nigra and locus ceruleus and in lipofuscin granules in human cerebral cortex, also observed that the diamine silver stain for the histochemical demonstration of melanin produced a deposition of reduced silver on the dense, particulate substructural component of the neuromelanin granule. Moses et al. (1966) further demonstrated that the lobular, lipid-like component of neuromelanin and lipofuscin granules was absent from melanin granules in several tissues. Similar ultrastructural observations in the Japanese monkey, *Macaca fuscata yakui,* have been made of substructurally tripartite neuromelanin granules in substantia nigra and locus ceruleus and of substructurally dipartite lipofuscin granules in cerebral cortex (Hirosawa, 1968). A tripartite substructure in substantia nigra neuromelanin granules was also seen in squirrel monkey (*Saimiri sciureus*) (Schwyn, King, and Fox, 1970). Roy and Wolman (1969) may even have further reduced the distinction between neuromelanin and lipofuscin in humans, having reported a tripartite substructure to be present in granules of cerebral cortical lipofuscin as well as in granules of substantia nigra neuromelanin.

The partial similarity in the ultrastructure of neuromelanin and neuronal lipofuscin is paralleled by the localization of lysosomal hydrolase activities in both pigments (Anderson and Song, 1962; Koenig, 1964, 1965; Samorajski, Keefe, and Ordy, 1964; Novikoff, 1967; Barden, 1969, 1970, 1971a; Siakotos and Koppang, 1973). Neuronal lipofuscin granules have also been postulated to form by the gradual transformation of primary lysosomes (Sekhon and Maxwell, 1974) and from autophagic vacuoles believed to incorporate small vesicles containing acid phosphatase activity (Brunk and Ericsson, 1972). As lipofuscin and neuromelanin granules have a closely related ultrastructure and manifest lysosomal hydrolase activities, and as the formation of lipofuscin granules has a lysosomal basis, the inference is clear that the formation of neuromelanin granules also has a lysosomal basis.

REPORTS OF COPPER IN PIGMENTED NUCLEI, AND AN ELECTRON PROBE MICROANALYSIS OF NEUROMELANIN AND LIPOFUSCIN DEMONSTRATING SULFUR-CONTAINING PIGMENTS

An apparent close neuroanatomic association of neuromelanin and copper was thought by investigators of the time (Tingey, 1937; Warren, Earl, and Thompson, 1960) to be suggestive evidence for a biochemical neuromelanogenic mechanism incorporating a tyrosinase-like copper enzyme (Frieden, Osaki, and Kobayashi, 1965), as this seemed to be the logical inference to be drawn from the biochemical determinations of high concentrations of copper in neuromelanin-bearing nuclei. Warren et al. (1960), in their extensive neuroanatomic survey of copper in human brain by use of colorimetric spectrophotometry, found the highest concentration of copper in the locus ceruleus and the second highest concentration in the substantia nigra. These observations were subsequently confirmed by Cumings (1968)

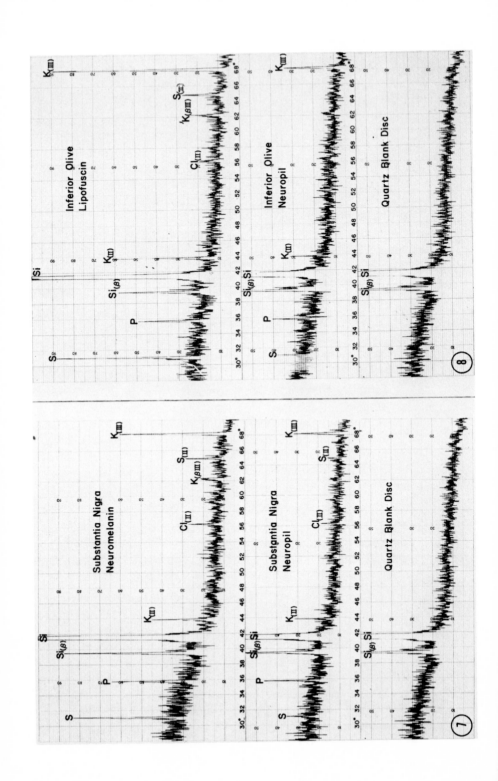

FIG. 7. Qualitative electron probe elemental scan of a single intracellular mass of human substantia nigra neuromelanin, an adjacent area of neural parenchyma (neuropil), and the supporting quartz disk blank. The fixed electron beam was utilized at a 1 μm diameter and the goniometer scanned continuously through two θ angles from 28° to 70°. Neuromelanin, when compared to neural parenchyma, contains a disproportionately high quantity of sulfur, as well as higher quantities of phosphorus, chlorine, and potassium. Peaks of K beta readings are so indicated, while peaks of K alpha readings have their order indicated only by Roman numerals. The quartz-supporting disk registered as silicon should be deleted from the scans of neuromelanin and neuropil. (From Barden and Martin, 1972, by permission of Plenum Press.)

FIG. 8. Qualitative electron probe elemental scan of a single intracellular mass of human inferior olive lipofuscin, an adjacent area of neural parenchyma (neuropil), and the supporting quartz disk blank conducted in the manner described for Fig. 7 and showing somewhat similar features.

whose estimations were made by atomic absorption spectrophotometry. Tingey (1937) chemically estimated the copper concentration to be greatest in human substantia nigra, in the absence of any estimation in the locus ceruleus, while in the pigment-free substantia nigra of ox he found the concentrations to be relatively low and no greater than in other regions of ox brain. Efforts undertaken by histochemical means to demonstrate the localization of copper in relation to neuromelanin in rhesus monkey substantia nigra were mostly unsuccessful, as copper was detected in neuromelanin in only one of six rhesus monkeys (Barden, 1967) and further efforts to detect additional endogenous copper in neuromelanin of rhesus monkey and human by means of histochemical unmasking procedures were entirely unsuccessful (Barden, 1969).

This contrast, between copper concentrations made evident by chemical and physical chemical methods and its near absence as demonstrated by histochemical procedures, served to induce an electron probe microanalysis of neuromelanin, intraneuronal lipofuscin, and associated neuropil in human brain (Barden and Martin, 1972). Our electron probe microanalysis incorporated a Philips AMR-3 Electron Probe Microanalyzer and registered those elements having an atomic number greater than 11, in addition to not having recorded for carbon, nitrogen, and oxygen. Sulfur, phosphorus, chlorine, and potassium were detected in the pigments and associated neuropil. Sulfur concentrations were disproportionately elevated in neuromelanin and some masses of inferior olive lipofuscin when these were compared to neuropil and lipofuscin from other neuroanatomic regions, while concentrations of phosphorus, potassium, and chlorine remained proportionately similar although somewhat elevated in the pigments (Figs. 7 and 8). X-ray fluorescence emission of electron beam scans for sulfur in sections from several neuromelanin-bearing and lipofuscin-bearing neuroanatomic regions were visualized as oscilloscopic displays, the results of which are outlined in Table 1.

TABLE 1. *Summary of results of X-ray fluorescence emission following electron probe scans specific for sulfur in sections of human brain containing neuromelanin- or lipofuscin-bearing neurons*

Nuclear location of scanned neurons	Presence of elevated sulfur concentrations in individual intraneuronal pigment masses
Neuromelanin-bearing	
Dorsal motor vagal nucleus	all positive
Locus ceruleus	" "
Substantia nigra	" "
Lipofuscin-bearing	
Inferior olive	some positive
Hypoglossal nucleus	all negative
Red nucleus	" "

Barden and Martin, 1972.

Basophilia, at low pH, of melanins of skin, pia, and eye was considered by Lillie (1955) to be inferential tinctorial evidence for the presence of sulfur in the form of sulfuric or sulfonic acid groups although similar tinctorial results signifying the presence of sulfur could not be demonstrated in neuromelanin. By chemical analysis, sulfur has been repeatedly recorded in melanins obtained from various sources other than brain and the sulfur concentration of some of these melanins has reached nearly 12% (Nicolaus, 1968; Lillie, 1969).

Sulfur in lipofuscin, at concentrations ranging from about 1 to 2%, has also been revealed by chemical analysis (Rosenfeld, 1901a, 1901b; Hendley, Mildvan, Reporter, and Strehler, 1963). Our (Barden and Martin, 1972) electron probe microanalysis recording of a disproportionately increased concentration of sulfur in human inferior olive lipofuscin, and its presence, in the absence of any disproportionate elevation in lipofuscin of other human neuroanatomic nuclei, has received substantial confirmation from recent histochemical studies of human neuronal lipofuscin following the utilization of analytical tinctorial methods. Inferior olive lipofuscin oxidized with performic acid and stained with aldehyde fuchsin after formaldehyde fixation demonstrated 5,6-dihydroxy-indolylsulfonic acids derived from what was believed to be a native aromatic sulfur linkage (Wall, 1972). Of equal pertinence are the observations of Braak (1971) of lipofuscin in inferior olive and dentate nuclei tested with several histochemical reactions, among which performic acid-aldehyde fuchsin was considered to demonstrate a sulfur-containing melanin-like component and periodic acid-Schiff was considered to demonstrate an oxidized and polymerized lipid component. Both the melanin and lipid components were regarded to be linked in lipofuscin. Braak (1971) found that in inferior olive lipofuscin the presence of each of these components was demonstrated by strong staining reactions, while in the dentate nucleus their presence was determined to be minimal, at best, as only weak or negative staining reactions occurred there. On the basis of this, it appears that human neuronal lipofuscin can be tentatively subdivided into a lipofuscin containing a strongly oxidized and polymerized lipid and a high sulfur melanin, and a lipofuscin containing a weakly oxidized lipid and a low sulfur content.

DISTRIBUTION, LOCALIZATION, AND SIGNIFICANCE OF AGE-ACCUMULATED COPPER AND IRON IN RELATION TO NEUROMELANIN AND TO THE ACTIVITIES OF THIAMINE PYROPHOSPHATASE AND TWO LYSOSOMAL HYDROLASES, ACID PHOSPHATASE AND NONSPECIFIC ESTERASE

An age-correlated increase in the concentrations of copper and iron, as in the case of neuromelanin, has been demonstrated by chemical and histochemical methods. The copper content of whole fetal human brain was chemically estimated to be less than one-third that of adult brain (Warren et al., 1960). By histochemical staining, copper was demonstrated in the diencephalon of three chronological age groups of rats that included a young group of 1 to 2 months, a mature group of 6 to 18 months, and a senescent group of 24 months or more (Kaneta, 1966). Copper, not detected in the young group of rats, was detected in the mature group in which granules of copper were stained in the stratum periventricular hypothalami, fimbria hippocampi, and habenular nucleus. In senescent rats, a marked increase in the content of copper granules was found in the stratum peri-ventriculare hypothalami, a modest increase was found in the fimbria hippocampi, and an absence of an increase was noted in the habenular nucleus. Hallgren and Sourander (1958) chemically estimated ferritin iron, as defined by Diezel (1955), in human brain and reported gradual increases during the first 20 to 30 years of life in the globus pallidus and the prefrontal, sensory, and cerebellar cortex as well as gradual increases up to 50 to 60 years of age in the putamen and caudate nucleus. The thalamus was out-standing in that a gradual decline in the content of ferritin iron followed a gradual 35 year increase. In a similar and subsequent study, Sundermann and Kempf (1961) chemically analyzed the iron concentrations of a large number of human brains and observed protracted chronological increases in iron concentration in the globus pallidus, putamen, and caudate nucleus. They also observed an increase in the iron content of the thalamus and cerebral cortex up to 40 to 50 years followed by a small reduction in the iron content toward the senium. By macroscopic histochemical staining of slices of human brain, Guizzetti (1915) demonstrated increasingly intense staining reactions for iron beginning postnatally at 1 month in the globus pallidus, at 9 months in the substantia nigra, at 2 years in the red nucleus, and at 3 years in the dentate nucleus. Macroscopic histochemical staining of human brain slices was also reported by Spatz (1922a) who detected iron post-natally at 6 months in the globus pallidus. With increasing chronological age the intensity of the staining reaction increased in the globus pallidus as well as in other iron-accumulating regions, including the pars reticularis of the substantia nigra, and the red nucleus, dentate nucleus, caudate, putamen, and subthalamic nucleus. Microscopic histochemical demonstrations of stained iron in the form of granules in neuropil, glial cells, and neurons were reported by Muller (1922), Spatz (1922a, 1922b), and Spatz and Metz (1926).

Our demonstration of the presence of sulfur rather than copper in neuro-melanin (Barden and Martin, 1972) left unresolved those biochemical demonstrations of an association of copper with neuromelanin (Tingey, 1937; Warren et al., 1960). This disparity then served to stimulate a survey of the histochemical distribution and localization of copper in brain of aging rhesus monkey and dog which, for purposes of comparison, also included a survey of the histochemical distribution and localization of iron (Barden,

1971*a*). The localization of these metals in relation to thiamine pyrophosphatase-positive and -negative glial cells was achieved by use of combined
staining methods. In this same study, other combined staining methods were
utilized for the demonstration of one or the other metal and the activity of
either lysosomal hydrolase, acid phosphatase, or nonspecific esterase. It was
found that copper, identified indirectly by its pseudoperoxidase activity with
diaminobenzidine and hydrogen peroxide as substrate and identified directly with **DMABR** or rubeanic acid, appeared in the form of extraneuronal
granules whose distribution in the brain of aging rhesus monkey and dog is
given in Table 2. It was also found that iron, identified indirectly in the

TABLE 2. *Distribution of copper*

Aging dog

Pons
  locus ceruleus
  parapeduncular nucleus
  central gray
Midbrain
  inferior colliculus
  interpeduncular nucleus
  central gray
  ventromedial substantia nigra
  ventral tegmental area

Metathalamus
  medial geniculate body
Hypothalamus
  posterior periventricular hypothalamic
    nucleus
  ventromedial hypothalamic nucleus
  periventricular gray
  anterior hypothalamic nucleus
  medial preoptic area
  ovoideus nucleus

Aging rhesus

Pons
  locus ceruleus

Hypothalamus
  ventromedial hypothalamic nucleus

Barden, 1971*a*.

TABLE 3. *Distribution of iron*

Aging rhesus

Cerebellum
  Cortex: granule cell layer
    (near Purkinje cells)
  dentate nucleus
  emboliform nucleus
  globose nucleus
  fastigal nucleus
Pons
  lateral vestibular nucleus
Midbrain
  substantia nigra
  superior colliculus

Thalamus
  pulvinar
  paratenial nucleus
  medial nucleus
  nucleus reuniens
Corpus striatum
  globus pallidus
  putamen
  caudate nucleus

Aging dog

Corpus striatum
  globus pallidus

Barden, 1971*a*.

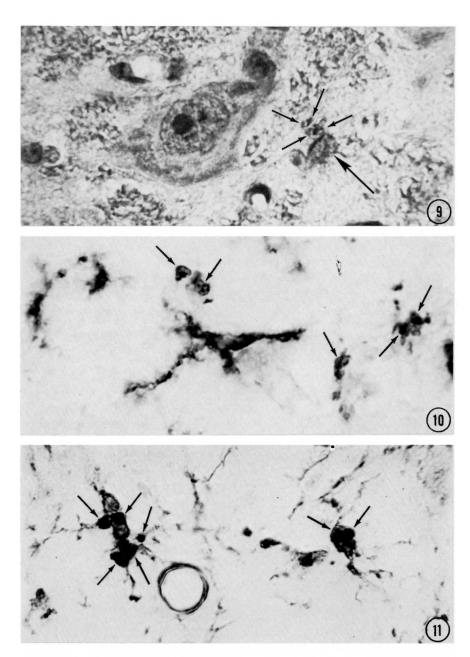

FIGS. 9–11. Cryostat sections of blocks from brains perfused with formol-phosphate. ×1079.

FIG. 9. This section of the locus ceruleus of an aging dog has been stained for copper with DMABR and counterstained with hematoxylin. A neuron is seen with a wide, weakly stained, perinuclear region containing several lightly stained neuromelanin granules at

manner utilized for copper and identified directly with acidified ferrocyanide, the Perls reaction, occurred most frequently as extraneuronal granules and less frequently in the form of small, diffusely stained extraneuronal bodies of about the same size as the granules. The combined distributions of iron as granules and as a diffuse stain in the brain of aging rhesus monkey and dog is given in Table 3. From comparisons of the distributions of copper and iron given in Tables 2 and 3 it can be seen that, while both metals occur in both species, copper is the predominant metal in brain of aging dog and iron is the predominant metal in brain of aging rhesus monkey. These metals are entirely independent of one another in their distribution; for in the single instance where they seem to topographically coincide in the substantia nigra, in actuality, the metals occupy different neuroanatomic subdivisions of the substantia nigra, with copper, in dog, localized to the ventromedial apex of the pars compacta near the ventral surface and with iron, in rhesus monkey, localized to the pars reticularis and along the ventral border of the compacta contiguous to the reticularis.

Counterstaining of DMABR-stained sections with hematoxylin demonstrated DMABR-stained copper granules in direct contact with hematoxylin-stained glial nuclei (Fig. 9), while counterstaining of Perls reaction-stained sections with neutral red demonstrated Perls reaction-stained iron granules and diffusely stained bodies in direct contact with the neutral red-stained glial nuclei or, rarely, as anatomically independent granules staining in the neural parenchyma. When sections stained for thiamine pyrophosphatase activity, which stains the Golgi apparatus of neurons and the cell membrane of some but not all glia, as discussed by Barden (1971*a*), were counterstained for copper with DMABR, granules of DMABR-stained copper were observed to localize free in the neural parenchyma independent of the thiamine pyrophosphatase-positive glia (Fig. 10). On the other hand, in sections stained for thiamine pyrophosphatase activity and counterstained with Perls reaction for iron, ferrocyanide-positive iron granules were almost always localized to thiamine pyrophosphatase-positive glial cell bodies and/ or their processes (Fig. 11), and ferrocyanide-positive, diffusely stained

---

one pole. A glial cell nucleus is in close apposition to the neuron and several glial nuclei occur in the neural parenchyma. One glial nucleus (*large arrow*) has several smaller DMABR-stained copper granules associated with it (*small arrows*).

FIG. 10. This section of the ventromedial hypothalamic nucleus of an aging dog has been stained for thiamine pyrophosphatase (TPPase) activity and counterstained for copper with DMABR. A TPPase active glial cell is visualized by lead rhodizonate. DMABR-stained copper granules (*arrows*) lie free in the neural parenchyma.

FIG. 11. This section of the substantia nigra, pars reticularis of an aging rhesus monkey, has been stained for TPPase activity and counterstained for iron with Perls reaction. Two TPPase active glial cells are visualized by lead sulfide. One glial cell is in association with a small blood vessel. Prussian blue-stained iron granules (*arrows*) occur in each glial cell body and the proximal portion of one process.

bodies were localized to thiamine pyrophosphatase-negative glial cells. These results have demonstrated that two or possibly three types of glia can be characterized in the following manner: thiamine pyrophosphatase-positive, iron granule-containing glial cells and thiamine pyrophosphatase-negative, copper granule-containing or diffusely stained iron-containing glial cells. Unfortunately, it was not possible to pursue efforts by histochemistry or by histologic staining methods to better identify and equate these various histochemically defined glia with the known glial types of routine histology.

In the case of combined staining for metals and lysosomal hydrolase activities, acid phosphatase and nonspecific esterase were each localized to neurons and their accumulated pigments, neuromelanin and lipofuscin, while copper and iron were localized to the neural parenchyma unassociated with the enzyme activities. This disparate arrangement was found to prevail not only for the larger accumulations of metals, but it was also maintained where the metal accumulations were minimal in amount. The interpretation given to these results was that copper and iron accumulate in glial cells in the absence of an associated lysosomal mechanism. In brain, this demonstrable absence of a lysosomal metal-accumulating mechanism was unexpected, as this was unlike the previously reported condition in liver (Goldfischer et al., 1966) wherein both copper (Goldfischer and Bernstein, 1969) and iron (Goldfischer, Novikoff, Albala, and Biempica, 1970) were found to accumulate in the lysosomal peribiliary lipofuscin granules of the parenchymal cells. The glial cell metal-accumulating mechanism remains to be elaborated.

Not only was there a complete disparity between the localizations of metals and lysosomal hydrolase activities, but it was also apparent that there was an absence of correlation between the topographic distribution of these metals and the distribution of neuromelanin. The distribution of neuromelanin in rhesus monkey includes the dorsal motor nucleus of the vagus, locus ceruleus, substantia nigra, and nucleus paranigralis, while in dog this pigment is distributed in the locus ceruleus, substantia nigra, and hypothalamus (Barden, 1971a). Table 4 demonstrates that the absence of correlation among the three substances copper, iron, and neuromelanin is so unequivocal that each is shown to occur in one or more neuroanatomic loci in the absence of the other two. This can be observed, in the case of copper, in the hypothalamus of rhesus monkey and the interpeduncular nucleus of dog, in the case of iron in the globus pallidus, caudate and putamen of rhesus monkey, and globus pallidus of dog, and in the case of neuromelanin in the dorsal motor nucleus of the vagus and the nucleus paranigralis of rhesus monkey. On the basis of these apparently independent distributions and localizations, consideration of a causal association between one or both metals and neuromelanin does not appear warranted.

The functions, if any, of the granular and diffuse accumulations of iron

TABLE 4. *Presence of copper, iron, and neuromelanin in selected regions of aging brain*

Animal	Substance	Dorsal vagus nucleus	Locus ceruleus	Substantia nigra	Midventral midbrain nuclei	Hypo-thalamus	Globus pallidus	Caudate and/or putamen
Rhesus	copper		X			X		
	iron			X			X	X
	neuromelanin	X	X	X	X			
Dog	copper		X	X	X	X		
	iron						X	
	neuromelanin		X	X		X		

Barden, 1971a.

and the granular accumulations of copper are not known. Their respective, overall topographic distributions do not coincide with the topographic distributions of any other specialized biochemical system of brain. Perhaps these metal accumulations merely represent the nondisposable end-products of metabolic activities of those metabolically specialized glial cells that accumulate them rather than the accumulations themselves being active components of metabolic activities.

BIOGENIC AMINES AND NEUROMELANIN

Demonstration of catecholamine histofluorescence in neuromelanin-bearing neurons (Barden and Barrett, 1972, 1973; Olson, Nyström, and Seiger, 1973 b) logically proceeded from the suggestions of several investigators who anticipated this association on the basis of evidence from histochemistry (Bazelon, Fenichel, and Randall, 1967; Barden, 1969, 1971 b) and biochemistry (Friede, 1953; Fellman, 1958; Vander Wende and Spoerlein, 1963; Marsden, 1965 b, 1969; Ishii and Friede, 1968; Nordgren, Rorsman, Rosengren, and Rosengren, 1971).

Bazelon et al. (1967) selectively stained neuromelanin in adult human brainstem with acidified silver nitrate and by examination of serial sections observed that neuromelanin-bearing neurons were distributed not only in large concentrations in the substantia nigra and associated midbrain nuclei but that these pigmented neurons also extended as a somewhat distorted column the entire length of the brainstem from the mesencephalon to the nucleus retroambigualis. They described the pattern of coincidence between the topographic distribution of neuromelanin-bearing neurons in human brainstem and that of catecholamine neurons in brain of rat as demonstrated by Dahlstrom and Fuxe (1965) with the Falck-Hillarp histofluorescence method. Consideration of the possibility that neuromelanin forms from catechol derivative precursors led Barden (1969) to devise model systems to test for this possibility, developed, in part, on the basis of the proposal furnished by Duffy and Tennyson (1965) that neuromelanin was melanized lipofuscin and, in part, on the basis of the proposal of Goldfischer et al. (1966) that melanin in liver peribiliary lipofuscin granules formed by means of the nonenzymatic process of a metal catalyzed pseudoperoxidation. Toward this didactic goal, a model was devised in which a neuromelanin-like pigment could be pseudoperoxidatively formed from neuronal lipofuscin following the impregnation of the lipofuscin with iron sulfide prior to its exposure to DOPA in the presence of hydrogen peroxide. The applicability of this must be rejected, however, as the idea of a metal-catalyzed pseudoperoxidative process being implicated in neuromelanogenesis has since been discounted as metals have been shown not to be endogenous to neuromelanin (Barden, 1971a; Barden and Martin, 1972).

With further regard to the association of neuromelanin and catecholamines,

Barden (1971*b*) stressed the need for evidence of this on more firm a basis than that of comparative topographic distributions and model systems and he recommended that direct demonstration of an association of pigment and catecholamine be attempted in the same animal. This matter was partially resolved through a biochemical analysis of human substantia nigra neuro-melanin by Nordgren et al. (1971) who were able to recover DOPA and dopamine from acid hydrolysates of the pigment. Concurrent demonstration of neuromelanin and catecholamine in the same neuron was reported by Barden and Barrett (1972, 1973) by means of alternated tungsten white light and near-ultraviolet fluorescent microscopic methods in which neuro-melanin was identified by its characteristic bright- and dark-field optical properties (Barden, 1969, 1971*a*) and catecholamines were demonstrated through utilization of the Falck-Hillarp histofluorescence method (Corrodi and Jonsson, 1967; Fuxe and Jonsson, 1973). This combined localization of neuromelanin and catecholamine was demonstrated in large neurons in the vicinity of the fornix of dog hypothalamus. Barden and Barrett (1973) determined that, as neuromelanin progressively accumulated in catecholamine-containing neurons, those neurons, initially entirely cate-cholamine-containing, manifested a gradual reduction in catecholamine histofluorescence and a gradual, very nearly linear, and inversely propor-tionate accumulation of neuromelanin. Four pairs of dogs were utilized in their study whose ages were 5 weeks, 3 months, 1 year, and of indeterminate advanced maturity, the advanced age of which, in the last instance, was estimated primarily by the presence of well-worn and missing teeth. While only catecholamine histofluorescence was seen in some perifornical neurons in 5-week-old dogs (Fig. 12), in some similarly distributed catecholamine-containing neurons of 3-month-old dogs neuromelanin was additionally demonstrable and was observed to occur in a range of accumulations ex-tending from its near absence to an accumulation more plentiful in its ap-pearance than the associated catecholamine (Figs. 14 to 18; see also Figs. 1 to 5, Barden and Barrett, 1973). Catecholamine histofluorescence was found not present in neuromelanin-bearing neurons in 1-year-old and aging dogs. However, fluorescent study of additional, more recently prepared sections from the original blocks of hypothalamus of our 1-year-old and aging dogs has presently demonstrated a small amount of green catechola-mine histofluorescence in the perikarya of several neurons bearing very large accumulations of neuromelanin (Fig. 13).

Neuromelanin characteristically manifests the capacity to scatter tungsten light in the dark-field (Figs. 14 and 17) and to absorb in the near ultraviolet (Fig. 13). The capacity of neuromelanin to absorb in the near ultraviolet is temporally labile, as a yellow fluorescence will eventually be induced during relatively protracted exposures to the near ultraviolet. An induced fluores-cence can be observed to develop within a few minutes in the smaller, usually younger accumulations of neuromelanin (Fig. 15) and not for 15

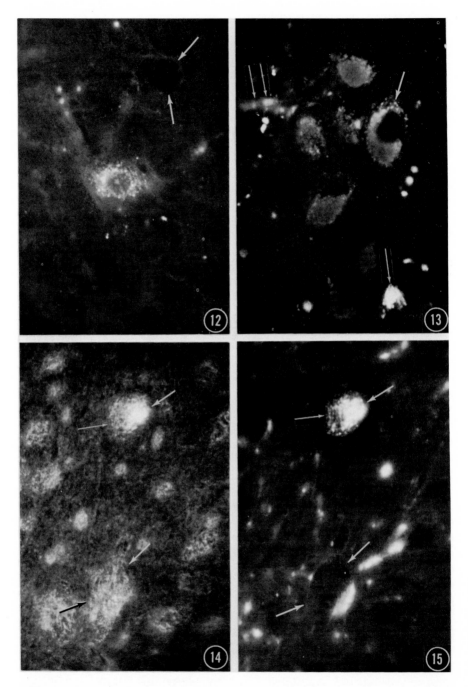

FIGS. 12–15. Neurons in the perifornical region of dog hypothalamus treated according to the Falck-Hillarp histofluorescence method for biogenic amines. ×552.

min or more in the largest masses of the oldest animals (Fig. 13). This gradually developed ultraviolet light induction of yellow fluorescence in neuromelanin is considered different from the yellow autofluorescence of lipofuscin (Fig. 13) which requires no induction period for its appearance. Moreover, the induction of yellow fluorescence in neuromelanin is not dependent on paraformaldehyde pretreatment for the demonstration of catecholamines, as protracted exposure to near-ultraviolet light, even in the absence of any such pretreatment, will induce a yellow fluorescence in this pigment (Barden, 1969; Barden and Barrett, 1973).

Recently, Olson et al. (1973*b*) applied the Falck-Hillarp histofluorescence method to postmortem brain of aging patients and observed catecholamine histofluorescence in a small proportion of neuromelanin-bearing neurons in the substantia nigra and locus ceruleus. In a related study, Olson, Boréus, and Seiger (1973*a*) exposed human fetal brain to the Falck-Hillarp procedure and observed catecholamine histofluorescence in cell bodies in the embryonic locus ceruleus and in cell bodies forming a broad flattened ventral mesencephalic nigral cell complex. The results of these studies of human fetal and aging substantia nigra and locus ceruleus substantially parallel those results we have reported for dog hypothalamus. Nevertheless, with regard to aging brain, Olson et al. (1973*b*) have also described the presence of some fluorescent lipofuscin in neuromelanin-bearing neurons when such neurons were viewed in near-ultraviolet light for the demonstration of catecholamine histofluorescence. On the basis of our observations of

---

FIG. 12. Catecholamine fluorescence in near-ultraviolet (UV) light in a 5-week-old dog. A neuron, in the center, exhibits a punctate pattern of green catecholamine fluorescence, here appearing as white, in its perikaryon, in addition to a negative nucleus and a moderately fluorescent nucleolus. Several loci of green fluorescence also occur in the neural parenchyma. The perikaryon of a catecholamine-free neuron lies between the arrows.

FIG. 13. This is a section from an aging dog viewed in near-UV light displaying an unusually large cluster of several partially absorbant neuromelanin-bearing neurons, a yellow (here appearing as white) autofluorescent lipofuscin-bearing neuron (*small arrow*), green (here appearing as dull white) catecholamine fluorescence in the neural parenchyma (*double arrows*), and small, scattered, and spherical foci of autofluorescent lipofuscin. One neuromelanin-bearing neuron also displays a very restricted amount of punctate catecholamine fluorescence immediately adjacent to its large mass of neuromelanin (*large arrow*).

FIG. 14. Dark-field, white light view of a pair of neurons in a 3-month-old dog. The upper neuron, demarcated by arrows, displays a mass of light scattering neuromelanin (*large arrow*). The lower neuron, also demarcated by arrows, does not possess neuromelanin.

FIG. 15. Near-UV light view of the section shown in Fig. 14. The upper neuron, demarcated by arrows, here displays green catecholamine fluorescence in its perikaryon (*small arrow*) and yellow fluorescence in its mass of neuromelanin (*large arrow*) induced during the approximately 15 min time period required for viewing and for photography. The lower neuron, also demarcated by arrows, does not display fluorescence. Catecholamine fluorescence is seen in portions of processes in several loci in the neural parenchyma.

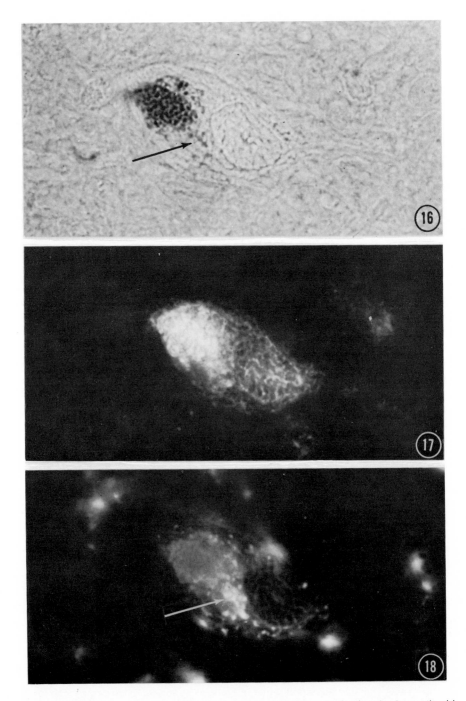

FIGS. 16–18. A neuron in the perifornical region of the hypothalamus of a 3-month-old dog treated according to the Falck-Hillarp histofluorescence method for biogenic amines. ×1,125 (*orig. magn.*). (From Barden and Barrett, 1973, by permission of the Williams & Wilkins Company.)

similarly treated and viewed neuromelanin in dog hypothalamus, it is suggested that the fluorescence of lipofuscin reported in human neuromelanin-bearing neurons, in actuality, is an ultraviolet light-induced fluorescence of some but not all neuromelanin granules in the perikarya of these irradiated neurons.

Akin to the age-correlated reduction of green catecholamine histofluorescence in perifornical neuromelanin-bearing neurons of dog hypothalamus, catecholamine fluorescence in processes in the perifornical region was also diminished with age (Barden and Barrett, 1973). On the other hand, we observed no age-correlated diminution of a very plentiful catecholamine histofluorescence in the median eminence and lower portion of the wall of the third ventricle. Biochemical studies of brain have also demonstrated topographically localized age-correlated reductions in catecholamine levels as well as reductions in the activities of enzymes controlling amine turnover. Finch (1973) measured a 22% reduction in striatal dopamine in the aging male mouse when mature mice were compared to senescent mice, while similar comparisons of norepinephrine levels in brainstem, cerebellum, and hypothalamus remained unchanged with advanced age. The efficiency of the utilization of tyrosine and L-DOPA in the hypothalamus, striatum, brainstem, and cerebellum was found by Finch (1973) to be 1.6 times greater in mature than senescent mice. Among several enzyme activities in control of catecholamine turnover in the caudate nucleus of rat, McGeer, Fibiger, McGeer, and Wickson (1971a) observed the rate-limiting enzyme, tyrosine hydroxylase, to display the greatest decline with age. A similar age-correlated decline in the activity of tyrosine hydroxylase in human caudate was reported by McGeer, McGeer, and Wada (1971b).

PHYSICAL BIOCHEMISTRY AND SELECTED HISTOCHEMISTRY OF NEUROMELANIN

Neuromelanin has been subjected to an analysis by several spectrophotometric methods and the results have indicated the presence of a

---

FIG. 16. High-power, bright-field view of a neuron in which a relatively large mass of neuromelanin granules has accumulated. Arrow points to a nonneuromelanin-bearing region of the perikaryon adjacent to the mass of neuromelanin in which catecholamine fluorescence occurs in near-UV light as shown in Fig. 18.

FIG. 17. Same field as in Fig. 16, here shown in dark-field white light and illustrating the light-scattering capacity of this mass of neuromelanin.

FIG. 18. Same field as in Fig. 16 shown in near-UV light. Weak fluorescence is seen in the mass of neuromelanin, whereas bright green (here shown as white) catecholamine fluorescence occurs as concentrated (*arrow*) and scattered loci elsewhere in the perikaryon. This large mass of neuromelanin was more resistant to the acquisition of a near-UV light-induced yellow fluorescence than the smaller mass of neuromelanin previously illustrated in Fig. 15. Under the same conditions that prevailed for viewing and for photography of Fig. 15, neuromelanin here has only a pale fluorescence.

melanin component in addition to a close similarity between it and lipofuscin. By use of Pollister type microspectrophotometry, Pakkenberg (1966) observed closely related visible light absorption curves in sections of human substantia nigra neuromelanin and inferior olive lipofuscin. Van Woert, Prasad, and Borg (1967) reported that the electron paramagnetic resonance and infrared absorption spectra of human substantia nigra neuromelanin were similar to those of the insoluble, lipid-extracted residuum of human cardiac lipofuscin, Amphiuma liver melanin, and synthetic melanins prepared from L-DOPA, dopamine, L-norepinephrine, and epinephrine. The infrared spectrometric observations of Van Woert et al. (1967) were confirmed by Maeda and Wegmann (1969) who, additionally, obtained infrared spectra from neuromelanin in human locus ceruleus identical to that of neuromelanin in human substantia nigra.

When Van Woert et al. (1967) compared the fluorescence of isolated, non-extracted human cardiac lipofuscin and substantia nigra neuromelanin at 365 nm, fluorescence occurred in lipofuscin but not in neuromelanin. They further observed an absence of fluorescence in the insoluble, chloroform-methanol extracted residuum of cardiac lipofuscin and attributed this absence to their having extracted the chemical source of the fluorescence of cardiac lipofuscin, polymerized degraded fatty acids. On the basis of its melanin-like absorption in ultraviolet light and its several melanin-like spectroscopic properties, Van Woert et al. (1967) concluded that the insoluble, lipid-extracted residuum of cardiac lipofuscin was similar to cutaneous melanin in which an absence of a comparable lipofuscin-like component occurs naturally (Moses et al., 1966; Fitzpatrick et al., 1967). Moreover, Van Woert et al. (1967) regarded neuromelanin to be a pigment composed entirely of melanin, similar to cutaneous melanin and the insoluble, lipid-extracted residuum of cardiac lipofuscin, and without an integrally associated lipid lobule-containing lipofuscin component. Recently, however, Van Woert and Ambani (1974) in their review of neuromelanin acknowledged the presence of such a lipid component in the brain pigment.

Histochemical studies of related phenomena in neuromelanin of human substantia nigra (Barden, 1969) and dog hypothalamus (Barden, 1971a) gave results comparable to one another but which have been given an interpretation different from the one offered by Van Woert et al. (1967). In the histochemical studies, if a section of dog hypothalamus containing neuromelanin were viewed by various forms of illumination, untreated dog hypothalamic neuromelanin was golden-brown in color in transmitted white light (Fig. 19), strongly light scattering in the dark-field (Fig. 20), and absorbant in near-ultraviolet light (Fig. 21), while neuromelanin in this very same section after it was bleached overnight in 10% hydrogen peroxide was no longer visible in transmitted white light (Fig. 22), no longer light scattering in the dark-field (Fig. 23), and fluorescent yellow in near-ultraviolet light (Fig. 24). Moreover, those optical properties of untreated human sub-

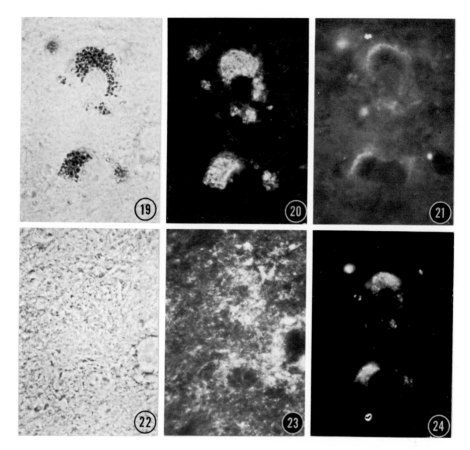

FIGS. 19–24. Neuromelanin in a fresh, unstained cryostat section of aging dog hypothalamus; same field in each figure. ×680. (From Barden, 1971a, by permission of the editor-in-chief, *Journal of Neuropathology and Experimental Neurology*.)

FIG. 19. Two neuromelanin-bearing neurons viewed in the bright-field. The neuromelanin granules are large and clearly distinct.

FIG. 20. Same field as shown in Fig. 19, here viewed in dark-field white light. Neuromelanin scatters light.

FIG. 21. Same field as shown in Fig. 19, here viewed in near-UV light. Neuromelanin absorbs in the near-UV light except near the periphery of the pigment masses which are shown to be slightly fluorescent.

FIG. 22. Same field as shown in Fig. 19. The section shown has now been treated overnight with 10% hydrogen peroxide. Neuromelanin has become bleached and is no longer visible in the bright-field. The procedure has also produced some shrinkage of the section.

FIG. 23. Same field as shown in Fig. 19 with treatment as in Fig. 22. In dark-field white light, neuromelanin no longer scatters light and is barely visible.

FIG. 24. Same field as shown in Fig. 19 with treatment as in Fig. 22. In the near-UV, neuromelanin is now fluorescent yellow.

stantia nigra lipofuscin were not unlike bleached neuromelanin, in that lipofuscin does not scatter light in the dark-field and is autofluorescent yellow in near-ultraviolet light (Barden, 1969). Table 5 is a comparison of these and other previously described histochemical properties of neuromelanin and lipofuscin. These histochemical results have been interpreted as having revealed an underlying fluorescent lipofuscin component in neuromelanin whose fluorescence is normally quenched by the existing melanin but whose existence has been revealed through the oxidative bleaching of neuromelanin. Bleaching of melanin with hydrogen peroxide and other oxidants degrades the melanin polymer by formation of soluble pyrrolecarboxylic acids (Mason, 1959), while hydrogen peroxide bleaching of lipofuscin has no effect on its property of autofluorescence (Barden, 1969).

The different viewpoints offered here in regard to pigmentary substructure can be weighed against the interpretation given to the ultrastructure of neuromelanin and lipofuscin granules as seen by electron microscopy and as analyzed through biochemistry. Under the preceding topic of ultrastructure, mention was made of the nonlipid lobule component of the tripartite neuromelanin granule that is composed of electron-dense, irregularly distributed patches of melanin deposited on a granular or linear matrix. As the matrix of the neuromelanin granule is morphologically identical to the matrix of cortical and pontine lipofuscin granules, it is suggested that the source of the spectroscopic properties of melanin recorded in granules of neuromelanin and cardiac lipofuscin were those of the deposits of melanin found in the matrix of both types of granules. Malkoff and Strehler (1963) and Siakotos and Koppang (1973) have shown that human cardiac lipofuscin granules morphologically consist of numerous, tightly packed, electron-dense, spheroidal components, while chemical analysis has demonstrated that the

TABLE 5. *Some characteristic histochemical and optical properties of neuromelanin and lipofuscin*

Test	Human and rhesus substantia nigra neuromelanin	Dog hypothalamic neuromelanin	Human and rhesus inferior olive lipofuscin
Ferrous ion uptake[a]	+	+	−
Cupric ion uptake	+	+	−
Light scattering	+	+	−
Autofluorescence	−	−	+
Fluorescence: UV induced	+	+	inapplicable
Fluorescence: bleaching induced	+	+	inapplicable
Periodic acid-Schiff	−	−	+
Schmorl reaction	+	+	+
Acid phosphatase	+	+	+
Nonspecific esterase	+	+	+

Barden, 1969, 1970, 1971*a*.
[a] Lillie, 1957*a*.

lipid solvent—insoluble residuum of human cardiac lipofuscin granules is essentially proteinaceous (Björkerud, 1964) and may also have a melanin moiety (Siebert, Diezel, Jahr, Krug, Schmitt, Grünberger, and Bottke, 1962). It is further suggested that the chemical composition of the matrix of neuromelanin may be proteinaceous in the manner of cardiac lipofuscin. If this were to be the correct interpretation, the neuromelanin granule would consist of melanin, protein, and lipid components rather than entirely melanin as suggested by Van Woert et al. (1967), or melanin and lipid as suggested by Van Woert and Ambani (1974).

GENESIS OF NEUROMELANIN

The presence of lysosomal hydrolase activities in neuromelanin has been discussed in a previous section and the absence of the mitochondrial enzyme activities, cytochrome oxidase (Barden, 1969) and succinic dehydrogenase (Friede, 1962), rule out any typical mitochondrial function for these lysosomal residual bodies. Evidence from electron microscopic reports, however, has been interpreted to indicate both a direct and an indirect mitochondrial origin for neuromelanin granules. These reports, one in which Hirosawa (1968) studied the Japanese monkey and the other in which Schwyn et al. (1970) studied squirrel and rhesus monkeys as well as man, offered proposals for neuromelanogenesis based on very similar electron microscopic evidence, which, taken together, are mutually complementary.

In neuromelanin-bearing neurons of the substantia nigra and locus ceruleus of the Japanese monkey, intramitochondrial inclusion bodies were seen which occurred singly or multiply in individual mitochondria and which ranged in size from small to as large as the interior space of the enveloping mitochondrion. Typical, tripartitely substructured neuromelanin granules, unmodified lysosomes, and lysosomes manifesting numerous irregular patches of dense substance were also seen. These various morphological configurations were considered by Hirosawa (1968) to signify that neuromelanin granules were derived from lysosomes which sequestered excess catecholamine present in the perikaryal milieu. He suggested that excess catecholamine was present, as numerous defective mitochondria were unable to maintain sufficient levels of monoamine oxidase activity to destroy the catecholamine remaining from normal metabolic requirements. Hirosawa (1968) noted that the absence of excessive levels of catecholamine in neuromelanin-forming neurons would greatly reduce the sequestration of these amines into lysosomes wherein, in theory (Barden, 1969), they would become oxidized to melanin. Schwyn et al. (1970) also reported inclusion body-containing mitochondria in neurons of the substantia nigra of squirrel and rhesus monkeys much like that described in the Japanese monkey. They observed that in some instances there was a pinching-off of that portion of the mitochondrion containing a large inclusion and, in addition, an association of the pinched-off mitochondrial inclusion with elongated, partially enveloping saccules of rough endoplasmic reticulum. Some rhesus monkey substantia nigra neurons did not contain neuromelanin granules and in those cells numerous typical lysosomes were observed. Unlike Hirosawa (1968), who specifically denied the occurrence of a gradual transformation from mitochondria to lysosomally derived neuromelanin, Schwyn et al. (1970) strongly favored the idea of a mitochondrial contribution to these lysosomal pigment granules. These latter workers also observed previously undescribed concentrations of small, vesicular structures in human substantia nigra neuromelanin granules which otherwise manifested typical tripartite substructures. Whereas they made no suggestion as to the contents of the small vesicles, it is here suggested that if the small vesicles were to be catecholamine-containing structures, their catecholamine content could become oxidized in this hydrolytic, lysosomal environment and polymerized into the melanin observed as electron-dense patches on the lipofuscin matrix of neuromelanin granules.

The similarity between neuromelanin and lipofuscin may have been further revealed by the above-described association of pinched-off mitochondrial fragments with saccules of rough endoplasmic reticulum (Schwyn et al., 1970). Novikoff, Novikoff, Quintana, and Davis (1973) have reported that lipofuscin granules of human hepatocytes form in a close spacial association with saccules of smooth endoplasmic reticulum. Formation of neuronal lipofuscin from degenerating mitochondria has recently been well documented (Duckett and White, 1974; Gopinath and Glees, 1974; Palladini, Mele, Bugiani, and Tarquini, 1974).

An overall sequence for neuromelanogenesis can be based on the following direct and indirect observations as well as hypothetical considerations. Neuromelanin-bearing neurons arise from catecholamine-containing neurons in neuromelanin-producing species and contain an inversely related combination of catecholamine and neuromelanin (Barden and Barrett, 1972, 1973; Olson et al., 1973b). Neuromelanin granules are lysosomally derived as they manifest acid hydrolase activities (Barden, 1969). In neuromelanin-bearing neurons, some mitochondria give rise to degenerating fragments filled with an inclusion (Hirosawa, 1968; Schwyn et al., 1970). These mitochondrial fragments may become autophagically incorporated into either lysosomes or their neuromelanin granule derivative during any stage of the pigment granule's formation (Barden, 1970; Schwyn et al., 1970; Gopinath and Glees, 1974) or, alternatively, they may be subjected to modification during an association with saccules of endoplasmic reticulum (Schwyn et al., 1970; Novikoff et al., 1973) prior to their incorporation into lysosomes or neuromelanin granules. Catecholamine enters the lysosome or neuromelanin granule either from solution in the cytosol or, perhaps, in the form of those numerous, concentrated, small vesicles demonstrated in human substantia nigra neuromelanin granules by Schwyn et al. (1970). Within the lysosome or neuromelanin granule, catecholamine, which may be free or vesicle-bound, and mitochondrial fragments containing inclusions, which may be native or modified, are hydrolyzed, oxidized, polymerized, copolymerized, and in a syneresis-like manner separated to form a lipofuscin matrix with an associated globular lipid (Barden, 1969, 1970; Sekhon and Maxwell, 1974). Melanin, derived from oxidized and polymerized catechol derivatives (Swan, 1963; Blois, 1965), is deposited as electron-dense patches on the lipofuscin matrix (Barden, 1969; Singer, Cate, Ross, and Netsky, 1974). During the formation of neuromelanin, sulfur-containing compounds concentrate in the granules (Barden and Martin, 1972), perhaps in combination with polymerized catechol compounds as pheomelanin (Rachlin and Enemark, 1969; Prota, 1972) or, perhaps, in combination with other polymerized constituents of the pigment granules (Koeppen, Barron, and Cox, 1971).

EVOLUTIONARY SIGNIFICANCE OF NEUROMELANIN

In the mammalia, the neuromelanin content of the locus ceruleus and/or the substantia nigra is minimally represented in a relatively small number of species included among nine of the lower orders (Marsden, 1961c), is increased in quantity in a few of the carnivores (Brown, 1943; Barden, 1971a), and is best represented in the primates. Among the primates, it is found in lesser quantities in the lower forms (Scherer, 1939; Lillie and Yamada, 1960; Moses et al., 1966; Hirosawa, 1968; Schwyn et al., 1970; Barden, 1970) and in greater quantities in the great apes (Scherer, 1939; Adler, 1942), culminating in man who manifests the greatest amount (Olszewski and Baxter, 1959; Bazelon et al., 1967). This comparative distribution of neuromelanin, with its obvious positive correlation with the higher primates, and with man in particular, has led Marsden (1965b) to advance a hypothesis to explain its phylogenetic significance. It was postulated that a phylogenetic transition occurs in brain catecholamine metabolism from neurotransmitter synthesis to neuromelanin synthesis: Marsden's evidence of transition having been based on the parallel distribution of catecholamines in rodent brainstem and neuromelanin in primate and carnivore brainstem. It was further postulated that the phylogenetically recent acquisition of catecholamine metabolism by prosencephalically derived structures has been paralleled by a suppression and concomitant shunting of mesencephalic and rhombencephalic catecholamine metabolism to metabolically innocuous neuromelanin formation. Essential to this hypothesis is the concept of encephalization (Noback and Shriver, 1969), wherein the evolution of vertebrate brain is determined by the extent to which dominance by recently expanded prosencephalic centers are exerted over formerly predominant mesencephalic and rhombencephalic centers.

Marsden's concept of neuromelanin phylogeny was first challenged by

Gfeller (1965) who pointed out that catecholamines in the prosencephalon are transported there from cell bodies located in the more caudal regions of the brain, and alternatively suggested that the amount of neuromelanin in a species might correlate with the duration of postnatal development preceding adulthood. Subsequently, Barden (1971a) reasoned that the presence of neuromelanin in dog hypothalamus, whose existence Marsden may not have been aware of, must be considered as evidence incompatible with this hypothesis. If Marsden's hypothesis were pursued to its logical conclusion, neuromelanin in dog hypothalamus, the most rostral neuroanatomic localization of neuromelanin in any mammalian species, would serve as evidence that the telencephalon exerts a greater dominance over the diencephalon in carnivores than it does in primates. This interpretation would reasonably compel the dubious conclusion that prosencephalic evolution is more advanced in carnivores than it is in primates. Other objections are based on other supporting evidence. Sarnat and Netsky (1974) observed that comparisons of neuromelanin pigmentation among various mammals such as those reported by Marsden (1961c) cannot be accomplished without knowledge of the animals' ages relative to their respective life-spans. To this can be added the objection that the silver staining method utilized by Marsden (1961c), the Masson-Fontana ammoniacal silver technique for a 24 hr staining period, is lacking in specificity. According to Lillie (1957b; 1965), staining with alkaline silver produces blackening of skin and eye melanins in 2 to 10 min, blackening of neuromelanin in 2 to 15 min, and blackening of lipofuscin in 18 to 24 hr. Consequently, a more specific staining method such as the ferrous or the cupric ion uptake method, discussed in a previous section, or the 24 hr silver technique utilized by Bazelon et al. (1967) at pH 3 would be required to differentiate neuromelanin from lipofuscin, both of which are known to occur in substantia nigra (Sachs, 1943; Barden, 1969). It would seem that before judgment can be made regarding the evolutionary significance of neuromelanin, more convincing evidence of its comparative distribution is required in conjunction, perhaps, with an explanation for its absence from the substantia nigra and other comparative neuromelanogenic regions of the brain of nonneuromelanin-bearing mammalian species.

REFERENCES

Adler, A. (1939): Melanin pigment in the central nervous system of vertebrates. *J. Comp. Neurol.,* 70:315–330.

Adler, A. (1942): Melanin pigment in the brain of the gorilla. *J. Comp. Neurol.,* 76:501–507.

Anderson, P. J., and Song, S. K. (1962): Acid phosphatase in the nervous system. *J. Neuropathol. Exp. Neurol.,* 21:263–283.

Barden, H. (1967): Loss of Golgi thiamine pyrophosphatase during accumulation of lipofuscin and neuromelanin in aging neurons. *J. Histochem. Cytochem.,* 15:768–769.

Barden, H. (1969): The histochemical relationship of neuromelanin and lipofuscin. *J. Neuropathol. Exp. Neurol.,* 28:419–441.

Barden, H. (1970): Relationship of Golgi thiaminepyrophosphatase and lysosomal acid phosphatase to neuromelanin and lipofuscin in cerebral neurons of the aging rhesus monkey. *J. Neuropathol. Exp. Neurol.,* 29:225–240.

Barden, H. (1971*a*): The histochemical distribution and localization of copper, iron, neuro-melanin and lysosomal enzyme activity in the brain of aging rhesus monkey and the dog. *J. Neuropathol. Exp. Neurol.,* 30:650–667.

Barden, H. (1971*b*): Distribution of neuromelanin and catecholamines in the brainstem. *Lancet,* 2:923.

Barden, H., and Barrett, R. (1972): Demonstration of catecholamine fluorescence in neuro-melanin-bearing perikarya of neurons in dog hypothalamus. *J. Histochem. Cytochem.,* 20:448.

Barden, H., and Barrett, R. (1973): The localization of catecholamine fluorescence to dog hypothalamic neuromelanin-bearing neurons. *J. Histochem. Cytochem.,* 21:175–183.

Barden, H., and Martin, E. (1972): Electron probe microanalysis of neuromelanin and lipo-fuscin. In: *Pigmentation: Its Genesis and Biologic Control,* edited by V. Riley, pp. 631–638. Appleton-Century-Crofts, New York.

Bazelon, M., Fenichel, G. M., and Randall, J. (1967): Studies on neuromelanin. I. A melanin system in the human adult brainstem. *Neurology (Minneap.),* 17:512–519.

Björkerud, S. (1964): Studies of lipofuscin granules of human cardiac muscle. II. Chemical analysis of the isolated granules. *Exp. Mol. Pathol.,* 3:377–389.

Blois, M. S. (1965): Random polymers as a matrix for chemical evolution. In: *The Origins of Prebiological Systems and of their Molecular Matrices,* edited by S. W. Fox, pp. 19–38. Academic Press, New York.

Braak, H. (1971): Uber das Neurolipofuscin in der Unteren Olive und dem Nucleus dentatus cerebelli im Gehirn des Menschen. *Z. Zellforsch. Mikrosk. Anat.,* 121:573–592.

Brown, J. O. (1943): Pigmentation of substantia nigra and locus coeruleus in certain carnivores. *J. Comp. Neurol.,* 79:393–405.

Brunk, U., and Ericsson, J. L. E. (1972): Electron microscopical studies on rat brain neurons. Localization of acid phosphatase and mode of formation of lipofuscin bodies. *J. Ultrastruct. Res.,* 38:1–15.

Calligaris, G. (1908): Beitrag zum Studium der Zeller des Locus coeruleus und der Substantia nigra. *Monatsschr. Psychiat. Neurol.,* 24:339–353.

Citkowitz, E., and Holtzman, E. (1973): Peroxisomes in dorsal root ganglia. *J. Histochem. Cytochem.,* 21:34–41.

Cooper, E. R. A. (1946): The development of the substantia nigra. *Brain,* 69:22–33.

Corrodi, H., and Jonsson, G. (1967): The formaldehyde fluorescence method for the histo-chemical demonstration of biogenic monoamines. A review on the methodology. *J. Histo-chem. Cytochem.,* 15:65–78.

Côté, L. J., and Fahn, S. (1969): Some aspects of the biochemistry of the substantia nigra of the rhesus monkey. In: *Progress in Neuro-Genetics,* International Congress Series No. 175, pp. 311–317. Excerpta Medica, Amsterdam.

Cumings, J. N. (1968): Trace metals in the brain and in Wilson's disease. *J. Clin. Pathol.,* 21:1–7.

D'Agostino, A. J., and Luse, S. A. (1964): Electron microscopic observations on the human substantia nigra. *Neurology (Minneap.),* 14:529–536.

Dahlstrom, A., and Fuxe, K. (1965): Evidence for the existence of monoamine-containing neurons in the central nervous system. I. Demonstration of monoamine in the cell bodies of brain stem neurons. *Acta. Physiol. Scand. (Suppl.),* 65(232):1–55.

DeDuve, C. (1973): Biochemical studies on the occurrence, biogenesis and life history of mammalian peroxisomes. *J. Histochem. Cytochem.,* 11:941–948.

Diezel, P. B. (1955): Iron in the brain: A chemical and histochemical examination. In: *Bio-chemistry of the Developing Nervous System,* edited by H. Waelsch, pp. 145–152. Academic Press, New York.

Duckett, S., and White, R. (1974): Cerebral lipofuscinosis induced with tellurium: Electron dispersive X-ray spectrophotometry analysis. *Brain Res.,* 73:205–214.

Duffy, P. E., and Tennyson, V. M. (1965): Phase and electron microscopic observations of Lewy bodies and melanin granules in the substantia nigra and locus caeruleus in Parkinson's disease. *J. Neuropathol. Exp. Neurol.,* 24:398–414.

Fellman, J. H. (1958): Epinephrine metabolites and pigmentation in the central nervous system in a case of phenylpyruvic oligophrenia. *Neurol. Neurosurg. Psychiatry,* 21:58–62.

Fenichel, G. M., and Bazelon, M. (1968): Studies on neuromelanin. II. Melanin in the brainstem of infants and children. *Neurology (Minneap.)*, 18:817–820.

Finch, C. E. (1973): Monoamine metabolism in the aging male mouse. In: *Development and Aging in the Nervous System*, edited by M. Rockstein, pp. 199–218. Academic Press, New York.

Fitzpatrick, T. B., Miyamoto, M., and Ishikawa, K. (1967): The evolution of concepts of melanin biology. In: *Advances in the Biology of Skin, Vol. 8*, edited by W. Montagna and F. Hu, pp. 1–30. Pergamon Ltd., New York.

Fitzpatrick, T. B., and Quevedo, W. C., Jr. (1966): Albinism. In: *The Metabolic Basis of Inherited Disease* (2nd ed.), edited by J. B. Stanbury, J. B. Wyngaarden, and D. S. Fredrickson, pp. 324–340. McGraw-Hill, New York.

Foley, J. M., and Baxter, D. (1958): On the nature of pigment granules in the cells of the locus coeruleus and substantia nigra. *J. Neuropathol. Exp. Neurol.*, 17:586–598.

Forno, L. S., and Alvord, E. C. (1974): Depigmentation in the nerve cells of the substantia nigra and locus ceruleus in parkinsonism. In: *Advances in Neurology, Vol. 5: Second Canadian-American Conference on Parkinson's Disease*, edited by F. H. McDowell and A. Barbeau, pp. 195–202. Raven Press, New York.

Friede, R. (1953): Uber die mutmassliche Bedeutung des Melanins in der Substantia nigra. *Arch. Exp. Pathol. Pharmakol.*, 118:286–289.

Friede, R. L. (1962): The relation of the formation of lipofuscin to the distribution of oxidative enzymes in the human brain. *Acta Neuropathol.*, 2:113–125.

Friede, R. L. (1966): *Topographic Brain Chemistry*. Academic Press, New York.

Frieden, E., Osaki, S., and Kobayashi, H. (1965): Copper proteins and oxygen. *J. Gen. Physiol. (Suppl.)*, 49 (1) Pt. 2:213–252.

Fuxe, K., and Jonsson, G. (1973): The histochemical fluorescence method for the demonstration of catecholamines. Theory, practice and application. *J. Histochem. Cytochem.*, 21:293–311.

Gfeller, E. (1965): Brain pigment and catecholamines. *Lancet*, 2:739.

Goldfischer, S., and Bernstein, J. (1969): Lipofuscin (aging) pigment granules of the newborn human liver. *J. Cell Biol.*, 42:253–261.

Goldfischer, S., Novikoff, A. B., Albala, A., and Biempica, L. (1970); Hemoglobin uptake by rat hepatocytes and its breakdown within lysosomes. *J. Cell Biol.*, 44:513–530.

Goldfischer, S., Villaverde, H., and Forschirm, R. (1966): The demonstration of acid hydrolase, thermostabile reduced diphosphopyridine nucleotide tetrazolium reductase and peroxidase activities in human lipofuscin pigment granules. *J. Histochem. Cytochem.*, 14:641–652.

Gopinath, G., and Glees, P. (1974): Mitochondrial genesis of lipofuscin in the mesencephalic nucleus of the V nerve of aged rats. *Acta Anat.*, 89:14–20.

Guizzetti, P. (1915): Principali risultati dell' applicazione grossolona a fresco delle reazioni istochimiche del ferro sul sistema nervoso centrale *Riv. Patol. Nerv. Ment.*, 20:103–117.

Gutner, I. I. (1954): On the deposition of melanin in the nerve cells of the brain in the dog. *Dokl. Akad. Nauk. S.S.S.R.*, 97:531–533; cited in (1958): *Biol. Abstr.*, 32:12250.

Hallgren, B., and Sourander, P. (1958): The effect of age on the non-haemin iron in the human brain. *J. Neurochem.*, 3:41–51.

Hanaway, J., McConnell, J. A., and Netsky, M. G. (1970): Cytoarchitecture of the substantia nigra in the rat. *Am. J. Anat.*, 129:417–438.

Hendley, D. D., Mildvan, A. S., Reporter, M. C., and Strehler, B. L. (1963): The properties of isolated human cardiac age pigment. II. Chemical and enzymatic properties. *J. Gerontol.*, 18:250–259.

Hirosawa, K. (1968): Electron microscopic studies on pigment granules in the substantia nigra and locus coeruleus of the Japanese monkey (*Macaca fuscata yakui*). *Z. Zellforsch. Mikrosk. Anat.*, 88:187–203.

Holtzman, E., Teichberg, S., Abrahams, S. J., Citkowitz, E., Crain, S. M., Kawai, N., and Peterson, E. R. (1973): Notes on synaptic vesicles and related structures, endoplasmic reticulum, lysosomes and peroxisomes in nervous tissue and the adrenal medulla. *J. Histochem. Cytochem.*, 21:349–385.

Hornykiewicz, O. (1966): Dopamine (3-hydroxytyramine) and brain function. *Pharmacol. Rev.*, 18:925–964.

Howell, J. S. (1959): Histochemical demonstration of copper in copper-fed rats and in hepatolenticular degeneration. *J. Pathol. Bacteriol.*, 77:473–484.

Hruban, Z., Vigil, E. L., Slesers, A., and Hopkins, E. (1972): Microbodies, constituent organelles of animal cells. *Lab. Invest.*, 27:184-191.

Ishii, T., and Friede, R. L. (1968): Tissue binding of tritiated norepinephrine in pigmented nuclei of human brain. *Am. J. Anat.*, 122:139-144.

Kaneta, N. (1966): Histochemical studies on the diencephalon of senescent rats. *Tohoku J. Exp. Med.*, 90:249-260.

Koenig, H. (1964): Studies of brain lysosomes. In: *Response of the Nervous System to Ionizing Radiation*, edited by T. J. Haley and R. S. Snider, pp. 403-412. Little, Brown, Boston.

Koenig, H. (1965): Histochemical studies of lysosomes and lipofuscin granules in the nervous system. In: *Fifth International Congress on Neuropathology*, International Congress Series No. 100, pp. 476-477. Excerpta Medica, Amsterdam.

Koeppen, A. H., Barron, K. D., and Cox, J. F. (1971): Striatonigral degeneration. *Acta Neuropathol.*, 19:10-19.

Kusunoki, T., Ishibashi, H., and Masai, H. (1967): The distribution of monoamine oxidase and melanin pigment in the central nervous system of amphibia. *J. Hirnforsch.*, 9:63-70.

Lillie, R. D. (1955): The basophilia of melanins. *J. Histochem. Cytochem.*, 3:453-454.

Lillie, R. D. (1957a): Ferrous ion uptake., *Arch. Pathol.*, 64:100-103.

Lillie, R. D. (1957b): Metal reduction reactions of the melanins: Histochemical studies. *J. Histochem. Cytochem.*, 5:325-333.

Lillie, R. D. (1965): *Histopathologic Techinic and Practical Histochemistry*, (3rd ed.). McGraw-Hill, New York.

Lillie, R. D. (1969): Histochemistry of melanins. In: *Pigments in Pathology*, edited by M. Wolman, pp. 327-351. Academic Press, New York.

Lillie, R. D., and Yamada, H. (1960): On the yellow brown pigments of the substantia nigra, locus caeruleus and dorsal vagus nucleus of a monkey (*Macaca mulatta*). *Okajimas Folla Anat. Jap.* 36:181-183.

Lovenberg, W., Weissbach, H., and Udenfriend, S. (1962): Aromatic L-amino acid decarboxylase. *J. Biol. Chem.*, 237:89-93.

MacMillan, P. C., and Brandt, W. H. (1966): Possible role of a peroxidative system in melanin synthesis in Verticillium. *Antonie van Leeuwenhoek*, 32:202-211.

Maeda, T., and Wegmann, R. (1969): Infrared spectrometry of locus coeruleus and substantia nigra pigments in human brain. *Brain Res.*, 14:673-681.

Malkoff, D. B., and Strehler, B. L. (1963): The ultrastructure of isolated and in situ human cardiac age pigment. *J. Cell Biol.*, 16:611-616.

Mann, D. M. A., and Yates, P. O. (1974): Lipoprotein pigments—Their relationship to aging in the human nervous system. II. The melanin content of pigmented nerve cells. *Brain*, 97:489-498.

Marsden, C. D. (1961a): Tyrosinase activity in the pigmented cells of the nucleus substantiae nigrae. I. Monophenolase and diphenolase activity. *Quart. J. Microsc. Sci.*, 102:407-412.

Marsden, C. D. (1961b): Tyrosinase activity in the pigmented cells of the nucleus substantiae nigrae. II. Further observations on monophenolase activity. *Quart. J. Microsc. Sci.*, 102:469-474.

Marsden, C. D. (1961c): Pigmentation in the nucleus substantiae nigrae of mammals. *J. Anat.*, 95:256-261.

Marsden, C. D. (1965a): The development of pigmentation and enzyme activity in the nucleus substantiae nigrae of the cat. *J. Anat.*, 99:175-180.

Marsden, C. D. (1966): Oxidative enzymes responsible for conversion of 3,4-dihydroxyphenylalanine to melanin in the small intestine of rodents. *J. Histochem. Cytochem.*, 14:182-186.

Marsden, C. D. (1969): Brain melanin. In: *Pigments in Pathology*, edited by M. Wolman, pp. 395-420. Academic Press, New York.

Marsden, D. (1965b): Brain pigment and its relation to brain catecholamines. *Lancet*, 2:475-476.

Mason, H. S. (1959): Structure of melanins. In: *Pigment Cell Biology*, edited by M. Gordon, pp. 563-582. Academic Press, New York.

McGeer, E. G., Fibiger, H. C., McGeer, P. L., and Wickson, V. (1971a): Aging and brain enzymes. *Exp. Gerontol.*, 6:391-396.

McGeer, E. G., McGeer, P. L., and Wada, S. A. (1971b): Distribution of tyrosine hydroxylase in human and animal brain. *J. Neurochem.*, 18:1647-1658.

Moses, H. L., Ganote, C. E., Beaver, D. L., and Schuffman, S. (1966): Light and electron microscopic studies of pigment in human and rhesus monkey substantia nigra and locus coeruleus. *Anat. Rec.*, 155:167–183.

Muller, M. (1922): Uber physiologisches Vorkommen von Eisen in Zentralnervensystem. *Z. Gesamte Neurol. Psychiat.*, 77:519–535.

Nagatsu, T., Levitt, M., and Udenfriend, S. (1964): Tyrosine hydroxylase. The initial step in norepinephrine biosynthesis. *J. Biol. Chem.*, 239:2910–2917.

Nicolaus, R. A. (1968): *Melanins.* Hermann, Paris.

Nieto, D., Nieto, A., and Briones, M. J. (1967): Filogenia y ontogenia de la substantia nigra. *Neurol. Neurocir. Psiquiatr.*, 8:33–55.

Noback, C. R., and Shriver, J. E. (1969): Encephalization and the lemniscal systems during phylogeny. *Ann. N.Y. Acad. Sci.*, 167:118–128.

Nordgren, L., Rorsman, H., Rosengren, A. M., and Rosengren, E. (1971): Dopa and dopamine in the pigment of substantia nigra. *Experientia*, 27:1178.

Novikoff, A. B. (1967): Lysosomes in nerve cells. In: *The Neuron,* edited by H. Hyden, pp. 319–377. Elsevier, Amsterdam.

Novikoff, A. B., and Novikoff, P. M. (1973): Microperoxisomes. *J. Histochem. Cytochem.*, 11:963–966.

Novikoff, A. B., Novikoff, P. M., Quintana, N., and Davis, C. (1973): Studies on microperoxisomes. IV. Interrelations of microperoxisomes, endoplasmic reticulum and lipofuscin granules. *J. Histochem. Cytochem.*, 21:1010–1020.

Okun, M. R., Donnellan, B., Lever, W. F., Edelstein, L. M., and Or, N. (1971a): Peroxidase-dependent oxidation of tyrosine to dopa to melanin in neurons. *Histochemie*, 25:289–296.

Okun, M. R., Donnellan, B., Patel, R. P., and Edelstein, L. M. (1973): Subcellular demonstration of peroxidatic oxidation of tyrosine to melanin using dihydroxyfumarate as cofactor in mouse melanoma cells. *J. Invest. Dermatol.*, 61:60–66.

Okun, M. R., Patel, R. P., Donnellan, B., Lever, W. F., Edelstein, L. M., and Epstein, D. (1971b): Dopa compared with dihydroxyfumarate as co-factor in peroxidase-mediated oxidation of tyrosine to melanin. *Histochemie*, 27:331–334.

Olson, L., Boréus, L. O., and Seiger, A. (1973a): Histochemical demonstration and mapping of 5-hydroxytryptamine- and catecholamine-containing neuron systems in human fetal brain. *Z. Anat. Entwicklungsgesch.*, 139:259–282.

Olson, L., Nyström, B., and Seiger, A. (1973b): Monoamine fluorescence histochemistry of human post mortem brain. *Brain Res.*, 63:231–247.

Olszewski, J., and Baxter, D. (1959): *Cytoarchitecture of the Human Brain Stem.* Lipincott, Philadelphia.

Pakkenberg, H. (1966): The pigment in the substantia nigra in parkinsonism. Microspectrophotometric comparison with other sources of human pigment. *Brain Res.*, 2:173–180.

Palladini, G., Mele, R., Bugiani, O., and Tarquini, D. (1974): La lipofuscinose due systeme nerveux. Une etude experimentale. *J. Neurol. Sci.*, 23:541–549.

Parkes, J. D., Vollum, D., Marsden, C. D., and Branfoot, A. C. (1972): Cafe-au-lait spots and vitiligo in Parkinson's disease. *Lancet*, 2:1373.

Patel, R. P., Okun, M. R., Edelstein, L. M., and Epstein, D. (1971): Biochemical studies of peroxidase-mediated oxidation of tyrosine to melanin: Demonstration of the hydroxylation of tyrosine by plant and human peroxidases. *Biochem. J.*, 124:439–441.

Pilcz, A. (1895): Beitrag zur Lehre von der Pigmententwicklung in den Nervenzellen. *Arb. Neurol. Inst. Wien*, 3:123–139.

Prota, G. (1972): Structure and biogenesis of phaeomelanins. In: *Pigmentation: Its Genesis and Biologic Control,* edited by V. Riley, pp. 615–630. Appleton-Century-Crofts, New York.

Rachlin, S., and Enemark, J. (1969): Studies of catecholamines. I. Sulfur analogs of norepinephrine. *J. Med. Chem.*, 12:1089–1092.

Riley, P. A. (1966): The synthesis and distribution of tyrosinase. A histochemical interpretation. *Br. J. Dermatol.*, 78:551–571.

Rosenfeld, M. (1901a): Uber das Pigment der Hamochromatose des Darmes. *Arch. Exp. Pathol. Pharmacol.*, 45:46–50.

Rosenfeld, M. (1901b): Uber das Verhalten des Melanoidins und des jodhaltigen Spongomelanoidins im thierischen Organismus. *Arch. Exp. Pathol. Pharmacol.*, 45:51–55.

Roy, S., and Wolman, L. (1969): Ultrastructural observations in parkinsonism. *J. Pathol.*, 99:39–44.

Russell, G. V. (1955): The nucleus locus coeruleus (dorsolateralis tegmenti). *Tex. Rep. Biol. Med.*, 13:939–988.

Sachs, H. W. (1943): Uber die Autogenen Pigmente, besonders das Lipofuscin und seine Abgrenzung von Melanin. *Beitr. Pathol. Anat.*, 108:272–314.

Samorajski, T., Keefe, R., and Ordy, J. M. (1964): Intracellular localization of lipofuscin age pigments in the nervous system. *J. Gerontol.*,19:262–276.

Sansone, F. M. (1967): Histochemical studies of the substantia nigra. *Anat. Rec.*, 157:386.

Sarnat, H. B., and Netsky, M. G. (1974): *Evolution of the Nervous System.* Oxford University Press, New York.

Saunders, B. C., Holmes-Seidle, A. G., and Stark, P. (1964): *Peroxidase. The Properties and Uses of a Versatile Enzyme and some Related Catalysts.* Butterworths, Washington.

Scherer, H. J. (1939): Melanin pigmentation of the substantia nigra in primates. *J. Comp. Neurol.*, 71:91–95.

Schwyn, R. C., King, J. S., and Fox, C. A. (1970): Pigments in the red nucleus and substantia nigra in man and in representative old and new world monkeys. *Bol. Estud. Med. Biol.*, 26:139–160.

Sekhon, S. S., and Maxwell, D. S. (1974): Ultrastructural changes in neurons of the spinal anterior horn of ageing mice with particular reference to the accumulation of lipofuscin pigment. *J. Neurocytol.*, 3:59–72.

Siakotos, A. N., and Koppang, N. (1973): Procedures for the isolation of lipopigments from brain, heart and liver, and their properties: A review. *Mech. Ageing Dev.*, 2:177–200.

Siebert, G., Diezel, P. B., Jahr, K., Krug, E., Schmitt, A., Grünberger, E., and Bottke, I. (1962): Isolierung und Eigenschaften von Lipofuscin aus Herzgewebe des Menchen. *Histochemie*, 3:17–45.

Singer, P. A., Cate, J., Ross, D. G., and Netsky, M. G. (1974): Melanosis of the dentate nucleus. *Neurology (Minneap.)*, 24:156–161.

Spatz, H. (1922a): Uber den Eisennachweis im Gehirn, besonders in Zentren des extrapyramidal-motorischen Systems. *Z. Gesamte Neurol. Psychiat.*, 77:261–390.

Spatz, H. (1922b): Uber Stoffwechseleigentumlichkeiten in den Stammganglien. *Z. Gesamte Neurol. Psychiat.*, 78:641–648.

Spatz, H., and Metz, A. (1926): Untersuchungen uber Stoffspeicherung und Stofftransport im Nervensystem II. Die drei Gliazellarten und der Eisenstoffwechsel. *Z. Gesamte Neurol. Psychiat.*, 100:428–449.

Srebro, Z., and Cichocki, T. (1971): A system of periventricular glia in brain characterized by large peroxisome-like-cell organelles. *Acta Histochem.*, 41:108–114.

Sundermann, A., and Kempf, G. (1961): Uber den physiologischen Eisengehalt einiger Stammherniganglien und seine Abhangigkeit vom Lebensalter. *Z. Alternsforsch.*, 15:97–105.

Swan, G. A. (1963): Chemical structure of melanins. *Ann. N.Y. Acad. Sci.*, 100:1005.

Tingey, A. H. (1937): The iron, copper and manganese content of the human brain. *J. Ment. Sci.*, 33:452–460.

Uzman, L. L. (1956): Histochemical localization of copper with rubeanic acid. *Lab. Invest.*, 5:299–305.

Van Der Ploeg, M., and Van Duijn, P. (1964a): The influence of peroxidases on the dopa-system. *J. R. Microsc. Soc.*, 83:405–423.

Van Der Ploeg, M., and Van Duijn, P. (1964b): 5,-6-Dihydroxy indole as a substrate in a histochemical peroxidase reaction. *J. R. Microsc. Soc.*, 83:415–423.

Vanderwende, C. (1964): Studies on the oxidation of dopamine to melanin by rat brain. *Arch. Int. Pharmacodyn. Ther.*, 152:433–444.

Vanderwende, C., and Spoerlein, M. T. (1963): Oxidation of dopamine to melanin by an enzyme of rat brain. *Life Sci.*, 6:386–392.

Van Woert, M. H., and Ambani, L. M. (1974): Biochemistry of neuromelanin. In: *Advances in Neurology, Vol. 5: Second Canadian-American Conference on Parkinson's Disease*, edited by F. H. McDowell and A. Barbeau, pp. 215–223. Raven Press, New York.

Van Woert, M. H., Prasad, K. N., and Borg, D. C. (1967): Spectroscopic studies of substantia nigra pigment in human subjects. *J. Neurochem.*, 14:707–716.

Wall, G. (1972): Uber die Anfarbung der Neurolipofuscine mit Aldehydefuchsinen. *Histochemie*, 29:155–171.

Warren, P. J., Earl, C. J., and Thompson, R. H. S. (1960): This distribution of copper in human brain. *Brain*, 83:709–717.

Aging. Volume 1, edited by H. Brody, D. Harman, and J. M. Ordy. Raven Press, New York © 1975.

Age and Lipids of the Central Nervous System: Lipid Metabolism in the Developing Brain

*,**Govind A. Dhopeshwarkar and * †James F. Mead

*Laboratory of Nuclear Medicine and Radiation Biology, and **Division of Environmental and Nutritional Sciences, School of Public Health, and †Department of Biological Chemistry, School of Medicine, University of California at Los Angeles, California, 90024

The development and growth of the CNS can be divided into several distinctive periods, each characterized by a unique event. For example, the first period, in which rapid neuronal proliferation occurs, is usually of a very short duration; e.g., in the rat, it is almost completed by the third post-natal day and in the human by the 25th week of gestation (Davison and Dobbing, 1968). The second period is designated "growth spurt" and lasts for 3 weeks after birth in rats and for about 2 years in man. It is in this period that the CNS matures with axonal and dendrite growth and more importantly, as far as lipids are concerned, glial multiplication and myelination occur. The third and the fourth periods would be characterized by maturation and aging. By far the greatest attention of most lipid biochemists has been focused on the second period, rightly so, because of the profound changes occurring in brain lipids mainly associated with the process of myelination. Except for a few attempts to study this in various species (Davison and Dobbing, 1968), most of the work is restricted to rats, mice, and humans. Moreover, because of this profound change in lipid metabolism during this rather short period, designated "critical" period of growth and development by Dobbing (1972), systematic studies have been undertaken at many laboratories, including our own, to examine uptake and turnover of lipids in the brain during this period of the life-span. These studies include lipid composition of the brain as related to age, rates of synthesis, and catabolism of complex lipids and fatty acids starting at birth and on through the critical periods of growth and old age. Effects of nutrition, diet, and environmental aberration on such physiological processes as aging are now drawing the attention of the researchers in this field. Whether such insults are the cause of temporary or permanent behavioral abnormalities, premature aging, or death, is still being debated, but it is now believed that such impacts, if started early enough, would cause certain irreversible damage.

CORRELATION BETWEEN AGE AND BRAIN LIPIDS

A very comprehensive and detailed study of brain lipids in rats has been done by Wells and Dittmer (1967). In addition to a dramatic increase, almost twofold, in the lipid content of the brain between birth and 4 weeks, these workers found that the newborn rat brain has detectable amounts of sterol esters but that within about a week the sterol esters decrease to undetectable amounts. This unique behavior is not shared with any other lipid component in the brain. During this early period, gangliosides, on the other hand, increased appreciably. In the next period, from 10 to 20 days, cerebroside, sphingomyelin, triphosphoinositide, phosphatidic acid, and galactosyl-diglyceride show an approximately two- to threefold increase in concentration. This increase continues up to a month and a half but at a slower rate. Another typical phospholipid that increases dramatically during this period of active myelination is ethanolamine plasmalogen (1-alk-1'-enyl, 2-acyl ethanolamine phosphoglyceride).

Similar studies on human brain autopsy material have been done by Stallberg-Stenhagen and Svennerholm (1965), Svennerholm (1968), Svennerholm and Stallberg-Stenhagen (1968), and Rouser and Yamamoto (1969). These workers found that in the frontal lobe, 18:0 decreased with age from 80% of total fatty acids in the newborn to 40% in adult. In contrast to this, long-chain fatty acids (chain length 22 to 26 carbons) increased from 10 to 50% during the same age interval. In the child brain, cerebroside contained lower amounts of the long-chain fatty acids (22 to 26 carbons) but it was found that odd-chain fatty acids increased from infancy to 10 to 15 years of age.

Some very long-chain fatty acids, up to 34 carbon atoms, were found in adult human brain sphingolipids (Pakkala, Fillerup, and Mead, 1966). The highly unsaturated 20:4 ω6 series and 22:6 ω3 series make up large portions of the total fatty acids of phosphatidylethanolamine (Sun and Horrocks, 1968). The α-hydroxy fatty acids are associated mainly with glycolipids (Bowen and Radin, 1968) and the odd-chain fatty acids are present in substantial amounts in polyphosphoinositides (Kerr and Reed, 1963) and also in cerebrosides (Kishimoto and Radin, 1959a).

Largely because of the more spectacular changes in the brain lipids during the developmental stages, the postdevelopmental aging period has been neglected. Such studies that have been carried out, however, have shown that there is very little change in the relative amounts of the lipid components. There is a rapid increase in total lipid during the developmental period followed by a very long course of slowly declining total lipid without significant changes in the relative proportion of any one lipid [Fillerup and Mead (1967); Rouser and Yamamoto (1969); Sun and Samorajsky (1972)]. It appears, then, that in the aging brain, as neurons and accompanying myelin are gradually lost, the total lipid complement decreases. In other words, the units concerned with the decrease in lipid are relatively large.

However, certain changes occur during aging in the fatty acids of the brain lipids and these may be very significant. First, as shown by Gellhorn and Benjamin (1966), fatty acid desaturation decreases with age, leading to an increased proportion of saturated fatty acids in the lipids of the elderly. Second, chain-length in the saturated fatty acids, particularly in the glyco-lipids, increases, leading to lipids with very long hydrocarbon chains. Possibly this very slow replacement process gradually molds a more stable structure (O'Brien, 1965) in the slow maturation of the glial cell plasma membrane into mature myelin. Accompanying this process, and perhaps resulting from it, are the formation and accumulation of α-hydroxy and odd-chain fatty acids in the sphingolipids (Kishimoto and Radin, 1959b). This process may result from degradative systems for the very long-chain fatty acids, which are not readily activated or attacked by the usual β-oxi-dation (Mead and Levis, 1962, 1963). In any event, the α-hydroxy acids thus formed may also contribute to myelin stability in presenting an ad-ditional hydroxyl group in a strategic position for forming strong hydrogen bonds in the apolar interior of the myelin membrane. No advantage has been considered for the odd-chain fatty acids and they may simply be the products of the α-oxidation process reincorporated into lipid.

These reactions do not seem to increase with age and the increasing proportions of these fatty acids may simply reflect the added stability of the products of a slow steady process.

The changes in the brain lipids with age are thus seen to reflect both the metabolism of the brain itself and the accessibility of the brain to lipids from the diet—a function of the various transport processes sometimes called the blood-brain barrier system.

BLOOD-BRAIN BARRIER SYSTEM AND AGE

Inability of trypan blue to permeate brain tissue in the adult animal, as against free staining in fetal neonatal brains, was attributed to development of the blood-brain barrier with increasing maturity (Davson, 1956). This was then chosen as an argument for explaining greater incorporation of many compounds, including cholesterol and fatty acids, in the developing brain as compared to that of the mature adult animal. This concept immediately leads to questions such as: How does the older brain get essential nutrients? Does the brain depend for the rest of life upon the vital supplies it received in the very early stage of development? Does the need for essential nutrients decrease as the species ages? Is the brain largely a closed metabolic system tending to conserve the supply of essential nutrients? What is the nature of the turnover of such essential nutrients?

Taking essential fatty acids such as linoleic (18:2 $\omega6$) and linolenic (18:3 $\omega3$) as examples of essential nutrients that the mammalian system is incapable of synthesizing *in vivo*, we first sought to answer these questions in the following way.

UPTAKE OF ESSENTIAL FATTY ACIDS BY THE ADULT BRAIN

Four-month-old adult rats were given $1\text{-}^{14}C$-linoleic (all *cis* 9, 12-octa-decadienoic acid) and $1\text{-}^{14}C$-linolenic acid (all *cis* 9, 12, 15-octadecatrienoic acid) by mouth and sacrificed 4 and 24 hr after the dose. Brain fatty acids were separated and decarboxylated (Dhopeshwarkar, Subramanian and Mead, 1971*a*, 1971*b*). Table 1 shows the results. From the label distribution data it is evident that $1\text{-}^{14}C$-linoleate and linolenate were taken up directly into the brain following oral administration. Had these fatty acids been degraded to acetate prior to uptake by the brain, the results would have been similar to those following $1\text{-}^{14}C$-acetate administration. The major elongation desaturation products of 18:2 and 18:3 are 20:4 and 22:6, respectively. Their label distribution is exactly as one would predict from a precursor-product relationship. This, then, shows that as far as essential fatty acids are concerned, there seems to be no barrier effect even in fully grown adult animals. It also dispels the doubt that animals must rely on the supply of essential fatty acids received during the very early stages of development (Dhopeshwarkar and Mead, 1973).

TABLE 1. *Relative carboxyl activity (% RCA) in brain fatty acids following administration of tracer*

Tracer	Interval (hr)	Fatty acid isolated from brain lipids			
		18:2 (% RCA)	20:4 (% RCA)	18:3 (% RCA)	22:6 (% RCA)[a]
L-^{14}C-Acetate	4	—	84.1	—	70.2
L-^{14}C-Linoleate	4	92.0	28.1	—	68.4
L-^{14}C-Linolenate	4	—	—	91.0	23.0
L-^{14}C-Acetate	24	—	83.3	—	81.9
L-^{14}C-Linoleate	24	88.0	3.5	—	72.4
L-^{14}C-Linolenate	24	—	81.7	92.4	12.4

[a] $\% \text{ RCA} = \dfrac{\text{radioactivity in }-\text{COOH}}{\text{radioactivity in total fatty acids}} \times 100.$

The evidence showing greater uptake of radioactivity from administered fatty acids in the adult brain as compared to the liver, provided the tracer is injected intracarotidly (Dhopeshwarkar and Mead, 1973), indicates that there is a competition between the liver and the brain for the uptake of fatty acids. Thus, material injected intracarotidly is readily taken up by the adult brain, which indicates that the aging process does not necessarily interfere in fatty acid uptake. However, no data are yet available on how this uptake is affected in the later aging process, e.g., at 2 to 3 yr.

FATTY ACID TURNOVER

Two fatty acids, palmitic and linolenic acids, were chosen for the turnover studies. Palmitic acid, a typical saturated fatty acid commonly found in most tissues including the brain, is also the main product of fatty acid synthetase. On the other hand, linolenic acid is the precursor of docasahexaenoate (22:6 ω3), a highly unsaturated fatty acid found abundantly in the brain. Essentiality of linolenic acid to the brain is still a matter of speculation but recent work by Bernsohn and Spitz (1974) has hinted that linolenic acid may have a biochemical function, distinct from that of linoleic acid, in restoring certain membrane-bound enzymes. Figure 1 shows the uptake of palmitate and linolenate into the brain of 13-day-old rats and its retention during further aging. It can be observed that whereas radioactivity from linolenate decreases continuously as the interval between dose and sacrifice increases, the radioactivity from palmitate does not decrease even after a long period of 30 days. One possible reason for this persistence of radioactivity in the brain following 1-^{14}C-palmitate injection, is reutilization of labeled 16:0 acyl groups for lipid biosynthesis as observed by Sun and Horrocks (1973). The persistence of radioactivity in the carboxyl carbon of palmitate over a long period observed in our earlier studies (Dhopeshwarkar, Subramanian, and Mead, 1973) supports this hypothesis. It is also possible that the palmitate and its elongation products are primarily incorporated into the myelin fraction, which has a relatively slow turnover rate (Davison, 1972).

The polyenoic fatty acids, as components of ethanolamine phospho-

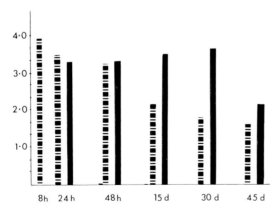

FIG. 1. Percent uptake of radioactivity in brain lipids at different intervals following intraperitoneal injection of 1-^{14}C-linolenic and 1-^{14}C-palmitic acid given to 12 to 13-day-old rats. Percent uptake $= \dfrac{\text{cpm/g brain wet weight}}{\mu\text{Ci dose given/g body weight}} \times 100$. Broken bars: after L-^{14}C 18:3; solid bars: after 1-^{14}C 16:0.

glycerides, would be largely associated with the glial and neuronal membranes (Fewster and Mead, 1968), and during the "critical" period of growth and glial proliferation the polyenoic acids could have a rapid metabolic turnover resulting in loss of radioactivity. It is clear from these data that the retention of ^{14}C radioactivity in the brain over an extended period depends on the nature of the injected tracer, even though both of the tracers used here were fatty acids.

INTERCONVERSION OF FATTY ACIDS IN THE BRAIN

Both palmitic and linolenic acids can be incorporated directly into other fatty acids and at the same time give rise to acetate by β-oxidation. This acetate can then be utilized in several ways, such as *de novo* synthesis of saturated fatty acids (16:0 and part of 18:0), chain elongation of existing fatty acids, and synthesis of cholesterol. Thus, individual brain fatty acids were isolated and the radioactivity determined following administration of 1-^{14}C-palmitate and L-^{14}C-linolenate separately. Figure 2 shows the relative specific activity (counts per min/mg × percent composition by gas/liquid chromatography) of brain fatty acids following intraperitoneal injection of 1-^{14}C-palmitate. As expected, palmitate was the most highly radioactive fatty acid in the brain 24 hr after the injection, although there is a rapid decrease in radioactivity as the interval between dose and sacrifice increased. The injected palmitate must have undergone oxidation to acetate to be reutilized for the synthesis of stearate (Mead and Fulco, 1961; Kishimoto, Davies, and Radin, 1965) and the polyunsaturated fatty acids 20:4

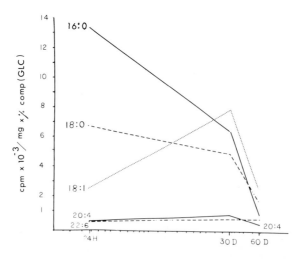

FIG. 2. Relative specific activity (cpm/mg × percent composition by gas/liquid chromatography) of brain fatty acids at different intervals following intraperitoneal injection of L-^{14}C-palmitic acid.

ω6 and 22:6 ω3 by the chain-elongation process. Thus within the short period of 24 hr, 18:0 attained relatively high radioactivity; at this time, although 18:1 had low radioactivity, this activity increased within the next 30 days to the point that it was the most highly active of the brain fatty acids, including the original tracer 16:0. The radioactivity of 20:4 and 22:6 must be the result of radioactive acetate (produced by oxidation of tracer 16:0) utilization for elongating nonradioactive (dietary) fatty acids 18:2 ω6 and 18:3 ω3. The total radioactivity of these polyunsaturated fatty acids was low because the 18 carbon atoms, counting from the methyl end, are non-radioactive and only the odd carbon atoms arising from acetate units contribute the radioactivity.

Figure 3 is a similar curve obtained with 1-^{14}C-linolenic acid as a tracer. The most surprising result of this experiment was that palmitate was the most radioactive component although 1-^{14}C-linolenic acid was the injected tracer. Since 18:3 ω3 is converted to 22:6 ω3, one would have expected 22:6 to be the most highly active component. It was only after 48 hr that the radioactivity of 22:6 increased appreciably. At this point the radioactivity of palmitate was already declining. During the first 8 hr, 22:6 and 18:1 had almost the same amount of radioactivity but in the next 48 hr 18:0 and 18:1 seem to share almost equal amounts of radioactivity. Fifteen days after the tracer (approximately at the end of the "critical" period of growth), as in the palmitate experiment, 18:1 attained high radioactivity. A gradual decrease in radioactivity of all the fatty acids, except 22:6, continued until the end of the 45 day period. Thus, the oxidative degradation of palmitate

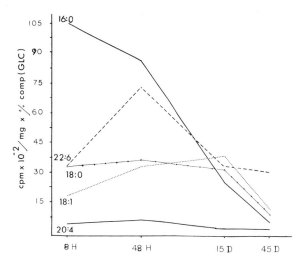

FIG. 3. Relative specific activity (cpm/mg × percent composition by gas/liquid chromatography) of brain fatty acids at different intervals following intraperitoneal injection of L-^{14}C-linolenic acid.

is a continuous process, but that of 22:6 (or 18:3) seems to be made up of two parts. One part, probably involving the free acid, is quickly degraded to acetate, which serves as starting material for *de novo* synthesis of palmitate (the major end-product of fatty acid synthetase) and the other part, presumably involving fatty acids in the form of complex polar lipids, is degraded at a slower rate. It is not clear whether linolenate is converted to 22:6 before or after incorporation into complex lipids.

Radioactivity in the carboxyl carbon compared to the rest of the molecule (% RCA) is indicative of the pathways (*de novo*, chain elongation, etc.) of biosynthesis. Persistence of radioactivity in the carboxyl carbon of brain palmitate (following 1-^{14}C-palmitic acid injection) over a long period of time shows that the original tracer is not completely oxidized even after 2 months (Table 2). If it was oxidized to acetate completely, the resynthesized palmitate would have equal distribution of radioactivity in the odd-numbered carbon atoms giving 12.5% RCA (or $\frac{1}{8}$). However, part of the injected acid must have been degraded to acetate because chain-elongated products have radioactivity in the carboxyl carbon in addition to formation of radioactive cholesterol. The 24-hr % RCA value for stearate is low and close to the theoretical *de novo* synthesis value ($\frac{1}{9}$ or 11.1%); however, the other two % RCA values indicate synthesis by chain elongation of injected palmitate. The % RCA for 20:4 and 22:6 is what one would predict from known reactions of 18:2 → 20:4 and 18:3 → 22:6.

When 1-^{14}C-linolenic acid was used as a tracer, no starting material could be found in the brain even in the early time period of 8 hr. However, the end-product of linolenic acid, docasahexaenoic acid (22:6 ω3), on decarboxylation, consistently showed a low % RCA. At the start, C-1 of 18:3 contained all the radioactivity and since the entire molecule is incorporated directly into 22:6, C-5 of 22:6 should have high activity and the carboxyl carbon

TABLE 2. *Percent distribution of radioactivity in brain fatty acids*

	Interval between dose and sacrifice						
	Tracer (L-^{14}C-palmitic acid)			Tracer (L-^{14}C-linolenic acid)			
Fatty acid	24 hr (% RCA)	30 days (% RCA)	60 days (% RCA)	8 hr (% RCA)	48 hr (% RCA)	15 days (% RCA)	45 days (% RCA)
16:0	78.4	70.4	60.3	13.4	12.8	14.3	20.7
18:0	9.4	4.6	6.6	19.5	14.0	7.6	12.8
18:1	11.2	4.8	6.0	21.5	15.2	10.1	11.9
20:4	57.1	55.4	47.3	55.4	85.6	98.8	81.1
22:6	69.5	57.7	76.2	5.0	5.6	3.2	2.8

$$\% \text{ RCA} = \frac{\text{radioactivity in —COOH}}{\text{radioactivity in total fatty acids}} \times 100.$$

should have a lower proportion of radioactivity; this low activity comes from the C_2 acetate units. In other words, the carboxyl carbon of 18:3 (starting material) or C_5 of 22:6, retained radioactivity even after 45 days.

The calculation of half-life or turnover rate of different fatty acids in terms of ^{14}C radioactivity is complicated, not only because of the inter-conversions and reutilization of the acyl groups in overall brain metabolism (Sun and Horrocks, 1973), but also because of the heterogenous nature of the brain tissue with different regions of the brain having unique composi-tion and metabolism (Shrinivas Rao and Subba Rao, 1973). Examining curves 2 and 3, it is apparent that the half-life of palmitate (taking the 24 hr point as that of highest specific activity) would be approximately 30 days. However, it should be pointed out here that the decrease in radioactivity is by no means linear over the 2-month period of study. The half-life of lino-lenate has to be computed from the curve for 22:6; similarly, taking the 48 hr point as that of highest specific activity, the $T^{1/2}$ for 18:3 is approximately 15 days. This may be interpreted as a greater need of a continuous supply of linolenic acid arising from a shorter half-life or higher turnover as compared to palmitate, but the brain does not depend on the exogenous supply of palmitate, which can be formed *de novo* from acetate. It would be interest-ing to study this process over a longer aging period and to establish the requirements throughout life.

INCORPORATION INTO COMPLEX LIPIDS

It is assumed that the half-life of most fatty acids, as free fatty acids, in the brain is very short. For example, Sun and Horrocks (1969) found that the half-life of free palmitic acid was less than 5 min. The incorporation into multicomponent complex lipids would result in complicated metabolic turn-over. In order to obtain information about metabolic turnover of the complex lipids, with respect of ^{14}C-acyl groups, each component of the brain lipids was isolated by column chromatographic procedures and its purity tested by thin-layer chromatography (Rouser, Kritchevsky, Heller, and Lieber, 1963). Figures 4, 5, and 6 give the radioactivity in terms of counts per minute/micromole/gram of brain tissue. Examining the curve for cholesterol and cerebroside (Fig. 4), one can observe that the radioactivity of cholesterol (originating from radioactive acetate, itself a degradation product of tracer fatty acid) shows an increase up to 48 hr after injection irrespective of whether it was palmitate or linolenate that was injected, but thereafter the radioactivity of cholesterol shows radical differences. When the injected tracer was palmitate, the cholesterol derived from its breakdown gained in radioactivity continuously up to 30 days. However, it was reduced by half during the same period when the injected tracer was radioactive linolenate. At first it is difficult to understand why the radioactivity of cholesterol should depend on the injected tracer when the cholesterol originates from the acetate

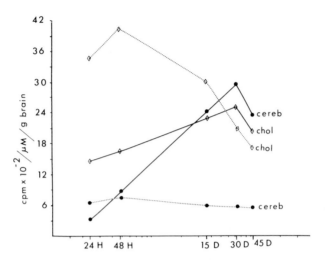

FIG. 4. Relative specific activity (cpm/μmole/g brain wet weight) of cholesterol (chol) and cerebrosides (cereb) at different intervals following injection of 1-¹⁴C-palmitic acid (solid line) and 1-¹⁴C-linolenic acid (broken line).

pool derived by the breakdown of either linolenate or palmitate. However, closer examination shows that the ¹⁴C-radioactivity in the brain following linolenate injection, decreased over a period of 30 days, unlike the radioactivity from palmitate. This indicates that the breakdown and reutilization of acetyl and acyl ¹⁴C activity from palmitate occurred over a longer period

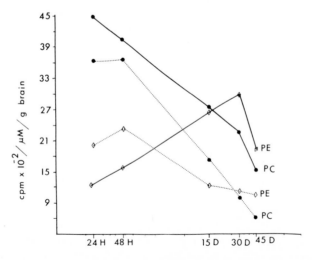

FIG. 5. Relative specific activity (cmp/μmole/g brain wet weight) of phosphatidylcholine (PC) and phosphatidylethanolamine (PE) at different intervals following injection of 1-¹⁴C-palmitic acid (solid line) and 1-¹⁴C-linolenic acid (broken line).

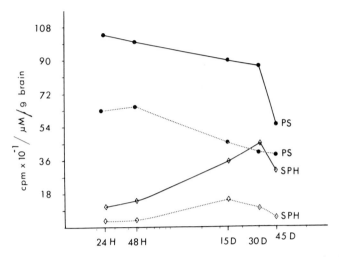

FIG. 6. Relative specific activity (cpm/μmole/g brain wet weight) of phosphatidylserine (PS) and sphingomyelin (SPH) following injection of 1-^{14}C-palmitic acid (solid line) and 1-^{14}C-linolenic acid (broken line).

of time, as compared to similar reactions originating from 1-^{14}C-linolenate. The persistence of the radioactive acetate pool could contribute to increasing activity of brain cholesterol, particularly because of the slow turnover rate of the bulk of cholesterol in the brain (Spohn and Davison, 1972).

The conversion of radioactive palmitate to stearate and longer chain fatty acids observed by Kishimoto and Radin (1966) could explain the higher radioactivity of brain cerebroside, the fatty acyl groups of which are characterized by such long-chain fatty acids. In the 1-^{14}C-linolenate experiment, although palmitate was highly active in the early period of 8 hr, the cerebroside content of the brain of 13-day-old suckling rats is very low; and thus, the product counts per minute/micromole/gram is numerically low. Fifteen days after the tracer (28-day-old rats) the cerebroside content is high but radioactivity of saturated acids is low; and so again, the product is low.

The radioactivity of brain phospholipid (phosphatidylcholine and phosphatidylethanolamine) after 1-^{14}C-palmitate and linolenate is shown in Fig. 5. Twenty-four hours after injection, it was observed that phosphatidylcholine was the most highly active component irrespective of the tracer. Regarding the 1-^{14}C-palmitate experiment, it is conceivable that phosphatidylcholine has maximum radioactivity because 16:0 is the major saturated fatty acid of phosphatidylcholine. When 1-^{14}C-linolenate was injected, because a high proportion of polyunsaturated fatty acids are found in phosphatidylethanolamine (Sun and Horrocks, 1968), it would have been expected that phosphatidylethanolamine would be the most active component. However, Fig. 5 shows that again, it is phosphatidylcholine that is the most radioactive component 24 hr after tracer injection. In the next 48 hr the radioactivity of 22:6 increased considerably as well as the radioactivity of phosphatidylethanolamine. The unexpected continued increase in radioactivity of phosphatidylethanolamine following injection of radioactive palmitate remains a puzzle.

Fig. 6 shows the similarity in the curves for phosphatidylserine and sphingomyelin. Radioactivity of phosphatidylserine was higher than that of sphingomyelin, irrespective of the tracer used. The increase in sphingomyelin radioactivity up to 30 days after injection of palmitate could be for reasons similar to those considered earlier for cerebrosides.

SUMMARY

The lipids of the CNS exhibit marked changes during the early period of life. For example, in the rat, the period of maximum changes in brain lipids is between the first and third week after birth. After about $1^1/_2$ months these variations level off. During the rest of the aging period it appears that as neurons and accompanying myelin are gradually lost, their total lipid component decreases. However, the fatty acid pattern is definitely affected during this aging period. This reflects in a decrease in unsaturation with age resulting in an increased proportion of saturated fatty acids of progressively increased chain length. There is also an accumulation of α-hydroxy and odd-chain fatty acids. The physiological implications of these changes are still not known, but it is generally believed that they add to the stability of the myelin, and this could be a reason for a very gradual age-dependent decrease in myelin lipids.

A study was undertaken to examine during the critical period of growth and development, the uptake and metabolic fate of ^{14}C-labeled palmitate, the most common saturated fatty acid, and a possible essential fatty acid, linolenic acid, which is the precursor of highly unsaturated docosahexaenoic acid found abundantly in brain ethanolamine glycerophosphatides. Although both compounds are fatty acids, the radioactivity from these was not retained to the same extent. Radioactivity from linolenic acid was lost much more rapidly. In fact, linolenic acid was rapidly oxidized to acetate, which was used for resynthesis of palmitate, and the palmitate became the most highly radioactive fatty acid. Thus, although a portion of the essential fatty acid was retained over the 2 month period, a considerable amount was oxidized and the acetate utilized for synthetic processes. Further work is needed to determine the implication of these and other results in terms of the role of essential fatty acids in the developing brain.

ACKNOWLEDGMENTS

Investigations discussed in this chapter and conducted in our laboratory were supported in part by Contract AT(04-1)GEN-12 between the Atomic Energy Commission and the University of California and by the U.S. Public Health Service Research Career Award No. GM-K6-19, 177 from the Division of Central Medical Sciences, National Institutes of Health.

The authors are very grateful for the excellent technical help from Mrs. Carole Subramanian in our investigation. We extend our sincere thanks to Mrs. Joyce Adler for her invaluable assistance in the preparation of this chapter.

REFERENCES

Bernsohn, J., and Spitz, F. J. (1974): Linoleic and linolenic acid dependency of some brain membrane bound enzymes after lipid deprivation in rats. *Biochem. Biophys. Res. Commun.,* 57:293–298.

Bowen, D. M., and Radin, N. S. (1968): Hydroxy fatty acid metabolism in the brain. In: *Advances in Lipid Research, Vol. 6,* edited by R. Paoletti and D. Kritchevsky, pp. 255–272. Academic Press, New York.

Davison, A. N. (1972): Biosynthesis of the myelin sheath. In: *Lipids, Malnutrition and the Developing Brain, CIBA Foundation Symposium,* edited by K. Elliott and J. Knight, pp. 73–90. Associated Scientific Publishers, Amsterdam.

Davison, A. N., and Dobbing, J. (1968): The developing brain. In: *Applied Neurochemistry,* edited by A. N. Davison and J. Dobbing, p. 253. Blackwell, Oxford.

Davson, H. (1956): *Physiology of the Cerebrospinal Fluid,* pp. 231–235. Churchill, London.

Dhopeshwarkar, G. A., and Mead, J. F., (1973): Uptake and transport of fatty acids into the brain and the role of the blood-brain-barrier system. In: *Advances in Lipid Research, Vol. 11,* edited by R. Paoletti and D. Kritchevsky, pp. 109–142. Academic Press, New York.

Dhopeshwarkar, G. A., Subramanian, C., and Mead, J. F. (1971a): Fatty acid uptake by the brain. IV. Incorporation of 1-^{14}C linoleic acid into the adult rat brain. *Biochim. Biophys. Acta,* 231:8–14.

Dhopeshwarkar, G. A., Subramanian, C., and Mead, J. F. (1971b): Fatty acid uptake by the brain. V. Incorporation of 1-^{14}C linolenic acid into adult rat brain. *Biochim. Biophys. Acta,* 239:162–167.

Dhopeshwarkar, G. A., Subramanian, C., and Mead, J. F. (1973): Metabolism of 1-^{14}C palmitic acid in the developing brain: Persistence of radioactivity in the carboxyl carbon. *Biochim. Biophys. Acta,* 296:257–264.

Dobbing, J. (1972): Vulnerable period of brain development. In: *Lipids, Malnutrition and the Developing Brain, CIBA Foundation Symposium,* edited by K. Elliott and J. Knight, pp. 9–20. Associated Scientific Publishers, Amsterdam.

Fewster, M. E., and Mead, J. F. (1968): Fatty acid and fatty aldehyde composition of glial cell lipids isolated from bovine white matter. *J. Neurochem.,* 15:1303–1312.

Fillerup, D. L., and Mead, J. F. (1967): The lipids of the aging human brain. *Lipids,* 2:295–298.

Gellhorn, A., and Benjamin, W. (1966): Fatty acid biosynthesis and ribonucleic acid function in fasting, aging and diabetes. *Adv. Enzyme Regul.,* 4:19–41.

Kerr, S. E., and Reed, W. W. C. (1963): The fatty acid component of polyphosphoinositide prepared from calf brain. *Biochem. Biophys. Acta,* 70:477–478.

Kishimoto, Y., Davies, W. E., and Radin, N. S. (1965): Turnover of fatty acids of rat brain gangliosides, glycerophosphatides, cerebrosides and sulfatides as a function of age. *J. Lipid Res.,* 6:525–531.

Kishimoto, Y., and Radin, N. S. (1959a): Isolation and determination methods for brain cerebrosides, hydroxy fatty acids and unsaturated and saturated fatty acids. *J. Lipid Res.,* 1:72–76.

Kishimoto, Y., and Radin, N. S. (1959*b*): Composition of cerebroside acids as a function of age. *J. Lipid Res.,* 1:79–82.

Kishimoto, Y., and Radin, N. S. (1966): Metabolism of brain glycolipid fatty acids. *Lipids,* 1:47–61.

Mead, J. F., and Fulco, A. J. (1961): Distribution of label from 1-^{14}C acetate in brain stearic acid. *Biochim. Biophys. Acta,* 54:362–364.

Mead, J. F., and Levis, G. M. (1962): α-Oxidation of the brain fatty acids. *Biochem. Biophys. Res. Commun.,* 9:231–234.

Mead, J. F., and Levis, G. M. (1963): A 1-carbon degradation of long chain fatty acids of brain sphingolipids. *J. Biol. Chem.,* 238:1634–1636.

O'Brien, J. S. (1965): Stability of the myelin membrane. *Science,* 147:1099–1107.

Pakkala, S. G., Fillerup, D. L., and Mead, J. F. (1966): The very long chain fatty acids of human brain sphingolipids. *Lipids,* 1:449–450.

Rouser, G., Kritchevsky, G., Heller, D., and Lieber, E. (1963): Lipid composition of beef brain, beef liver, and the sea anemone: Two approaches to quantitative fractionation of complex lipid mixtures. *J. Am. Oil Chem. Soc.,* 40:425–454.

Rouser, G., and Yamamoto, A. (1969): Chemical architecture of the nervous system, Lipids. In: *Handbook of Neurochemistry, Vol. 1,* edited by A. Lajtha, pp. 121–169. Plenum, New York.

Shrinivasa Rao, P., and Subba Rao, K. (1973): Fatty acid composition of phospholipids in different regions of developing human fetal brain. *Lipids,* 8:374–377.

Spohn, M., and Davison, A. N. (1972): Cholesterol metabolism in myelin and other subcellular fractions of rat brain. *J. Lipid Res.,* 13:563–570.

Stallberg-Stenhagen, S., and Sveenerholm, L. (1965): Fatty acid composition of human brain sphingomyelins: Normal variation with age and changes during myelin disorders. *J. Lipid Res.,* 6:146–155.

Sun, G. Y., and Horrocks, L. A. (1968): The fatty acid and aldehyde composition of the major phospholipids of mouse brain. *Lipids,* 3:79–83.

Sun, G. Y., and Horrocks, L. A. (1973): Metabolism of palmitic acid in the subcellular fractions of mouse brain. *J. Lipid Res.,* 14:206–214.

Sun, G. Y., and Samorajski, T. (1972): Age changes in the lipid composition of whole homogenates and isolated myelin fraction of mouse brain. *J. Gerontol.,* 27:10–17.

Svennerholm, L. (1968): Distribution and fatty acid composition of phosphoglycerides in normal human brain. *J. Lipid Res.,* 9:570–579.

Svennerholm, L., and Stallberg-Stenhagan, S. (1968): Changes in fatty acid composition of cerebrosides and sulfatides of human nervous tissue with age. *J. Lipid Res.,* 9:215–225.

Wells, M. A., and Dittmer, J. C. (1967): A comprehensive study of the postnatal changes in the concentration of the lipids of developing rat brain. *Biochemistry,* 6:3169–3175.

Aging. Volume 1, edited by H. Brody,
D. Harman, and J. M. Ordy. Raven
Press, New York © 1975.

Life-Span Neurochemical Changes in the Human and Nonhuman Primate Brain

*J. Mark Ordy, *Bernice Kaack, and ***Kenneth R. Brizzee

*Delta Regional Primate Research Center, Covington, Louisiana 70433, and **Department
of Anatomy, Tulane University School of Medicine, New Orleans, Louisiana 70112*

BRIEF HISTORY AND CURRENT STATUS OF NEUROCHEMISTRY

Neurochemistry and Gerontology

As an interdisciplinary science, gerontology now includes sociology, psychology, physiology, biochemistry, and morphology. Biological gerontology is regarded as a relatively young discipline with a predominant interest in genetic, molecular, and cellular mechanisms of aging (Curtis, 1966; Kohn, 1971). This is in general accord with the current emphasis on genetic and molecular mechanisms throughout the fields of biology. However, in the growing discipline of neurobiology, the predominant emphasis on genetic, molecular, and cellular sources of aging may have an inhibitory effect on promising future research concerned with numerous other environmental influences on the brain in aging. Attempts to construct only genetic and molecular theories of aging for the brain *a priori* exclude reference to other levels of biological and social organization. These sources may also have an influence on the brain, at least on the rate of its aging since they presumably affect the median life-span of the individual. The organizational complexity essential to maintain life from molecular, cellular, organ, and organismic levels implies that age-dependent changes in the organization of the brain may be just as significant as the genetic, molecular, and cellular changes currently considered as the basic or exclusive sources of biological aging (Sacher, 1968; Dayan, 1972). Organizational complexity is a fundamental feature of the brain. The brain is uniquely characterized by tissue interdependence, organizational complexity, redundancy, and environmental modifiability. Biological aging may involve changes in all molecules, cells, tissues, and organs of the body (Kohn, 1971). However, the unique role of the brain in adaptation to the environment through learning and its integration of the entire body may play an important "pacemaker" role in the rate of aging. Since each postmitotic neuron is as old as the individual, it may also be essential to consider development, maturity, and aging as interrelated aspects of the total life-span (Ordy and Schjeide, 1973). The brain is the respository not only of the genetic or DNA-"programmed" capacities but also the experiences acquired throughout the life-span. It mediates the input of the physical and social environments into an output of adaptation during development, maturity, and senescence (Birren, 1965).

All of the neurosciences, including neurochemistry, have undergone a remarkable and explosive expansion in recent years. This rapid progress has occurred primarily in research on brain development rather than aging. There are many basic differences in the brain during development, maturity, and aging. However, since the differentiated postmitotic neurons of the mammalian brain are not replaced by cell division after birth, separation of the life-span into stages in neurobiological research imposes restrictions for relating long-term changes in such unique functions as memory to antecedent changes in the brain (Ordy and Schjeide, 1973). In long-term or life-span studies, it is now generally recognized that the mammalian brain undergoes a period of rapid growth, remains relatively stable throughout maturity, and then appears to decline in senescence. Some selective declines in sensory, cognitive, and motor capacities after maturity appear to be universal manifestations of aging (Birren, 1965; Schaie, 1968; Busse and Pfeiffer, 1969). However, these age declines can result from interactions among age-related changes in personality, role expectancies, altered psychosocial relations, as well as from DNA-programmed physiological, chemical, and morphological changes in the brain. Whatever the sources of age decline, the brain must play a critical role in aging since it regulates the behavioral adaptations to the environment through conditioning and learning. It is also concerned with reflex regulation or integration involving the physiology and chemistry of the total organism. Due to the neurosecretory role of the hypothalamic-pituitary-adrenal axis and the "trophic" function of the brain in neuromuscular coordination, interactions between DNA and environmentally determined age changes in the brain may influence or contribute to the declines of neuroendocrine, motor systems, and all other organs of the body. Finally, a phylogenetic source for attributing an important "pacemaker" role to the brain in aging is the significant correlation between brain weight and life-span in mammals (Sacher, 1959).

A survey of the current neurochemical literature has indicated only a very limited number of reviews dealing directly with chemical alterations in the brain in aging (Herrmann, 1971). Due to the current exclusive emphasis on genetic, molecular, and cellular mechanisms of aging (Sacher, 1968), only a few earlier and some recent clinical studies have concentrated on life-span changes in chemical composition, metabolism, and the chemical aspects of neurotransmission as possible sources of aging, particularly in the human brain (Himwich, 1959; Dayan, 1972). As another major consequence of the current overemphasis on genetic, molecular, and cellular mechanisms of biological aging, there has been a separation of behavioral, physiological, neurochemical, and morphological levels of observation in univariate neurobiological studies of aging as opposed to an increasing number of multivariate studies in developmental neurobiology (Himwich, 1970; Ordy and Schjeide, 1973). In view of the unique role of the brain in learning and its integrative functions throughout the life-span, it is only within a broad multidisciplinary framework that a "neurochemistry of gerontology" can contribute to clarification of basic chemical alterations in the brain and the chemical aspects of sensory, cognitive, and motor declines as the more obvious and significant behavioral manifestations of biological aging.

Neurochemistry and Neurobiology

The historical antecedents or origins for the new field of neurochemistry have included studies of (1) the chemical composition or architecture of the nervous system, (2) metabolic reactions or energy transformations, and (3) chemical aspects of such neural functions as excitation, conduction, and transmission. Important influences on neurochemistry have also come from such clinical fields as psychiatry, neurology, neuropathology, and from such basic sciences as pharmacology, physical chemistry, and biophysics (Tower, 1958). A continuation in the three areas of interest and the clinical and basic science influences on neurochemistry can be clearly recognized in the content and organization of the recent seven volumes of the *Handbook of Neurochemistry*. The handbooks contain reviews of the following areas: architecture and structural neurochemistry; metabolic reactions; turnover and control mechanisms; genetic and environmental alterations in chemical equilibrium and chemical aspects of neuropathology (Lajtha, 1969–1972). As one of the most recent disciplines in neuroscience, neurochemistry has now also begun to play a dynamic and vital role in such diverse areas as the roles of molecular and cellular mechanisms in learning (Schmitt, 1967), neural plasticity (Galambos, 1970), dynamics of synaptic modulation (Bloom, 1974), changes in RNA and protein during conditioning and learning (Hyden and Lange, 1970), and the role of biogenic amines in arousal, emotions, and mental illness (Kety, 1970). However, there has been a serious neglect of life-span or even long-term chemical evaluations of the human brain. In view of the scarcity of data and the great interest in the neurochemistry of the human brain, the aims of this neurochemical review and research program have been an examination of life-span changes in chemical composition, metabolism, and neurotransmitters as physiological regulators in the human and nonhuman primate brain. The primary emphasis has been on aging. However, since aging may represent, at least in part, a continuation of a developmental life-span program, major features of brain development and maturity have been included as antecedent, temporal, or sequential points of reference.

NEUROCHEMISTRY, HUMAN MEDIAN, AND MAXIMUM LIFE-SPANS; EXPERIMENTAL DESIGNS; NEUROCHEMICAL METHODS AND PROBLEMS

As in all of biological gerontology, where the focus is on aging as an extension of an ontogenetic program, a neurochemistry of gerontology requires a conceptual framework, appropriate experimental designs and chemical methods for assessment of the multiple sources of even the major sequential chemical changes that may occur in the brain throughout the life-span. Unlike some other DNA-programmed traits, biological aging in the brain must represent complex interactions between genetically and environmentally determined variables. Convenient starting points of reference for neurochemistry and aging include chronological age, average and maximum life-spans, and age-specific survival or mortality. Whereas major interest in biological gerontology is ultimately directed towards man, his long life-span, complex social environments, and limited application of invasive procedures have made rodents and other short-lived mammals more practical subjects in biological gerontology. For a wide range of reasons, there are only a very small number of experimental and clinical neurochemical studies of age differences in chemical composition, metabolism, or the chemical aspects of neurotransmission encompassing the entire life-span of man.

Human Median, Maximum Life-spans, Brain Mass, Reproduction

As in animal studies of aging, an evaluation of major life-span changes in neurochemistry of the human brain entails at least specification of chronological age, the median and maximum life-spans. Changes in brain weight during development, maturity, and aging can also serve as the more prominent chronological or temporal sequences in the life-span of man. Since maturity has also been associated with reproduction, two other major points of reference may include sex differences in the onset and termination of reproductive capacity. Figure 1 illustrates the chronological age, estimated median, and maximum life-spans, the major changes in brain weight, and the sex differences in duration of male and female reproductive periods of man.

The most frequently cited asymptotic average values of the human 20 to 30-year-old brain weight is 1,400 g for the male and 1,300 g for the female (Minckler and Boyd, 1968; Arendt, 1972). Compared to these asymptotic values of human brain weight during maturity, there are two other generally recognized major life-span changes in brain weight of man. As in most mammalian species, including man and nonhuman primates, the brain undergoes a period of rapid growth known as the "growth spurt" during perinatal

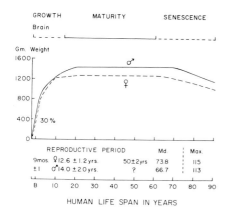

GROWTH   MATURITY   SENESCENCE

FIG. 1. Life-span changes in human brain weight. Major points of reference include chronological age, median and maximum life-spans, male and female reproductive periods. At birth, the brain weight of 350 g represents 30% of the 1,400 g asymptotic adult weight. Sex differences in brain weight appear throughout life. Brain weight values are based on literature references cited in the text.

development, it remains relatively stable throughout maturity, and then appears to decline in mass during senescence. The exact onset of decline in brain mass or any other feature may be difficult to establish in small and heterogeneous samples of human subjects. Chronological and biological ages may not coincide. There is a well-recognized large variability within cross-sectional and longitudinal samples. According to estimates from relatively large human samples, brain weight for males decreases from 1,400 g by 5% at age 70 to 10% by age 80, and by 20% by age 90 and above. According to these estimates, by age 90 human brain weight is reduced to the same level as that of a 3-year-old child (Minckler and Boyd, 1968). It is interesting to note that there is a significant sex difference or dimorphism in brain weight throughout the life-span in man. The maximum asymptotic female brain weight at maturity is significantly less (100 to 150 g). It attains this maximum adult value earlier at 18 to 20 years, in contrast to 25 to 30 years in the male, and the onset of decline also occurs earlier, between 60 and 70 in the female, as opposed to 70 and 80 in the male (Arendt, 1972).

Compared to other organs, the variability of brain weight in man has been reported to be low and to decrease from approximately ± 20% in early life to ± 10% after the fifth postnatal year (Minckler and Boyd, 1968). This life-span change in variability or lack of homogeneity of variance within and across chronological age samples poses some serious sampling difficulties for determining whether any feature of the brain in a sample of old subjects differs at statistically specified levels of confidence from samples of young and mature subjects (Norris and Shock, 1966).

In addition to life-span changes in brain mass, other gross morphological changes in the human brain with increasing age after 70 include atrophy, narrowing of the cerebral gyri, and widening and deepening of sulci between them (Andrew, 1971). The space between the cranial cavity and brain increases since the volume of the brain becomes smaller. There is a significant increase in the size of the ventricular system with age which has been attributed to an increased volume of cerebrospinal fluid (CSF) in the ventricles (Himwich, 1959; Arendt, 1972).

In view of the lack of quantitative morphological data, there is still considerable controversy concerning the onset, rate, regional, and species variations in cell and nerve fiber loss as well as the incidence of mitosis or cell renewal in the mammalian nervous system (Buetow, 1971). Although there is a marked variation among human subjects of the same chronological age, nerve cell and fiber numbers appear to decrease with age in the male and female, particularly in human subjects above 70 years of age. In man, significant variations in cell loss among cortical, subcortical, and other architectural or topographical regions have also been reported (Arendt, 1972). In some animal studies, similar trends in cell loss have been reported, generally only in the oldest subjects. However, other animal studies have reported negligible, if any, cell loss compared to man (Buetow, 1971).

Physiologically, life-span comparisons of EEG activity have indicated only negligible reductions of the occipital alpha rhythm from 10 to 12 cps to 8 to 10 cps in healthy males over 65 years of age (Obrist, 1965). Small but statistically significant changes in visual- and auditory-evoked responses reported after 40 years of age have suggested an earlier onset of functional decline in the human brain (Dustman and Beck, 1969).

Behaviorally, the generally recognized decline in speed of behavior with age in man and animals has been attributed to the onset of a primary or basic process of aging in the brain since it integrates the input and output in behavior (Birren, 1965). Although declines in sensory, cognitive, and motor functions may be ultimately associated with specific structural and functional changes in the brain, the neural basis of these declines and their significance in global personality adjustments in aging require clarification by multivariate studies that bridge the gap from behavioral to electrical, chemical, and morphological levels of observation (Ordy and Schjeide, 1973). Although requiring further experimental clarification, it is apparent that the changing variance, the increasing incidence of neuropathology, and mortality with age pose complex methodological sampling difficulties for estimating, at statistically significant levels of confidence, the exact onset and time course of structural and functional declines in the human brain in any heterogeneous sample of subjects evaluated during senescence (Norris and Shock, 1966; Schaie, 1970).

Longitudinal, Cross-sectional Designs

In behavioral life-span studies, the concept of chronological age has generally been treated as an independent or experimental variable. Since the concept of age may be generation-specific, and long-term aging studies may not be replicated, the logical status of chronological age as an experimental variable in longitudinal and cross-sectional designs has received some detailed scrutiny and generated considerable theoretical and methodological controversies (Schaie, 1970). In experimental life-span studies, the two most widely used methods for studying change in the brain over extended time intervals would include longitudinal and cross-sectional designs. Longitudinal samples yield age changes within subjects. Cross-sectional samples provide age differences among subjects. Animal life-span studies in which subjects are sacrificed for chemical and morphological evaluations are necessarily cross-sectional and provide age differences in the dependent variables. Even in carefully controlled animal studies, longitudinal age samples across the life-span may confound age changes with long-term environmental changes, and cross-sectional samples may confound age differences with generation differences. In life-span behavioral studies, several developmental life-span models of aging have been proposed in order to isolate or identify the contributions from chronological age compared to "cohort" controls and the time of measurement in the assessment of major sequences of aging (Schaie, 1970).

The selection of appropriate longitudinal and cross-sectional designs and the use of species with shorter life-spans have produced considerable progress in biological gerontology. However, many neurobiological aging studies using animal subjects have contributed primarily inconclusive or misleading findings since only vague descriptions of even the chronological ages were included, or the designation of age was unspecified or unknown. Generally, only small groups of "young, mature, and old" subjects are specified in a typical aging study. This lack of specificity even in chronological age undoubtedly represents a major source of the widely recognized large variance among subjects in longitudinal and cross-sectional designs. In better designed and controlled life-span animal studies of aging, various statistical univariate and multivariate models have now been proposed for evaluating long-term changes in neurobiological development, maturity, and aging (Ordy and Schjeide, 1973). However, for numerous and very obvious reasons, life-span neurochemical evaluations of the human brain have been restricted to accident victims and to clinical evaluations based on small sample descriptive cross-sectional designs. Whereas these neurochemical studies of the human brain represent a commendable beginning, only appropriate designs developed in animal studies can provide the reliable guides ultimately essential in a neurochemistry of gerontology for man.

Neurochemical Methods and Special Problems

The emergence of neurochemistry as one of the most rapidly growing disciplines among the neurosciences has resulted in part from theoretical stimulation from such adjacent disciplines as psychology, neurophysiology, neuropharmacology, morphology, and in part to the rapid development of a special chemical methodology for the evaluation of the chemical composition, metabolism, and the chemical aspects of neurotransmission in the nervous system. Due to the complexity of the nervous system, a variety of these special chemical methods have now been developed for evaluation of the nervous system, but they have been applied primarily in animal species (Fried, 1971). The application of these chemical methods for the evaluation of the human brain has been extremely sparse compared to the increasing number of animal studies. The alleged rapid postmortem changes in the human brain have been presumed to be a barrier rather than a challenge for neurochemical studies. The chemical values reported in the literature on composition, metabolism, and neurotransmitters in the human brain are generally fragmentary and inconclusive. Wide variations in the reported chemical values have been partly due to the presumed rapid postmortem autolysis in the brain and partly to older chemical techniques. Until recently, it has been generally assumed that the chemical evaluations that can be reliably determined in human brain samples obtained post-mortem are quite limited. A number of such constituents as myelin, lipids, cholesterol, cerebrosides, and proteins were considered to remain quite stable, if prepared and stored under proper temperature. Other chemical constituents, such as substrates and enzymes, were presumed to be highly labile without special precautions in the processing of brain samples following postmortem examination (Dickerson, 1968). More recently, several neurochemical studies have reported comparable values even for neurotransmitters and their associated enzymes in the human brain. Surprisingly, the human brain samples in these studies were obtained at various times ranging from less than 1 to 24 hr after death. Brain samples have been obtained from accident victims with no antecedent illnesses or from patients with various neurological disorders. According to these chemical studies, neither lapse of time between death and autopsy nor length of storage appeared to be insurmountable sources of error since they did not preclude statistical comparisons of significant age differences and regional variations in neurotransmitters and their associated enzymes (McGeer, McGeer, and Wada, 1971a; Nies, Robinson, and Ravaris, 1971; McGeer, McGeer, and Fibiger, 1973; Nies, Robinson, Davis, and Ravaris, 1973; Cote and Kremzner, 1974).

LIFE-SPAN CHANGES IN MAIN CHEMICAL CONSTITUENTS AS POSSIBLE SOURCES OF AGING IN THE HUMAN BRAIN

Molecular theories of aging have attempted to identify changes in DNA, RNA, protein, and subcellular organelles as primary sources of cellular aging. However, the cumulative loss of the highly differentiated postmitotic cells of the brain may alter intercellular interactions and reduce the physiological and neurochemical functions of relatively normal remaining cells. Although tissue constituents interact in all organs, in no other organ are the interactions as complex or as critical for normal function as in the brain. Consequently, recent trends in neurobiology include a more inclusive emphasis on the relationships among neurons, glia, neuropil, vascular elements, and the extracellular space or microenvironment in the integrative functions of the brain. Due to these complex interactions among brain tissue constituents, it seems likely that significant decreases in the main chemical constituents with age may alter the interactions among tissue constituents and also represent identifiable chemical sources of decline in function of the human brain.

Rank Order of Main Chemical Constituents of the Human Brain

The rank order of the main chemical constituents of the mean adult male human brain mass of 1,400 g includes: (1) water 76.2%; (2) extracellular space 20 to 25% volume, CSF 9% volume, and blood 3% volume; (3) total lipids 11.5%; (4) DNA, RNA, protein 9.5%; (5) soluble organic substances (free amino acids, oxygen, hormones, etc.) 1.5%; (6) inorganic salts (cations and anions) 1.0%; and (7) glycogen 0.3%. Regardless of the species, sex, and age, inorganic water comprises by far the highest proportion of brain weight, ranging from 70 to 92% of the total mass of the brain (McIlwain and Bachelard, 1971). Depending primarily on age, water constitutes 48 to 92% in gray matter of the total fresh weight and 65 to 90% in white matter (Katzman and Schimmel, 1969). Brain H_2O content is localized primarily intracellularly. The immediate extracellular or microenvironment of neurons and glia is an interstitial fluid which is separated from the blood by capillary walls and from the cerebrospinal fluid by the ventricles of the mammalian brain. The proportion of extracellular space and fluids of the total brain volume have been estimated as 20 to 25% by chemical methods (Pappius, 1969) and morphometrically at 20% in electron micrographs of the rat cerebral cortex fixed by freeze-substitution (Bondareff and Narotzky, 1972). After considerable controversy concerning the existence and size of the extracellular space in the brain, it is now generally recognized that extracellular space can represent between 15 and 25% of the total brain volume and that this space may be altered by age, physiological conditions, and various pathological states (Pappius, 1969).

The electrical activity of the brain is based on differential ion concentration of neurons and the extracellular fluids. As in the case of water, there are also gray and white matter differences in the distribution of inorganic ions or electrolytes of the brain. The distribution of electrolytes, including Na^+, K^+, Ca^{2+}, Mg^{2+}, and Cl^-, is characterized by an excess of inorganic cations over anions and is balanced by anions of large molecular weight. Glial cells have been considered high in electrolytes. It has been proposed that glial cells and the extracellular space are involved in the rapid movement of water between brain tissue and the blood compartment (Clausen,

TABLE 1. *Rank order of nine main chemical constituents or composition of average adult human male brain mass (1,439 g)*

Constituents	Average adult human male brain mass[a]		
	Rank	1,439 g	% weight-volume ($\square$)
H_2O	1	1,068	76.2
Total lipids	2	190	11.5
DNA, RNA, protein	3	140	9.5
Extracellular space	(4)	—	(25.0)
CSF	(5)	—	(9.0)
Blood	(6)	—	(3.0)
Soluble organic substance (Free amino acids, 34.25 moles/g	7	21	1.5
Inorganic salts: electrolytes (cations: Na, K, Ca; anions: Cl)	8	14	1.0
Carbohydrates (glycogen)	9	6	0.3

[a] The values of the "adult" male brain weight (1,439 g) and percent or volume ($\square$) constituents of total mass are based on published references. The values are approximations since they do not include specifications of exact chronological age, sample size, mean, standard deviation, or other statistics.

1969). Table 1 contains the rank order and the values of the main chemical constituents of the adult human brain as a point of reference for development and aging.

Chemical Constituents as Possible Major Sources of Age Decline in Brain Weight

In one of the earlier and more comprehensive reviews of life-span biochemical changes in the brain of man, an attempt was made to assign the loss of 233 g, from 1,394 g at 30 years to 1,161 g at 90, to such major chemical constituents as H_2O, lipids, proteins, electrolytes, and other chemical constituents of the brain (Himwich, 1959). It was estimated that of the total dry weight, lipids comprise 190 g and proteins 140 g. By 90 years of age, lipids decreased to 140 g and proteins to 100 g, representing a loss of 25% of total lipids and 28% of proteins. Figure 2 illustrates estimated life-span changes in the major chemical constituents of the human brain.

Life-span Changes in H_2O

Although inorganic water comprises 70 to 92% of the total human brain mass, there is still some doubt concerning the progressive decrease in water content of the human brain during senescence. According to earlier studies,

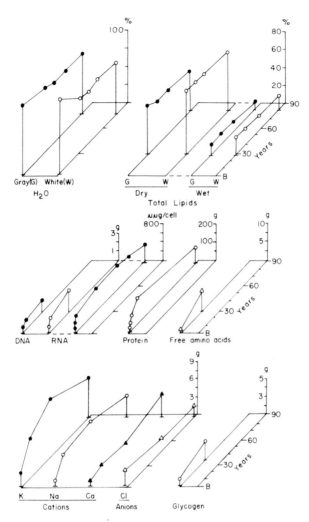

FIG. 2. Estimated life-span changes in the major chemical constituents of the human brain. Values are based on literature references cited in the text.

there is a decrease in water content from approximately 90% at birth to 76.8% at age 30, with a slight increase of water to 78.5% by age 80 (Himwich, 1959). In more recent studies, total brain H_2O was reported to decline from 90.2% in a 2-month-old infant to 80.9% in an 80-year-old subject (Fillerup and Mead, 1967). In another study, total brain H_2O was estimated to decrease from 85.9% at 3 weeks to 72.4% at 98 years (Rouser and Yamamoto, 1968). The uncertainty concerning the progressive loss of brain H_2O during human senescence requires clarification, since the rate of total body water loss for a given species has been observed to be so constant that it has been suggested as a law of biological aging (Calloway, 1971). The slight increase of brain H_2O to 78.5% by age 80 in man may represent an exception to the reported constant rate of total body water loss with age or it may simply reflect sampling variations. More careful methods for identification of the sources of sample variance should provide more definitive values concerning progressive changes in the major inorganic brain constituent (H_2O) during senescence.

Life-span Changes in Extracellular Space, Electrolytes

Although the extracellular space may range from 15 to 25% of the total brain volume, there have been no chemical studies of age differences in extracellular space of the human brain throughout the life-span. Based on electron micrographs, a significant decrease in extracellular space of the adult rat cerebral cortex has been reported from 20% of the volume at 3 to 10% in 26-month-old rats (Bondareff and Narotzky, 1972). Since the water content of the human brain comprises approximately four-fifths of the entire weight, some attempts have been made to determine whether the age-dependent changes in water content occur in extra- or intracellular compartments. According to earlier studies, intracellular H_2O and potassium remain relatively unchanged during growth and in maturity but may decline during senescence. Sodium and chloride, as extracellular constituents, decrease with extracellular H_2O during growth, remain relatively unchanged during maturity, and may increase during senescence. Nitrogen and phosphorus have been reported to decrease during senescence. Whereas sulfur and calcium decrease during development, they remain stable during maturity and increase during senescence (Himwich, 1959). Recent studies have reported decreases in calcium, chloride, and sodium and increases in magnesium, potassium, and phosphorus in the brain of newborn compared to adult human subjects (Altman and Dittmer, 1973). Since the differences in water content and electrolytes in gray and white matter are associated with the preponderance of myelin in white matter, future studies are essential to establish how the declines in lipids with age are related to the decline of intracellular potassium and water and the number of normally functioning neurons of the brain during senescence.

Life-span Changes in Lipids

In the chemical composition of the brain, lipids are unique since they constitute over half of the total dry weight. Myelin is also one of the most conspicuous morphological features of the nervous system. The composition, distribution, and turnover of lipids in the human brain throughout the life-span have received considerably more attention than other major constituents (Mokrash, 1969). Based on earlier crude methods and incomplete extraction procedures, it was reported that the lipids of the brain had a characteristic composition and varied significantly with age and various pathological conditions. Cholesterol, cerebrosides, and sphingomyelin were first identified as "myelin-type" constituents in studies of life-span changes in lipids of the human brain (Brante, 1949).

By using the composition of brain lipid expressed as percentage dry weight, decreases in total lipids of 9% in white and 11% in gray matter were reported in the human brain for subjects ranging from 26 to 80 years of age (Fillerup and Mead, 1967). In a more comprehensive study of human brain lipid composition at different ages, it was reported that the percent total lipids of fresh weight increased from 3.5% at birth to 10.5% at 33 years and then declined significantly to 7.5% by 98 years of age (Rouser and Yamamoto, 1969). As a broad generalization, human brain lipid composition appears to change continuously throughout life, but the greatest changes occur during the period of development. The changes during maturity appear to be considerably slower and the changes in senescence again become more rapid and appear to be the reverse of those during development (Rouser and Yamamoto, 1969). In recent years, there has been an increasing interest in the structure and function of myelin and other cellular and subcellular membranes in the nervous system (Johnston and Roots, 1972). However, these studies have not been concerned with life-span changes in subcellular and cellular membranes.

Life-span Changes in DNA, RNA, Protein Content of the Human Brain

During brain development, DNA and RNA have an essential role in protein synthesis essential for growth. In prenatal brain growth, both DNA and RNA increase during mitotic cell multiplication of neurons and glia. At birth or shortly after when mitosis of neurons terminates, there appears to be only a negligible increase in DNA, but RNA and protein continue to increase with cell enlargement. In the human brain, DNA and RNA increase rapidly and at the same rate until 10 months postnatally. DNA continues to increase but only gradually, presumably due to the increase in glia, while RNA and protein increase more rapidly for approximately 2 years (Dobbing and Sands, 1970). Thus far, it has not been established precisely at what point adult levels of DNA, RNA, and protein concentrations are attained in the human brain (Rappoport, Fritz, and Myers, 1969). When all cellular growth ceases, DNA, RNA, and protein concentrations appear to remain relatively constant throughout the life-span, although RNA and protein continue to undergo continuous turnover. The DNA content of the human brain has been reported to increase from 300 mg/brain fresh brain tissue at 4 days of age to 850 mg/brain by 1 year and 1,000 mg/brain at maturity. RNA increases from 400 mg/brain fresh brain tissue at 4 days of age to 1,400 mg/brain by 1 year and 2,550 mg/brain at maturity (Rappoport et al., 1969). Protein increases from 57 mg/g fresh tissue at 1 month of age to 62 mg/g at 9 months, from 75 mg/g at 15 months (Winick and Rosso, 1969) to 116 mg/g at 6 to 10 years, and reaches 136 mg/g in adults (Himwich, 1959).

Surprisingly, studies of changes in DNA, RNA, and protein content in the human brain from maturity to old age are few in number. Both increases and decreases in human brain DNA, RNA, and protein content have been reported from maturity to old age (Herrmann, 1971). According to some sources, DNA content of the human brain remains relatively constant from the age of 40 but may increase by the age of 90 (Timiras, 1972). This increase in DNA during senescence appears in contrast to the decrease in RNA, protein, and lipids. The alleged increase in human brain DNA content in senescence has been attributed to the proliferation of glial cells and an increase in pyknosis of neurons (Timiras, 1972). RNA and protein content of the human brain have been reported to increase up to the age of 40, remain relatively stable to age 60, and then begin to decline rapidly. However, this life-span change in human brain RNA and protein is complicated by short-lasting reversible fluctuations in RNA and protein that may result from increased functional demands throughout the life-span. RNA and protein have also been implicated in learning and memory (Hyden, 1967a).

Estimates of DNA content have also been utilized as chemical indices of cell numbers in the brain. Since the RNA content of neurons is considerably higher than that of glial cells, RNA/DNA ratios have also been used as chemical estimates of differential neuron/glial populations in different regions of the brain. Protein/DNA and protein/RNA ratios have been used as estimates of cellular protein concentrations and synthesis (Davison and Dobbing, 1968). More recently, quantitative neurochemical and morphometric histological and cytological evaluations have been combined at the laminar, cellular, and regional level to obtain concurrent chemical and anatomical indices of the human brain (Hess and Pope, 1972). Thus far, these quantitative neurochemical-morphometric methods have not been utilized for studying the "chemoanatomical" changes in the human brain during aging.

Increasing interest has been devoted recently to the comparatively high concentration of free amino acids in the mammalian brain. They serve not only as building blocks in protein synthesis and as possible intermediates in energy metabolism under some extreme conditions, but they can also serve as neurotransmitters in the CNS (Curtis and Johnston, 1970). Studies have shown significant differences in the composition of the free amino acid pool in the brain between newborn and adult mammalian species (Agrawal and Himwich, 1970). In the human brain, analysis of amino acids in protein-free extracts have indicated a concentration of 404.5 mg/100 g wet weight in a 3-year-old child (Okumura, Otsuhi, and Kameyama, 1960). The content of free amino acids in the adult human brain in the combined gray and white matter has been reported as 700 mg/100 g (Robinson and Williams, 1965; Davison and Dobbing, 1968). Changes in free amino acids in human brain from maturity to old age have not been reported.

Life-span Changes in Carbohydrate Content in the Human Brain

Although carbohydrate metabolism is of crucial importance for the energy requirements, the brain at any one time contains less than 1% of glycogen and glucose, as the two main carbohydrates. The glycogen content of the human brain has been estimated at 1.12 mg/100 g in adult subjects (Coxon, 1970). Regarding life-span changes in brain glycogen, its level in the cerebral cortex at birth has been estimated as one-fifth of that in the adult (Pocchiari, 1971). Glycogen is found in both neurons and glia and its concentration seems to be subject to variations in response to a variety of influences. The marked increases in glycogen content in the brain from birth to maturity are presumably correlated with increasing development of cortical function. Changes in glycogen content from maturity to senescence remain to be determined.

LIFE-SPAN CHANGES IN CIRCULATION AND ENERGY METABOLISM AS SOURCES OF AGING IN THE BRAIN

The "language" of neurons in sensory, cognitive, and motor functions is considered to be primarily electrical. The energy for the electrical activity is ultimately based on respiration or oxidative phosphorylation of glucose in mitochondria as the main substrate of cellular energy metabolism in the brain. It has been proposed that most of the brain's extremely high energy utilization may be associated with the active transport of ions to sustain and restore the membrane potentials discharged during excitation, conduction, and transmission (Sokoloff, 1972; Bachelard, 1970). Since the electrical activity in sensory, cognitive, and motor functions of the brain is ultimately based on energy metabolism, it seems possible that, if blood flow, O_2, and glucose to the brain are decreased during aging, the respiration rate may decrease, cell loss may occur, and various cerebral functions may become impaired as a direct consequence of age declines in cerebral blood flow and energy metabolism. However, over 90% of the O_2 is utilized by mitochondria (Moore and Strasberg, 1970). Consequently, age declines in intracellular energy metabolism may also result from decreased rates of mitochondrial oxidative phosphorylation as fundamental processes of intracellular aging.

Cerebral Blood Flow

As in all other organs, the basic functions of cerebral circulation are to provide substrates for energy metabolism, maintain the structural integrity of the organ, and remove products of metabolism. The blood content of the adult human brain comprises 3.5% of the total brain volume and flows through a 1,400 g adult human brain at a rate of 800 ml/min (McIlwain and Bachelard, 1971). Although the adult 1,400 g weight of the human brain is only 2.0% of the body, the volume of blood supply through the human brain is over 15% of the total basal cardiac output. A reduction in cerebral blood flow to half of its normal rate results in rapid loss of consciousness in the average mature human subject (Sokoloff, 1972).

There are several older studies of life-span changes in blood flow through the human brain that have indicated a gradual decline of cerebral blood flow from an average of 106 ml/100 g/min at 6 years of age to 62 ml at 21 years or maturity and 58 ml at 71 years in normal old subjects. Cerebral blood flow was decreased even more significantly to 48 ml/100 g/min in arterio-sclerotic and senile psychotic patients (Sokoloff, 1972).

Cerebral Oxygen Uptake

Compared with the rate of utilization, the oxygen stores of the brain are extremely small. Consciousness is lost within 10 sec if the cerebral blood flow is terminated and the sole source of O_2 is in the tissue and the remaining blood content of the brain. The high cerebral blood flow has to supply the brain's "avaricious appetite for oxygen" (Sokoloff, 1972). The brain as an organ, performs no unique mechanical, osmotic, or chemical work. The oxygen uptake of the human adult brain constitutes 20 to 25% of the total basal O_2 requirement of the human body (McIlwain and Bachelard, 1971). Several studies of life-span changes in O_2 uptake by the human brain have indicated a gradual decline from an average of 5.2 ml/100 g/min at 6 years to 3.5 at 21 and 3.3 at 71 years. Lower values of 2.7 ml/100 g/min were reported for a sample of 72-year-old senile psychotic patients (Sokoloff, 1972).

Glucose Utilization

Under normal conditions, glucose is the main or exclusive energy-yielding substrate for the brain's high rate of energy metabolism according to a variety of *in vitro* and *in vivo* metabolic studies (McIlwain and Bachelard, 1971). Comprising only 2.0% of the total human body weight, the brain utilizes approximately 25% of the total adult bodily consumption of glucose. According to one frequently cited source, the basal conscious human brain consumes 156 μmoles/100 g/min of oxygen (Sokoloff, 1972). Since CO_2 is the same, the respiratory quotient is almost 1.0 for the brain. For normal healthy young adult males, the average values reported in the literature have included 3.3 ml O_2/100 g/min and 5.4 mg glucose/100 g/min. The average cerebral blood flow cited in the literature includes 54 ml/100 g brain/min.

The O_2 and glucose consumption for the average 1,400 g human male brain have been estimated at 46 ml O_2 and 76 mg glucose/min (Sacks, 1969). Although almost 90% of the brain glucose is oxidized in glycolysis, glucose carbon is also incorporated into glycogen, lipids, amino acids, and proteins during metabolic turnover of these constituents (Balazs, 1970).

Owing to rapid anaerobic glycolysis during the postmortem period, glucose and glycogen levels reported in the literature for the human brain have varied considerably (Bachelard, 1969). From arteriovenous differences in glucose, O_2 uptake and CO_2 production (glucose utilization calculated on the basis of 6 moles O_2 required for complete oxidation of 1 mole of glucose), blood glucose levels of 9.8 mg/100 ml and rate values of 31 μmoles/ 100 g brain tissue/min have been reported for glucose utilization in the brain of normal young adult human male subjects (McIlwain and Bachelard, 1971; Sokoloff, 1972). Experimental studies of life-span changes in brain glucose utilization have not been reported for man. Blood glucose levels are known to increase from 50 mg/100 ml at birth to 85 mg by 8 years of age (Timiras, 1972). Since venous glucose levels have not been established, rates of glucose utilization by the human brain during development remain to be determined. The arterial blood glucose levels for normal adult human subjects are generally listed at 92.0 mg/100 ml (McIlwain and Bachelard, 1971). Although the basal metabolic rate is known to decline significantly from 30 to 90 years of age in man (Shock and Yiengst, 1955), the fasting blood sugar levels and acid-base balance are presumed to remain essentially unchanged throughout the life-span. However, when displacements in blood sugar levels are induced in glucose tolerance tests, the rate of return to resting levels has been reported to be significantly slower in old than in young human subjects (Andres, 1967; Timiras, 1972). In view of the conflicting findings, further metabolic studies are essential to establish possible declines in blood glucose, O_2 uptake, and rate of glucose utilization by the clinically normal human brain as well as the sources of declines in homeostatic regulation of blood glucose and the consequences to the brain during senescence. Figure 3 illustrates the reported life-span changes in blood flow, O_2, and blood glucose levels in the human brain.

Significance of Life-span Changes in Cerebral Blood Flow, O_2, and Glucose for Sensory-Cognitive-Motor Functions of the Human Brain

A cerebral oxygen consumption of 5.2 ml/100 g brain tissue/min in a 5 to 6-year-old represents a value of 60 ml/min for the 1,155 g brain or 50% of the total basal body O_2 consumption, a proportion significantly higher than the 20 to 25% in adults. This has been interpreted as a possible requirement for providing the extra energy associated with growth of the brain (Sokoloff, 1972). Despite many contrary clinical reports, the more prevalent current views are that cerebral blood flow, O_2 uptake, and blood glucose

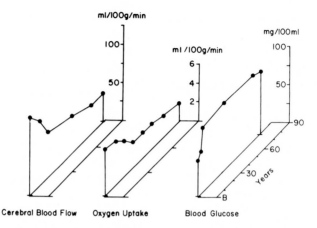

FIG. 3. Life-span changes in cerebral blood flow, O_2 consumption, and blood glucose in the human brain. Values are based on literature references cited in the text.

levels may not decline significantly in the brain of healthy normal human subjects from 50 to 72 years of age (Sokoloff, 1972; Timiras, 1972). However, in physiological, pathological, and behavioral studies with adult human subjects, significant correlations have been established among levels of consciousness, reflexes, EEG, a variety of psychiatric, convulsive, vascular disorders, and even mental activity (Sokoloff, 1972). More recent studies with old human subjects have also indicated significant correlations in decline of Verbal and Performance scores on the Wechsler Adult Intelligence Scale (WAIS), the EEG dominant frequency, and cerebral blood flow through the left parietal region of the brain in a sample of 260 old human subjects with a mean age of 69.8 years (Wang, Obrist, and Busse, 1974). Other studies have shown that intellectual impairment and brain deterioration are closely related to cardiovascular disease in old age (Wang and Busse, 1974a). In the same series of studies, brain impairments determined by psychometric, EEG, and neurological evaluations were found to be significantly correlated with decreased longevity in a sample of 265 subjects with a mean of 70.9 years of age (Wang and Busse, 1974b).

It has been proposed that the brain may play an important "pacemaker" role in aging since significant correlations have been established between brain weight and life-span for mammalian species (Sacher, 1959). It has also been suggested that the structural and/or pathological changes in the cerebral vascular system may play the critical "pacemaker" role in the brain during aging (Sokoloff, 1959). The unique and extreme metabolic dependence of the human brain on continuously high blood flow, oxygen, and glucose make it highly probable that age declines in circulation and energy metabolism independent of neurological diseases may also be involved ultimately in psychological impairments, and in changes of electrical activity, as well as in some of the chemical and morphological alterations observed in the human brain during senescence. It has been proposed that cerebrovascular resistance may increase in senescence independent of neurological disorders (Sokoloff, 1959, 1972). Consequently, loss of neurons or accumulation of such metabolic by-products as lipofuscin with age may also be closely associated with increasing ischemia and anoxia. In addition to the decline in cerebral blood flow, O_2 uptake, and probable decrease in glucose levels or rates of utilization, age declines in oxidative phosphorylation of glucose in mitochondria have been proposed as fundamental intracellular mechanisms of aging (Oeriu, 1964). Differences in rate of phosphorylation with different substrates and stability of mitochondria in the brain between young and old rats have been reported (Weinbach and Garbus, 1959).

Life-span Changes in the Blood-Brain-CSF Barrier Systems

It is difficult to discuss life-span changes in cerebral circulation and energy metabolism of the brain as sources of aging without reference to changes in the so-called blood-brain barrier. Despite many misleading implications of this concept, the blood-brain barrier continues to provide an overall point of reference for evaluation of transport and exclusion mechanisms in the brain for many constituents supplied and removed by the bloodstream (Fenstermacher, Patlak, and Blasberg, 1974). The blood-brain barrier has been examined in terms of chemical, morphological, and electrical characteristics (Katzman, 1970). In the neurochemical literature, brain permeability "barrier" functions are invoked as mechanisms for the transport of substances essential for energy metabolism, the precursors of organic constituents synthesized within the brain, and the removal of metabolites (Dobbing, 1968).

The various permeability mechanisms that restrict or facilitate the entry of substances into the brain are still designated collectively as the blood-brain barrier, whereas the mechanisms between the blood and CSF constitute the blood-CSF barrier. Current problems included in permeability barrier mechanisms are diffusion, active and mediated transport, molecular size, lipid solubility, ionic dissociation, extracellular space, regional permeability differences in the brain, permeability of capillary endothelium, and the role of the blood-brain barrier in development, pathology, drugs, radiation, and other environmental hazards (Katzman, 1970, 1972). Regarding life-span changes, it is generally stated that the blood-brain barrier is absent in early life and develops only gradually during maturation. However, many of the mechanisms of the blood-brain barrier, including "tight junctions" in the capillary endothelium and the exclusion of protein molecules, are known to be present in newborn animals. However, it is now also known that labeled phosphates enter into the brain more rapidly during the brain "growth spurt" when the substances are required in greater quantities for the incorporation of new structures and for energy metabolism (Dobbing, 1968). In view of the recognized importance of brain permeability barriers for the maintenance of a constant chemical environment, it is surprising that few studies have examined changes in brain permeability barriers as major sources of aging in the mammalian brain during senescence. One of the most prominent characteristics of the brain to injury including trauma, drugs, radiation, tumors, infections, toxins, and other hazards is the apparent breakdown of the blood-brain barrier with the diffusion of protein molecules into brain tissue (Bakay, 1972). Although considerable interest has been focused on changes in the blood-brain barrier during development and in neuropharmacology for controlling the entry of substances into the brain, thus far, experimental studies have not been reported on changes in the blood-brain barrier in senescence. These studies would be extremely important since the blood-brain barrier does seem to contribute a critical regulatory mechanism for controlling substances circulating in the blood to provide the brain with the proper chemical environment essential for normal function. Intercellular material and cell contact interactions are important features in the organization of all organs. However, in no other organ are the intercellular interactions as complex and critical for normal function as in the brain. Studies of intercellular control of intracellular metabolism in the liver of rats during aging have shown changes in intracellular metabolism due to reductions in density of liver parenchymal cells with age (Bhargava, 1970). Since reductions in cell density of the brain with age are also presumed to occur in the human (Brody, 1955) and the mammalian brain (Buetow, 1971), the studies of age declines in intercellular control mechanisms in the liver provide convincing evidence for the inclusion of brain permeability barrier systems or the so-called blood-brain barrier as possible major sources of age decline in intercellular control of intracellular metabolism in the human brain during senescence.

LIFE-SPAN CHANGES IN METABOLIC TURNOVER OF DNA, RNA, PROTEIN, LIPIDS, AND CARBOHYDRATES IN THE MAMMALIAN BRAIN

Because of the explosive interest in molecular biology, it is not surprising that cellular theories of aging in biological gerontology have invoked almost exclusively biochemical explanations for intracellular aging. Particular emphasis has been placed on DNA, RNA, and protein. In the brain, these informational macromolecules are carriers of genetic and presumably of acquired information or memory. They are also centrally involved in the comparatively high rate of cellular metabolism or turnover of brain constituents. Until recently, problems of life-span changes in metabolic turnover in the brain in relation to environmental stimulation and memory remained completely unexplored. Since the postnatal brain comprises postmitotic cells and nonregenerative tissues, the term "turnover" has generally been associated only with mechanisms of synthesis and breakdown in energy metabolism. Metabolic activity and turnover, particularly of RNA and protein, have only recently been implicated in environmental modifiability and acquired memory. According to numerous recent animal studies, metabolic turnover of macromolecules may occur at high rates for most constituents of the mammalian brain and only some small, as yet undetermined components of the brain may remain permanent. If currently dominant genetic and molecular error accumulation theories of cellular aging and protein synthesis or breakdown and cell loss are also relevant as explanations for aging in the human brain, then age-dependent changes in RNA and protein turnover should become demonstrable in life-span studies of metabolic turnover in the brain. Thus far, cell loss appears to be a generally accepted, but as yet chemically and morphometrically unverified, feature of the human brain in senescence (Brody, 1955; Tomash, 1972). Studies of major life-span changes in metabolic turnover in the brain should be of direct relevance for the interpretation of major changes in acquired short-term memory, environmental modifiability of the chemical constituents, or the equilibrium of the brain and the chemical aspects of neurological disorders in senescence.

As an environmentally modifiable adaptive cybernetic control system, the unique features of the brain are its role as repository for inherited characteristics, the acquisition, consolidation, and storage of short-term information or learning and long-term memory lasting throughout life. In contrast to short-term and intermediate memory, frequently associated with electrical activity in neuronal networks, long-term memory appears to be relatively stable or permanent. This apparent permanent nature of long-term memory has made it reasonable to assume that at least some of the cellular and/or network storage mechanisms in the brain may also be relatively permanent. According to earlier views, the permanence of long-term memory may be associated with the nonrenewal or turnover of DNA in postmitotic cells of the brain (Verzar, 1968). As part of the intensive current interest in memory or information storage mechanisms in the brain, DNA, RNA, and protein have received increasing attention as macromolecular mechanisms of learning and memory (Glassman, 1974). Both the genetic memory and the acquired memory have now been attributed to the unique coding properties of DNA, RNA, and protein as the primary informational macromolecules of the brain. RNA and protein have become not only central neurochemical correlates of learning but also of environmental stimulation and diverse categories of change (Rappoport and Daginawala, 1970; Rose, 1970; Glassman, 1974). In view of the dominant emphasis of the molecular error accumulation in RNA and protein synthesis in aging, it seems surprising that life-span changes in short-term, intermediate, or long-term memory have not been associated more directly with changes in DNA, RNA, and protein content, their metabolic turnover, or some specific features of DNA-programmed or age-dependent accumulation of molecular errors in DNA, RNA, protein synthesis, and breakdown. Although still controversial, loss of short-term memory has been proposed as one of the more prominent manifestations of human aging (Keevil-Rogers and Schnore, 1969).

Almost all of the experimental information available on age-dependent error accumulation in protein synthesis is based on *in vitro* tissue culture studies. The information on metabolic turnover of DNA, RNA, protein, lipids, and carbohydrates in the "whole brain" is based on investigations with laboratory animals. However, some brief comments on the implications of the rapid recent developments in studies of age-dependent error accumulation in protein synthesis and metabolic turnover observed in tissue culture and the brain of mammalian species and their implications for age-dependent changes in learning and memory in relation to possible molecular error accumulation and changes in metabolic turnover in the human brain during aging appear relevant. Numerous animal studies have also indicated age differences in learning and memory after RNA administration and drugs that facilitate or inhibit protein synthesis (Solyom, Enesco, and Beaulieu, 1967). Other animal studies have shown quantitative and qualitative changes in RNA and protein related to age and different training or learning conditions (Hyden, 1967b; Dellweg, Gerner, and Wacker, 1968). More recently, studies of molecular error accumulation in protein synthesis and aging have been reported with human diploid cells (Ryan, Duda, and Cristofalo, 1974). Other reasons for some pertinent comments on age-dependent changes in metabolic turnover in the mammalian brain in this review on the human brain include the current exclusive focus on these molecular or intracellular sources of aging and cell loss as the major features of aging. Although molecular and other intracellular organelles must play an important role in the brain, it seems unlikely that they can provide complete explanations of aging in the brain without reference to any other level of organization, particularly to changes in such major tissue components as neuropil, extracellular space, or the microenvironment and vascularity. The focus on accumulation of molecular errors and cell loss can lead to a persistent underemphasis of age-dependent changes in intercellular organization as sources of declines in intracellular metabolism with age. Also, it is apparent that age-dependent error accumulation in RNA and protein turnover and cell loss in the brain must be considered in a broader context since the brain as an organ is uniquely characterized by tissue interdependence, redundancy, organizational complexity, and environmental modifiability. Since the primary focus in this chapter is the life-span neurochemical changes in the human brain, the brief comments in the following sections on major life-span changes in metabolic turnover in the mammalian brain in relation to environmental influences are restricted to the following (1) influence of molecular or intracellular error accumulation theories of aging on interpretation of aging in the human brain; (2) life-span changes in synthesis and breakdown or turnover of mammalian brain DNA, RNA, protein, lipids, and carbohydrates; (3) life-span changes in chemical equilibrium of the mammalian brain resulting from genetic and environmental interactions; and (4) intra- and extracellular changes as interdependent sources of the rate of decline in the mammalian brain during senescence.

Influence of Molecular or Intracellular Error Accumulation Theories of Aging on Interpretation of Aging in the Human Brain

According to current general molecular theories of aging, an organism's life-span is under direct genetic control. The DNA of the chromosomes contains the basic "genetic memories" for directing the life cycle of cells, organs, and the organisms. The behavioral, physiological, biochemical, and anatomical characteristics of an organism are determined by sequences or codes of nucleotides stored in DNA. The DNA molecules specify, through RNA transcription and translation into specific proteins, not only the phylogenetic instructions for the life-span of a species, but also the ontogenetic organization of the brain, forms of learning, adaptation, and the subsequent decline in brain structure and function during senescence (Ordy and Schjeide, 1973). According to current views of gene expression or the role of informational molecules in differentiation of the brain, a specific assortment of genes and enzymes are involved in the control of the ontogenetic program (Tyler and Tyler, 1970). In addition to the evidence on DNA-specified species-specific life-spans, other indirect evidence for a central role for DNA in evolution of the brain and behavior includes a decreasing reliance on instinctive patterns of behavior in phylogeny, evolutionary trends in increasing use of learning-set formation (Hodos, 1970), and the molecular and chemical order of behavioral and morphological relationships in the evolution of primates including man (Wilson and Sarich, 1969).

There are two contrasting views of postmaturity cellular aging as part of a life-span ontogenetic program: (1) Cellular aging in all organs, including the brain, is a direct consequence of a DNA-directed or preordained developmental life-span program. (2) Cellular aging is a result of an age-dependent random accumulation of molecular errors resulting in cell loss (Strehler, 1967). According to current views on DNA constancy as primary genetic informational and replicative material, it is renewed in mitosis only when the nucleus divides. Since the differentiated postmitotic macroneurons of the mammalian brain do not divide after birth, it has seemed reasonable to assume that postmaturity age declines in cell function and cell loss are ultimately due to alterations in nucleic acids and proteins as carriers of all cellular information. The two contrasting molecular theories of aging have invoked almost exclusively changes in regulatory mechanisms at the genetic level as primary sources of cellular aging. The accumulation of errors may be initiated or controlled at this level by specific regulatory genes. The errors in macromolecular mechanisms are either genetically determined and preordained in the primary structure of DNA, or there is an age-dependent randomly determined progressive, irreversible accumulation of these molecular errors in DNA to RNA information transfer or "readout" followed inevitably by altered protein synthesis, greatly amplified and detrimental metabolic declines of cells, and finally cell loss in tissues and organs, including the brain (Orgel, 1963; Hahn, 1971; Strehler, Hirsch, Gusseck, Johnson, and Bick, 1971). Essentially, cellular aging is programmed into DNA as part of a life-span developmental program, possibly as a result of evolutionary selection, or there is an increasing age-dependent random or stochastic accumulation of molecular errors in the repeated copying by RNA of the DNA code with decreasing specificity of translation in protein synthesis (Sinex, 1966; Strehler et al., 1971; Orgel, 1973). Considerable support has been reported for age-dependent accumulation of errors in amino acid analogue incorporation into protein, inactive enzymes, and shortened life-span in animal and tissue culture studies (Holliday, 1969; Orgel, 1973). Whereas some recent studies have reported increasing error accumulation with aging in human diploid cells (Holliday and Tarrant, 1972; Lewis and Tarrant, 1972; Cristofalo and Sharf, 1973), other studies have reported no change in error accumulation or total population doublings of human diploid cells as well as a difficulty in distinguishing between "mis-synthesis" of protein and changes in the rate of turnover (Ryan et al., 1974).

In the context of molecular error accumulation during aging, it has been proposed that free radicals can also damage both DNA and other cell structures. Free radicals can be produced by metabolic processes of cells, or they may come from the environment. Vitamin E, the natural lipid antioxidant, and other substances have been used as free radical inhibitors in studies of the rate of free radical reactions in amino acids and proteins (Harman, 1956). Recently a comprehensive summary of current molecular and cellular theories of aging and their common attempts to trace the major life-span changes to their molecular and cellular origins has now been published (Marx, 1974a,b).

It seems plausible that there may be a DNA-specified aging program in the cells of the brain which operates similar to a developmental program that appears to be strictly "time-locked" and independent of environmental influences during some embryonic or fetal stages (Sperry, 1968; Jacobson, 1970). However, regulatory mechanisms involved in DNA, RNA, and protein synthesis and breakdown are numerous and complex, and current knowledge on gene expression and environmental interactions in the brain, particularly on molecular and cellular renewal and repair during ontogeny including aging, is quite fragmentary and incomplete. According to current views, nuclear DNA of mature macroneurons is not subject to metabolic turnover. Cell replication does not occur and repair synthesis, if this does occur, has not been established (Mahler, 1972). General molecular error accumulation theories of cellular aging may have a different generality and validity for continuous, intermittent, and postmitotic cell populations in different organs (Hayflick, 1973). In the case of the postmitotic cells of the brain, it is becoming increasingly apparent that genetic and environmental influences on RNA and protein content and possibly turnover interact not only during development and maturity, but also in aging (Ordy and Schjeide, 1973).

Life-span Changes in Synthesis and Breakdown or Turnover of Mammalian Brain DNA, Protein, Lipids, and Carbohydrates

The term "turnover" in neurochemistry refers to synthesis and degradation in metabolism and the rate is generally evaluated by the incorporation of labeled precursors or in degradation from the decay of radioactivity. Under steady-state conditions, the two rates are presumably approximately equal and both can represent the rate of turnover of a particular nervous tissue constituent. The general scheme of DNA, RNA, and protein synthesis in the brain has been reviewed extensively (Barondes and Dutton, 1972). Briefly, genetic DNA directs transfer, messenger, and ribosomal RNA, which in turn direct the sequences of amino acid incorporation into proteins. Proteins are also enzymes which are involved in the metabolism of other proteins, lipids, and carbohydrates in the brain.

DNA, RNA, Protein Turnover

Although DNA constancy and DNA stability are closely related, DNA constancy refers to the quantity, whereas DNA stability refers to its turnover. According to most current views, nuclear DNA of mature macroneurons is not subject to metabolic turnover. In contrast, the half-life of mitochondrial DNA in the brain of the rat has been estimated at 31 days compared to 7.5 days in the liver (Gross, Getz, and Rabinowitz, 1969). According to at least one study, there may be at least a partial turnover of DNA in nondividing cells, but at a rate considerably less than has been reported for RNA and protein (Pelc, 1970). Animal studies have focused on changes in nucleic acids and their associated enzymes as primary sources of cellular aging. These genetic sources have included quantitative changes or loss of DNA, RNA, and protein per cell and organ, changes in their information content, particularly changes in transcription and translation enzymes involved in protein synthesis (Hahn, 1971). Loss of DNA, RNA, and protein per cell or organ have been proposed as sources for declining functional capacity with increasing age. With the exception of cellular RNA loss in the human spinal cord during the life-span, losses in DNA, RNA, and protein per cell with increasing age for different regions of the human brain have not been reported. Conflicting findings have been reported concerning regional variations in declines of DNA content in the human brain during aging. Increases in brain DNA content of very old human subjects have been reported and attributed to loss of cellular cytoplasm. Depending on region, decreases in DNA concentrations as well as increases in the human brain have been reported (Herrmann, 1971). Loss of DNA in the mammalian brain has generally been associated with the loss of cells. However, loss of neurons with increasing age has been reported to be compensated for by an increase in glial cells (Johnson and Erner, 1972). Consequently, cell loss appears to be a generally accepted but as yet morphometrically and chemically unverified feature not only of the human but also of the mammalian brain in aging (Tomasch, 1972). In view of the enormous redundancy of interneurons in neuronal networks and the highly significant differences in total numbers of sensory, inter-, and motor neurons in the brain, it remains to be determined whether the loss of DNA content per cell, region, and whole brain can be related to cell loss and declining functional capacity during senescence (Herrmann, 1971; Hahn, 1971).

The possibility that changes in RNA base composition, concentration, and turnover may be responsible for cellular aging has also received considerable attention (Balis, 1969). One study of life-span changes in cellular RNA in the human CNS has been reported. According to this study of RNA content of motor neurons in the spinal cord of man, RNA concentration increases from 402 $\mu\mu$g/cell at 3 months after birth to 640 $\mu\mu$g/cell up to the age of 40, remains relatively stable until 60, then declines to 420 $\mu\mu$g/cell after 80 years of age (Hyden, 1967a). Numerous animal studies have now indicated that short-lasting, reversible fluctuations in RNA content and/or turnover in different cell populations and regions of the brain may be superimposed upon the probable age-dependent life-span changes. Regarding RNA turnover, animal studies involving incorporation of precursors into RNA have indicated decreases with age in RNA turnover (Balis, 1969). Other animal studies have shown quantitative and qualitative changes in RNA and protein content and their turnover related to age and different training or learning conditions (Hyden, 1967b; Dellweg et al., 1968; Glassman, 1974). Since RNA content and turnover are highly dependent on various functional states including nutrition, circadian rhythms, and numerous other environmental challenges, it has been difficult to interpret genetic and environmental interactions in RNA content and turnover throughout the life-span (Ordy and Schjeide, 1973).

Proteins have a wide diversity of functions in the mammalian brain. This diversity of functions is based on the vast number of complex cellular and subcellular structures that can be organized by combining 20 different amino acids into long polymers. As in all cells, neuronal and glial proteins are synthesized on polysomes. They may remain free in the cytoplasm, be organized into organelles, or migrate in "fast or slow" axonal transport through extremely long axonal processes, far removed from the DNA and RNA of the cell perikarya (Barondos and Dutton, 1972). Since a decrease in protein content has been reported in the brain for man and other mammalian species, animal studies have attempted to examine changes in the rate of protein turnover as a function of age. The rate at which proteins are synthesized has been determined with the incorporation of labeled amino acids as precursors into protein, or by evaluating the rate of disappearance of the labeled precursors. According to animal studies, the rate of protein turnover in the mammalian brain increases during development, remains relatively constant during maturity, and then appears to decline in old animals. The rate of turnover appears to be subject to short-lasting reversible fluctuations which may be imposed upon the above-cited major life-span changes. The life-span changes appear to be similar to age-dependent and environmentally modifiable changes reported for RNA content and turnover (Balis, 1969; Marks and Lajtha, 1971). Since neurons synthesize and turn over proteins rapidly in perikarya, "slow" and "fast" mechanisms of axoplasmic transport have received increasing attention in animal studies (Davison, 1970). Age differences in "fast" axoplasmic transport have been reported in old cats and dogs (Ochs, 1973).

In recent years, the free amino acids in the mammalian brain have received increasing attention in protein synthesis and in their possible role as neurotransmitters (Guroff, 1972). The high concentration and rapid metabolism of glutamic and aspartic acids and their derivatives have been studied extensively since they are among the more significant features of brain metabolism. According to animal studies, glutamate and aspartate concentrations rise during development, remain stable during maturity, and then decline rapidly, depending on region and species (van den Berg, 1970). Although free amino acids, proteins, monoamines, and their associated enzymes have received increasing attention in studies of the developing brain in different mammalian species, there are only a few animal studies that have dealt with the postmaturity changes in amino acids, proteins, and monoamines (Agrawal and Himwich, 1970). According to a recent study, age-dependent declines in aspartic and glutamic acid, glutamine, alanine, glycine, taurine, phosphoethanolamine, and cystathioanine have been reputed in the cerebral cortex, cerebellum, brainstem, and spinal cord of rats 30 months of age compared to amino acid levels in the same regions at 2 months of age (Timiras, Hudson, and Oklund, 1973).

Free and protein amino acids in different regions of the human brain were reported for three adult human males based on biopsy specimens obtained within 6 hr after death (Robinson and Williams, 1965). In another study of the distribution of free amino acids in the human brain, distribution patterns of amino acids were compared among normal adult, pathological, and fetal brain (Okumura et al., 1960).

Lipid Turnover

Over half of the dry weight of the brain is composed of lipids. Although small amounts of gangliosides and phospholipids in cellular and subcellular membranes may be concerned with neurotransmission and metabolic processes, respectively, most of the lipids in the nervous system are an integral structural component of membranes. Most lipids of the nervous system present in cellular and subcellular membranes serve as selective permeability barriers either at the surface of cells or within cells in the cytoplasmic organelles. Any consideration of life-span changes in lipid composition or metabolism in the nervous system must also be related to various anatomical or cytoarchitectural features of the brain, since there are distinct differences in lipid content and turnover, not only in cell type but also in different pathways and centers of the mammalian brain. One of the major distinctions in brain lipids has been based on comparisons of their composition and turnover in gray matter, which is relatively low in myelin, and white matter, which is relatively high in myelin.

The changes in lipid composition and turnover in the human brain during development, maturity, and aging have been studied much more extensively than other constituents. As a broad generalization, human brain lipid composition and turnover appear to change rapidly during development, turnover relatively slowly during maturity but continuously throughout life. Lipid composition of the adult human brain appears to remain relatively constant even under conditions of severe starvation, where there may be a substantial change in other chemical constituents (Davison, 1968; Davison and Dobbing, 1968). Changes in human brain lipid composition and turnover during senescence appear to be the reverse of those reported during development (Rouser and Yamamoto, 1969). In both man and animals, there is a progressive deposition of lipids present largely or entirely in myelin during development. Observations on lipid composition of the whole human male brain from fetal stages to 98 years have provided an important step in the quantitative assessment of one of the major chemical constituents of the brain (Rouser and Yamamoto, 1969). In general, the lipid composition of the human brain is unique compared to other organs not only in terms of the high total lipid concentration, but also in the types of lipids that are present in different organelles, cell types, and regions of the brain. As in most mammalian species, the three major categories of lipids in the human brain include cholesterol, sphingolipids, and phospholipids. A relatively complete review of the lipid composition including major gangliosides of the normal adult human brain has been presented (Suzuki, 1972). The reported values in lipid composition, including the major gangliosides in the adult human brain, have been proposed as a frame of reference for evaluating changes in brain lipids during brain development and in certain neuropathological disorders. However, these normal adult values have not been used as points of reference in the evaluation of age-dependent changes in lipids of the human brain during senescence (Suzuki, 1972).

In animal studies, the turnover of lipids in the nervous system has generally been considered in the context of their role as structural components of membranes, and the possibility, that some amino acids and lipids may provide an additional source of energy in the brain in the absence of glucose under starvation and during some drug and pathological conditions (Davison, 1968). Utilization of lipids as sources of energy in most organs includes triglycerides and some fatty acids. Turnover of lipids depends on nutritional states. The turnover of structural lipids in membranes, particularly in the brain, appears to be relatively slow, and seems to depend primarily on the age and class of lipid. In all organs, fuel lipids, such as triglycerides, have relatively fast turnover rates on the order of 1 to 7 days. Lipids which form cellular and organelle membranes are classed as intermediate lipids, with turnover rates of 1 to 4 weeks, while structural lipids of membranes, such as myelin, have turnover rates of over a month (Burton, 1971). Myelin accounts for most of the mammalian brain lipid. Its stability after development and relatively slow turnover throughout life make it likely that as the major structural component of membranes, myelin is largely excluded from the other generally high metabolic activity of the nervous system. After early development, myelin membranes are known to contain low lipid-associated enzyme activity (Rouser and Yamamoto, 1969). Considerable progress has also been reported in the classification of hereditary neuropathological disorders and lipid metabolism in man (Wilson, 1968). Some neuropathological disorders arise from genetically determined changes in the level of an enzyme involved in lipid metabolism. Secondary changes in lipid metabolism may arise from changes in metabolic balance, tissue degeneration, and the loss of cells (Rouser and Yamamoto, 1969).

Carbohydrate Turnover

Under normal conditions, the basic and unique substrate for energy metabolism in the brain is glucose. The brain depends on glucose not only for energy but also as the major carbon source for the turnover of a variety of other simple and complex molecules. The principle source of lipid carbon in the brain is blood glucose. A large portion of the carbon appears rapidly not only in CO_2 but also in amino acids and their derivatives, particularly glutamic acid, glutamine, gamma-aminobutyric acid (GABA), and aspartic acid. Glucose metabolism in the brain is uniquely dependent on a high rate of mitochondrial respiration. The high energy requirements of the brain

have been related to neurotransmitter synthesis, electrical activity, maintenance of ionic gradients, the synthesis of protein and some lipid macromolecules in both neurons and glia, and to intracellular transport (Maher and
Lehrer, 1972).

Despite the "avaricious" metabolic appetite of the brain involving blood
flow, O_2 uptake, and glucose utilization, the brain has relatively little tissue
glycogen or "fuel" reserve and relies primarily on rapid utilization of glucose
contained in the bloodstream. Glucose and glycogen levels in brain tissue
are quite low for an organ so uniquely dependent on them as sources of
energy. The levels for the two main carbohydrates, glucose and glycogen,
reported in the literature for the human brain and for other species, vary
widely, partly due to methodological difficulties in evaluation, and in the
case of man, due to the rapid postmortem changes which occur after the
blood supply to the brain has ceased (Bachelard, 1969). In several studies,
glycolytic enzymes, cofactors, and metabolites in the human brain were
compared between gray and white matter in normal and pathological conditions. The order of depletion of energy reserves in tissue samples from
the cerebral cortex was p-creatine, adenosine triphosphate, and glucose
with glycogen depletion at a slower rate (Robinson and Phillips, 1964;
Kirsch and Leitner, 1967). The lability of glycolytic enzymes, cofactors,
and glycogen reported in the human brain has been verified in various
animal species (Coxon, 1970).

Regarding life-span changes, the major changes in glycolytic capacity of
the mammalian brain occur during development. Although age declines in
cerebral blood flow, O_2 consumption, and glucose utilization in the human
brain have been reported, these age declines have been attributed primarily
to changes in cerebral blood flow and pathology rather than normal aging
(Sokoloff, 1972). Some animal studies have reported declines in glucose
and glycogen metabolism in the brain of aged animals. However, cerebral
blood flow or cellular sources of the age-dependent metabolic declines in
the mammalian brain have not been established (Suzuki, 1972).

Changes in Chemical Equilibrium of the Brain Induced
by Environmental Stimulation

As an environmentally modifiable organ, the brain appears to be stable
and relatively permanent in some respects, but it is also subject to internal
and external environmental influences. The chemical equilibrium or homeostatic mechanisms of regulation are dynamic rather than static and they are
vulnerable to a wide range of genetic and environmental hazards. Such
effects on the brain include nutrition, drugs, stress, radiation, convulsion,
ischemia, temperature, diseases, and perhaps most important, the more
subtle effects of training and experience or memory in relation to specific
neurochemical correlates of sensory, cognitive, and motor functions (Lajtha,

1969–1972). Animal studies have examined the environmental modifiability or the chemical and morphological "plasticity" of the mammalian brain during development, maturity, and aging (Ordy and Schjeide, 1973). As a broad generalization, recovery of homeostatic equilibrium and repair of structures in the mammalian brain are probably greater in the embryo than fetus, are greater in the young than in the adult, and may also be greater in maturity than in senescence. Despite the overall apparent ontogenetic decrease in modifiability of behavior and the chemical and morphological "plasticity" of the mammalian brain, a chemical and morphological "plasticity" remains throughout the life-span (Ordy and Schjeide, 1973).

Intra- and Extracellular Changes in the Brain as Sources of the Rate of Decline During Senescence

The progressive and cumulative, but as yet chemically and morphometrically unverified loss of neurons in the brain with age in man is now generally accepted as a possible major factor in the decline of sensory, cognitive, and motor functions during senescence. Due to the highly significant differences in total number and redundancy among sensory, inter-, and motor neuronal networks, the differential consequences of cell loss in the human brain throughout the life-span for sensory, cognitive, and motor capacities require experimental clarification. The conflicting findings regarding age-dependent changes in such major constituents as brain weight, H_2O, lipids, proteins, and extracellular "space" determined by chemical and anatomical methods also require clarification.

In considering age-dependent chronological declines of functional capacity including memory of the human brain during senescence, it is apparent that the intra- and extracellular sources of aging may include changes in primary structures of DNA, RNA, and protein, their concentration or turnover, loss of subcellular organelles, loss of neurons, altered neuron-glia relationships, and finally altered intercellular network relations as suggested by recently reported decreases in dendritic spines in the cerebral cortex of old rats (Feldman, 1974). Since genetic and environmental influences interact, it is apparent that the rate of intra- and extracellular age-dependent changes in the brain can be identified most readily in carefully controlled animal life-span studies utilizing only the most sophisticated experimental designs.

LIFE-SPAN CHANGES IN NEUROTRANSMITTERS OR BIOGENIC AMINES, ASSOCIATED ENZYMES, AND METABOLITES IN THEIR ROLE AS PHYSIOLOGICAL REGULATORS OR CONTROL MECHANISMS

In contrast to the molecular or neurochemical focus on DNA, RNA, and protein as the unique genetic and acquired informational macromolecules of the brain, including their role as basic molecular or cellular sources of aging, neurophysiological theories have proposed that reflex integration, neuronal coding, learning, and memory may be associated with aggregate or global electrical "field" properties of neuron ensembles, networks, or circuits (John, 1972). The failure of the extensive classical brain lesions made even within so-called "point-to-point" pathways and centers in the mammalian brain to produce specific functional deficits has been used as a major argument against the primary emphasis on molecules, organelles, individual cells, or specific cellular connections as the basic units in neuronal coding or acquisition, transfer, storage, retrieval, and loss of information in the nervous system (Kandel and Spencer, 1968). Taking cognizance of interneuronal redundancy, particularly in the neocortex, aggregate-field hypotheses of learning have implied that existing connections in specific pathways and centers may have little or nothing to do with learning which may be associated primarily with global network properties, particularly the neuropil, rather than depend on intracellular chemical events in single cells. Although changes in such global "electrical field" activity as EEG are difficult to interpret in relation to cellular or regional origin, age changes in EEG activity, particularly the so-called alpha waves, have been recorded from the brain of old human subjects (Obrist, 1963; Wang, 1969). More localized age changes in visual, auditory, and somatosensory-evoked cortical potentials have also been reported in man after 40 years of age (Dustman and Beck, 1969). It seems likely that neurophysiological "aggregate field" hypotheses of memory changes in aging may consider changes in brain tissue interdependence, organizational complexity, network capacity, redundancy, and environmental modifiability as major sources of aging in the brain rather than cellular sources.

Neurotransmitters and Biogenic Amines in the Brain

Loss of short-term memory (Keevil-Rogers and Schnore, 1969), slowing of reflexes, and decreases in speed and accuracy are some of the most prominent and fundamental behavioral manifestations of human aging (Birren, 1965). These age changes may be attributable to structural and functional changes in neuronal network capacity, including neuromuscular coordination. Whereas age changes in chemical composition, energy metabolism, and rate of turnover in the brain are undoubtedly numerous and complex, age changes in neurotransmitters or biogenic amines and their associated enzymes must also represent important sources of aging. They are known to play an important role as physiological regulators or control mechanisms. The "language" of neurons is primarily electrical. Most of the recent neurophysiological studies of neuronal coding have directed their attention to neuronal membranes, particularly the synapse as the most likely cellular site of "plasticity" in information transfer among neurons and effectors.

Single unit iontophoretic studies have focused on specific neurotransmitters or biogenic amines to establish their role as physiological regulators in neuronal coding, memory, and reflex integration of the physiology and chemistry of all other organs in the body (Mandell, 1973). Through its structural and functional "asymmetry," the synapse provides the excitation and inhibition for other neurons and the effectors of the body (McLennan, 1970; Hall, Hilderbrand, and Kravitz, 1974). A number of chemical substances, generally referred to as neurotransmitters or biogenic amines, have been proposed to be involved in information transfer, or as physiological regulators among neurons and between the nervous system and the effectors. A major effort in the entire new field of neurochemistry has been devoted to the chemistry of synaptic transmission (Hall et al., 1974). The history and current status of the biochemical events involved in synaptic transmission have been reviewed extensively in numerous review articles, books, and several volumes of the *Handbook of Neurochemistry.*

Essentially, arrival of an action potential at the presynaptic terminal results in the release of a chemical transmitter, its diffusion across the synaptic cleft, and interaction with receptors in the postsynaptic cell membrane. Transmitter release and receptor interactions involve ionic permeability changes in membranes. The ions, their changes, and direction of movement determine whether a transmitter is excitatory or inhibitory. Mechanisms of inactivation or reuptake remove the transmitters from sites of action. The specific criteria proposed for the identification of acetylcholine (ACh) and norepinephrine (NE) as excitatory and inhibitory transmitters in isolated ganglia of the autonomic nervous system have also been extended and proposed for the identification of putative transmitters in the CNS (Cooper, Bloom, and Roth, 1970). These criteria include: enzymes in presynaptic terminals for synthesis, storage granules and release mechanisms in terminals, synaptic mimicry or postsynaptic receptor response to presynaptic iontophoretic application, and enzymes for inactivation or mechanisms of presynaptic reuptake. Based primarily on studies with various mammalian species and invertebrates, the following substances and their associated enzymes of synthesis and degradation have been tentatively identified as putative transmitters in the mammalian CNS: ACh, choline acetyltransferase (ChAc), and acetylcholinesterase (AChE) (Potter, 1970); the catecholamines norepinephrine (NE) and dopamine, tyrosine hydroxylase (TH), DOPA decarboxylase (DOD), and monoamine oxidase (MAO) (Aures, Hakanson, and Clark, 1970; Costa and Neff, 1970; Glowinski, 1970; Iverson, 1970; Quastel, 1970); serotonin (5-HT) and catechol-o-methyltransferase (Page and Carlsson, 1970); and the amino acids—GABA, glutamic acid, and glycine (Baxter, 1970; Cooper et al., 1970; Curtis and Johnston, 1970).

Although the putative neurotransmitters and their associated enzymes have been studied very extensively in the mammalian brain, relatively little is known concerning their distribution, concentration, and level of activity in the human brain. Neurotransmitter and enzyme values reported for the human brain are generally based on chemical evaluations of tissue samples obtained after variable intervals between death and autopsy. In many cases age, sex, and clinical state of the subjects have not been specified. Although to date only a very small number of studies have been reported on neurotransmitters in the human brain, Table 2 contains a summary of putative neurotransmitters and some associated enzyme values reported in the literature for different regions of the adult human brain in relation to comparable values reported for other mammalian species. These values in Table 2 for the adult human brain and for other species were selected from regions with the highest content and/or as the only values available in the published references.

Some age differences in cholinergic and monoaminergic transmitters and associated enzyme values have been reported for different regions of the human brain. Brain tissue samples were obtained from accident victims ranging in age from 15 to 60 years with no attendant history of neuro-

TABLE 2. *Neurotransmitter content and associated enzymes in the adult human brain[a]*

	Associated enzymes	
Neurotransmitter	Synthesis	Degradation
ACh 0.5–0.6 μg/g[b] (human cerebral cortex)	ChAc 0.39 nmoles/g/hr (human cortex)	AChE 0.29 nmoles/g/hr (human cortex)
Dopamine 2.45–3.75 μg/g (human caudate)	DOD 3.0 μmoles/g/hr (human caudate)	dopamine B oxidase 2.5–3.5 μmoles/g/hr (dog brain)
NE 0.35–0.60 μg/g (human hypothalamus)	dopamine B oxidase 2.5–3.5 nmoles/g/hr (dog brain)	catechol-O-methyl transferase or MAO 0.5 μmoles/g/hr (human hypothalamus)
5-HT 0.2–0.23 μg/g (human hindbrain)	5-hydroxytryptophan decarboxylase 3.0 moles/g/hr (human hypothalamus)	MAO 8.4 μmoles/g/hr (human hypothalamus)
GABA 2–4 nmoles/g (mammalian cortex)	GAD 1,640–1,656 nmoles/g/hr (human hypothalamus)	GABA-transaminase 9 nmoles/kg/hr (monkey occipital cortex)
Glutamate 10 mmoles/brain (mammalian brain)	glutamate dehydrogenase 0.59 mg/ml (beef liver)	GAD 1,640–1,656 nmoles/g/hr (human hypothalamus)

[a] Neurotransmitter and associated enzyme values for the adult human brain were selected from regions with highest content or as the only values available.
[b] Tower, D. B., and Elliott, K. A. C. (1952): *Am. J. Physiol.,* 168:747–759. Other values are based on published references cited in text.

pathology or other illnesses. The activities of TH, DOD, and glutamic acid decarboxylase (GAD) were examined in the substantia nigra, caudate nucleus, putamen, and hypothalamus. In the substantia nigra, TH, DOD, and GAD activity decreased significantly from 69 to 3, 1,250 to 60, and 5190 to 520 nmoles/g wet weight/hr, respectively. Similar significant reductions in TH, DOD, and GAD activity were observed in the caudate nucleus and putamen. In the hypothalamus, DOD declined from 375 to 22 and GAD from 1,640 to 560 nmoles/g wet weight/hr by 60 years of age. In contrast to the highly significant age declines of TH, DOD, and GAD in the substantia nigra, caudate nucleus, and putamen, TH activity in the hypothalamus was significantly lower throughout the life-span, ranging from 1 to 5 nmoles/g wet weight/hr, and this low activity did not change significantly with increasing age (Cote and Kremzner, 1974). In another study, the TH activity in the caudate nucleus of six healthy human subjects aged 5, 8, 17, 42, 55, and 57 decreased significantly from a high of 121 nmoles/g/hr in the 5-year-old to 19 nmoles/g/hr in the 57-year-old subject (McGeer et al., 1971a; McGeer and McGeer, 1973). The TH activity reported in this chapter was significantly higher than values reported for 12 different regions of five male psychiatric patients ranging from 43 to 91 years of age (Vogel, Orfei, and Century, 1969). It is interesting to note that TH activity in the caudate nucleus, putamen, and substantia nigra was relatively high compared to other regions in the human brain and that the basal levels and regional variations of TH activity in the human brain were comparable to those of two nonhuman primates, the baboon (*Papio papio*) and the rhesus monkey (*Macaca mulatta*) (Cote and Fahn, 1969; McGeer et al., 1971a). Comparisons have also been made among choline acetylase, AChE, GAD, and TH in brain tissue samples obtained from several cortical and subcortical regions of normal healthy adult accident victims and of patients with Huntington's chorea (McGeer et al., 1973), Parkinson's disease, and epilepsy (McGeer et al., 1971a; McGeer, McGeer, and Wada, 1971b).

Postmaturity declines in choline acetylase and AChE have been reported for the human cerebral cortex (McGeer et al., 1971a). Age declines in DOD have also been reported for different regions of the human brain (Lloyd and Hornykiewicz, 1970). Relatively small but statistically significant declines in dopamine, NE, and 5-HT have been reported for the caudate and hindbrain of the human CNS (Robinson, Nies, Davis, Bunney, Davis, Colburn, Bourne, Shaw, and Coppen, 1972; Nies et al., 1973). Dopamine reached near-adult levels by birth, increased to 3.75 g/g by 53 years, and decreased to 2.45 μg/g at 83 years (Bertler, 1961). Significant decreases in dopamine levels of the basal ganglia have been associated with the age-related increases in the incidence of Parkinson's disease (Hornykiewicz, 1972). In normal subjects, NE declined from 0.60 μg/g at 25 years of age to 0.35 μg/g at ages over 70. 5-HT decreased relatively little from 0.23 μg/g at 25 years to 0.20 μg/g at over 70 years (Nies et al., 1973).

In contrast to the age-related declines, several studies have now reported increased MAO activity with age in the hindbrain (Nies et al., 1973). Thus far, life-span changes in ACh have not been reported for the human brain. Only a few ACh values have been found in the literature for the mammalian brain. Using the frog rectus muscle for bioassay and a microchemical method, an ACh value of 19.1 μmoles/g/tissue has been reported for the whole adult mouse brain (Goldberg and McCaman, 1973). In the adult mammalian cerebral cortex, an ACh value of 121 to 147 nmoles/g protein has been reported (Potter, 1970). It has also been reported that the level of 5-hydroxytryptophan decarboxylase, the rate-limiting enzyme in 5-HT synthesis, is present in very low concentrations in the human brain compared to several lower mammalian species (Robins, Robins, Croninger, Moses, Spencer, and Hudgens, 1967). Figure 4 illustrates the major life-span changes in some neurotransmitters and associated enzymes in the human brain based on estimated values reported in the cited literature references.

The life-span age differences or inferred changes in neurotransmitter and associated enzyme values that have been reported for different regions of the human brain in the cited literature and some recent review articles must be considered fragmentary, tentative, and highly incomplete (Bender, 1970; McGeer, Fibiger, McGeer, and Wickson, 1971; Tryding, Tufvesson and Ilsson, 1972; Eisdorfer and Fann, 1973). However, it is apparent that generally neurotransmitter levels including synthesizing and degrading enzyme activity decline significantly in many regions of the human brain during aging. Whereas human and animal studies have clearly indicated significant declines in neurotransmitter levels and enzyme activity with increasing postmortem delay, it seems relevant to note that statistically significant age declines and regional differences can be inferred in the human brain from the published references. It also seems relevant to note that while species differences exist, neurotransmitter and enzyme values for different regions of the human brain appear to be comparable to values reported for several nonhuman primates (Pscheidt and Himwich, 1963; Ho, Taylor, Fritchie, Englert, and McIsaac, 1972; Maas, Dekirmenjian, Garver, Redmond, and Landis, 1973) and for some lower mammalian species (Hollander and Barrows, 1968; Epstein and Barrows, 1969; Ordy and Schjeide, 1973).

According to animal studies, major life-span changes in neurotransmitters and their enzymes include rapid increases in cholinergic and monoaminergic levels during development, including a possible role in cellular differentiation of the brain, in addition to their role in synaptic functions (Vernadakis, 1973). They remain stable, but responsive to environmental and functional changes during maturity and then decline during aging. In the cholinergic "ACh" system, it is now generally accepted that ChAc, the synthesizing enzyme, is a more reliable index of ACh than AChE, the hydrolyzing en-

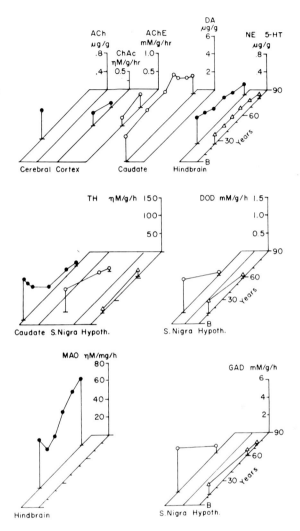

FIG. 4. Life-span changes in cholinergic, monoaminergic transmitters and associated enzymes in the human brain. Values are based on literature references cited in the text. DA-dopamine.

zyme. It has been reported that during aging of the chick cerebral cortex, ChAc declines, while AChE increases, suggesting loss or decline in function of cholinergic neurons and possibly memory (Vernadakis, 1973). The age declines in NE and 5-HT and their enzymes were considerably less and highly selective in different regions of the chick brain. Age declines in cortical AChE have also been reported for the rat (Hollander and Barrows, 1968) and the whole brain of the C57BL/10 mouse (Ordy and Schjeide, 1973). Animal studies of age differences in the monoaminergic systems

dopamine, NE, 5-HT have shown not only significant age declines in catecholamine levels in the hypothalamus and striatum of old C56BL/6J mice
but also in their rate of turnover, inferred from the reduced incorporation of
injected radioactive precursors into four different regions of the mouse
brain (Finch and Jonec, 1973).

It is apparent that there are major life-span changes in neurotransmitters
and their enzymes. However, evidence for the putative neurotransmitters
and their enzymes in synaptic activity, neural frequency coding by changes
in excitation, and inhibition in specific pathways and centers of the CNS in
relation to specific sensory-cognitive-motor responses is primarily circum-
stantial and based on neuropharmacological studies (Cooper et al., 1970)
and on significant correlations in multivariate studies (Ordy and Schjeide,
1973). In multivariate studies of human aging, attempts have been made to
correlate age declines in speed of behavior, as one of the most fundamental
manifestations of aging, with changes in such global electrical activity as
the EEG alpha cycle (Obrist, 1965), the alpha frequency of the human EEG
as the master timing mechanism of behavior (Surwillo, 1968), and the electrical activity in the autonomic and cardiovascular systems (Callaway, 1965).
More recently, significant differences have also been reported in biofeedback
conditioning of the EEG alpha rhythm (8 to 12 Hz) between 15 young (18 to
29 years) and 15 old (60 to 81 years) normal healthy human subjects (Woodruff and Birren, 1972). This recent study indicates the interesting and unique
prospects of environmental modifiability or "plasticity" of even the global
or network EEG alpha rhythm generally considered to be an intrinsic rhythm
of the brain. The behavioral studies have demonstrated declines in timing,
speed, and reaction time of old human and animal subjects. Electrophysiological studies have shown age changes not only in global but also in single
unit electrical activity of the brain (Sparks and Travis, 1967). Although
speculative, age declines in electrical activity of the brain may be related to
age declines in neuropil or synaptic density. Recent quantitative morphometric aging studies of dendritic spines, as the major synaptic receptor sites,
have indicated a significant 35% reduction of apical dendritic spines in layer
4 of the visual cortex in 29.5-month-old rats (Feldman, 1974). Whereas subcellular fractionation studies have been undertaken more recently to determine age changes in synaptosomes of different regions of the mouse brain
(Finch and Jonec, 1974), most of the previously reported neurochemical
studies of aging have been done on heterogeneous nervous tissue comprising neurons, glia, neuropil, extracellular material, and vascular elements.
Recent studies on isolated ganglia from *Aplysia californica* indicate realistic
future prospects of multivariate aging studies involving concurrent assessment of specific behavioral responses in relation to evaluation of single unit
electrical activity and protein turnover in specific identifiable single neurons
(Gainer and Barker, 1974).

The Hypothalamic-Pituitary-Adrenal Axis, Biogenic Amines, and Hormones in Adaptation and Aging

As interrelated, adaptive control systems, the brain plays a unique role in adaptation to the environment in reflexes, conditioning and learning, and the hypothalamic-pituitary-adrenal axis through homoestatic feedback regulation of metabolism in response to environmental challenges. Animal learning studies have focused on cholinergic mechanisms in cortical and subcortical regions. Monoaminergic mechanisms in the limbic system and the hypothalamic-pituitary-adrenal axis have received increasing attention in emotions, arousal, reactivity to stress, and the integration of biological drives (Kety, 1967). Behaviorally, learning has generally been defined as a relatively permanent change in behavior and the brain produced by reinforced practice. Learning or performance have also implied a dependence on biological drives and their reinforcement. Recently, learning and levels of motivation based on biological drives have been "linked" as an integrated, adaptive process through the hypothalamic-pituitary-adrenal axis. Numerous animal studies have shown a close temporal relationship in synthesis, storage, or release of hypothalamic catecholamines, pituitary adrenocorticotrophic hormone (ACTH) and adrenal catecholamines and corticosteroids in response to a wide range of environmental conditions. According to animal studies of life-span changes in neuroendocrines, hypothalamic catecholamines, pituitary ACTH, and adrenal hormones may not change markedly with age but decrease significantly in magnitude of response and rate of recovery after various categories of stimulation and stress (Friedman, Green, and Sharland, 1969; Hess and Riegl, 1970).

The capacity to adapt to an ever-changing environment is a fundamental characteristic of man and all animal species. The nervous and neuroendocrine systems play a major role in regulating the adaptation of the organism to the environment. Two of the most prominent biological characteristics of aging include a progressive decline in homeostatic adaptation to the environment and increasing probability of mortality. Although numerous authors have proposed a central regulatory role for hypothalamic nuclei, the pituitary, and adrenal glands in aging, very few experimental or clinical studies are available in the literature on age declines in homeostatic regulation in man and other mammalian species (Timiras, 1972).

GENETIC AND ENVIRONMENTAL INTERACTIONS IN THE BRAIN THROUGHOUT THE LIFE-SPAN

Current neurobiological theories of major sources of change in brain development, maturity, and aging range from genetic hypotheses of molecular neurobiology to mathematical or cybernetic models of the brain as an environmentally modifiable, adaptive control system (Ordy and Schjeide, 1973). In life-span studies of the brain, one of the major theoretical issues consists of the clarification of the respective roles of genetic and environmental sources and their interactions throughout the life-span. In contrast to most genetic traits, the quantitative assessment of the rate of aging is highly complex since it includes genetic sources where the exact quantitative contributions are not known and the environmental influences which are superimposed as interactions on the genetic program throughout the life-span. In most human and animal aging studies, chronological age, average or maximum life-span, and age-specific survival or mortality rather than rate of aging have been used as the more obvious dependent variables (Cook, 1972). For a variety of reasons, short-lived lower mammalian species rather than man have also been used as subjects. Consequently, relatively little information is available on environmental modification of the human brain, the rate of its aging, or the effects on average or maximum life-span, other than the reported effects of various environmental variables on human mortality. Since it is generally accepted that chronological and biological ages of heterogenous genetic population even in normally variable environments do not coincide, measuring the biological rate of human aging has become of considerable social importance and represents a challenge to biological gerontology (Comfort, 1972).

Environmental Modification of the Brain, Average Life-span, or Rate of Aging

The careful control of genetic and all environmental factors throughout the life-span covering several years is rather difficult to obtain even under ideal laboratory conditions for most mammalian species. Previously reported longitudinal and cross-sectional life-span studies have provided conflicting evidence on the relative roles of genetic and environmental variables on the brain and the rate of aging since they have been inferred primarily from changes or differences between control and experimental subjects in mortality, average or maximum life-spans (Strehler, 1967; Cook, 1972). Although carefully controlled genetic and environmental interaction studies involving the brain and the rate of its aging are few in number (Ordy and Schjeide, 1973), numerous human and animal studies do suggest that a wide range of environmental variables can influence the brain, the rate of aging, mortality, and at least the average life-span. Major environmental variables that have been considered to be of importance in affecting the brain and rate of aging in human and animal subjects are: (1) nutrition (McCay, Sperling, and Barnes, 1943), (2) exercise (Tiplady, 1972), (3) stress (Ordy, Samorajski, Zeman, and Curtis, 1967), (4) drugs, particularly alcohol and tobacco (Wallgren, 1971; Granich, 1972; Gentleman and Forbes, 1974), (5) accidents, primarily the effects of head injury (Liu, Wickstrom, Saltzberg, and Heath, 1973), (6) radiation (Egana, 1971; Ordy, Samorajski, Hershberger, and Curtis, 1971), (7) infectious diseases and immunological changes (Walford, 1969), (8) temperature (Cremer, 1971), (9) O_2 pressure, convulsions, ischemia, and a variety of other, more stable, environmental hazards (Timiras, 1972). Table 3 provides a summary and possible rank order of the major environmental sources that have been examined for their possible effects on the brain, the average life-span, or rate of aging, and on age-specific mortality.

Chemical Modification of the Brain, Average Life-span, or Rate of Aging

In recent years, numerous attempts have been made to alter the rate of aging in a variety of mammalian species with some specific chemical agent, in some cases presumed to affect the brain and/or the rate of aging as in-

TABLE 3. *Environmental modification of the brain, average life-span, or rate of aging*

Possible rank order of source	Effects on brain functions, average life-span	Proposed mechanisms in brain, body
Nutrition	sensory-cognitive-motor, increases-decreases	RNA, protein, neurotransmitters, enzymes, circulation, metabolism
Exercise	sensory-cognitive-motor, increases	RNA, protein, neurotransmitters, enzymes, circulation, metabolism
Stress	sensory-cognitive-motor, increases-decreases	brain-neuroendocrines, affective disorders, catecholamines
Drugs (alcohol, tobacco)	sensory-cognitive-motor, increases-decreases	DNA, RNA, protein, neurotransmitters, enzymes, circulation, metabolism
Accidents (head injury)	sensory-cognitive-motor, decreases	trauma, edema, circulation, metabolism
Radiation	sensory-cognitive-motor, increases-decreases	DNA, RNA, protein, neurotransmitters, enzymes, circulation, metabolism
Infectious diseases	sensory-cognitive-motor, increases-decreases	immunoregulation, RNA, protein, neurotransmitters, enzymes, circulation, metabolism
Temperature	sensory-cognitive-motor, increases-decreases	DNA, RNA, protein, neurotransmitters, enzymes, circulation, metabolism
O_2 pressure, convulsions, ischemia, etc.	sensory-cognitive-motor, increases-decreases	RNA, protein, neurotransmitters, enzymes, circulation, metabolism

Reported observations in the cited literature with human and animal subjects have indicated dynamic homeostasis of the nervous system to environmental sources based on chemical equilibrium between stability and plasticity.

ferred from changes or differences in average and rarely maximum life-spans (Kormendy and Bender, 1971; Granich, 1972; Hollander, 1972). Examples of major categories of chemical agents that have been used extensively include: magnesium pemoline and cycloheximide as stimulants and inhibitors of protein synthesis, respectively, the antioxidants butylated hydroxytoluene and meclofenoxate, various lipofuscin and collagen cross-link inhibitors, immunoregulators, vitamins, polyunsaturated fatty acids, and hormones. Table 4 summarizes the main categories of chemical agents

TABLE 4. *Chemical modification of the brain, average life-span, or rate of aging*

Chemical agent	Effect on brain, average life-span	Proposed mechanism in brain, body
Stimulants-inhibitors; magnesium pemoline, procaine amide, 5,5-diphenylhydantoin, triacyanoaminopropene, yeast-RNA, ribaminol, inosine-alkylamino alcohol complexes, cycloheximide, actinomycin-D	stimulants enhance, inhibitors reduce sensory-cognitive-motor functions; life-span changes not reported	DNA, RNA, protein, neurotransmitters, enzymes, circulation, metabolism, neuro-endocrines, effectors
Butylated hydroxytoluene	sensory-cognitive-motor functions ?; 45% increase of mouse mean life-span	antioxidant, inhibitor of free radicals, retard food intake
Meclofenoxate (Centrophenoxine®), magnesium orotate, kawain	sensory-cognitive-motor functions; increased life-span	antioxidant, lipofuscin inhibitor, reduced glycolysis, increased pentose shunt
Vitamin E, polyunsaturated fatty acids	sensory-cognitive-motor functions ?; life-span ?	antioxidants, free radicals, lipofuscin
Posterior pituitary hormones: oxytocin	sensory-cognitive-motor functions; decreased mortality in 24–30-month rats	electrolyte balance
Corticosteroids: hydrocortisone, prednisolone	sensory-cognitive-motor functions, emotions; increased mean life-span in mice	antiinflammatory, immunosuppressive, food intake
Azathioprine, cyclophosphamide	sensory-cognitive-motor functions; 50% increase in survival of mice	immunoregulators, immunosuppressive agents
Chelating agents: D-penicillamine; lathyrogens: -aminopropionitrile	sensory-cognitive-motor functions ?; no apparent effect on survival of rats	inhibitor of intramolecular cross-link formation in collagen

Reported observations in the cited literature on chemical modification of the brain, average life-span, or rate of aging are based on clinical studies with old human subjects, laboratory animals, and tissue culture.

that have been examined for their effects on the brain, life-span, or rate of aging.

As indicated in various sections of this chapter, it is apparent that numerous chemical agents, drugs, and environmental pollutants can influence the brain throughout the life-span (Granich, 1972). Although most neurobiological studies have concentrated on the effects of various chemical agents on the most vulnerable period of the brain during the perinatal "growth spurt," there has been some increasing interest in psychopharmacology and aging (Eisdorfer and Fann, 1973). In general, it has been reported that some of the chemical agents used in aging studies have had specific effects on sensory-cognitive-motor functions of the brain, as well as altered the average life-span of mammalian and lower vertebrate species. However, only a few studies have reported extensions of the maximum life-span after antioxidants in mice (Comfort, Youhotsky-Gore and Pathmanathan, 1971) and in *Drosophila* (Hochschild, 1971). Since both increases and decreases of average life-span can result from a wide range of influences, significant increases in maximum life-span by chemical and other agents provide the most compelling evidence for inhibition of aging.

Neurochemical Aspects of Some Primary Postmaturity Psychiatric, Neurological Disorders and Senile Dementias in Man

In recent years the neurochemical aspects of some genetic and primary postmaturity psychiatric, neurological disorders or lesions and senile dementias have received increasing attention (Wilson, 1968; Embree, Bass, and Pope, 1972; Hornykiewicz, 1972; Weil-Malherbe, 1972). These clinical disorders are characterized by mental deterioration, diffuse or discrete cortical and subcortical degeneration, and a variety of neurochemical changes in the brain. Table 5 summarizes the proposed chemical defects in cortical and subcortical regions in some psychiatric and neurological disorders and senile dementias.

According to neurochemical theories of the etiology of these diseases, the mental deterioration in some of these disorders may be associated in part with impairment of chemical transmission within the brain. The age-related increases in the incidence of these disorders and related syndromes may result from decreased synthesis and/or breakdown of neurotransmitters, their metabolites, or alterations in the synthesizing and degrading enzymes of the transmitters (Weil-Malherbe, 1972; Marx, 1974b). It is apparent that the age-related increase in the incidence of these neurological disorders makes the differentiation of basic neurochemical age changes and the neuropathological changes that may be superimposed upon them a difficult and challenging area of future clinical and basic research. The differentiation between "normal aging" and pathology represents one of the more important theoretical and clinical problems in biological gerontology.

TABLE 5. *Neurochemical aspects of some primary postmaturity neurological disorders or lesions and senile dementias*

Disorder	Effects on brain functions	Chemical defects in CNS
Psychoses, organic, affective disorders	psychopathology, hallucinations, delusions, etc.	CNS, ANS, limbic system, catecholamines, mineral metabolism, altered hormone levels
Senile dementias	mental deterioration	cortical, subcortical, decreased sulfatides, phospholipids
Alzheimer's disease	defective memory, disorientation	cortex, increased acid-polysaccharides, cerebrosides, decreased phospholipids
Huntington's chorea	mental deterioration, involuntary movement disorder	caudate, putamen, altered metabolism, enzymes, metals, transmitters, lipids
Creutzfeldt-Jakob disease	mental deterioration	cortex, decreased gangliosides, cerebrosides
Pick's lobar atrophy	mental deterioration	cortex, circumscribed atrophy, Pick's cells, sudanophilic and PAS-positive material, altered NADH and ATPase
Abiotrophies	mental deterioration	cortical, subcortical, enzymes, selective tissue degeneration
Parkinson's disease	extrapyramidal motor disturbances, akinesia, rigidity, tremor	basal ganglia, decreased dopamine, 5-HT, NE

Common features of the primary lesions or dementias: include mental deterioration, general or circumscribed degeneration of the cerebral cortex, basal ganglia, and the increasing probability of mortality in middle and late life.

ANS = autonomic nervous system; PAS = para-aminosalicylic acid; NADH = nicotinamide adenine dinucleotide.

NEUROBIOLOGY AND AGING IN NONHUMAN PRIMATES

Although of the same taxonomic order as man, it is surprising that nonhuman primates have been used so infrequently in neurobiological research on aging. Many of man's most distinctive sensory, learning, and motor capacities are shared only by higher diurnal primates (Chiarelli, 1973). There is an increasing encephalization or localization of distinctive sensory-cognitive-motor functions in the cortex of primates and man, e.g., Stripe of Genarri, striate area 17, visual cortex. This entails the use of nonhuman primates for specific structure-function studies throughout the life-span. An extensive reorganization of the brain may have occurred in primate evolution (Holloway, 1966, 1967). Life-span changes in specific sensory, associative, and motor functions of the brain may be identified more readily in visual and somatosensory neocortical regions where neuronal contact specificity has been demonstrated to be uniquely precise (Hubel and Wiesel, 1968). Complex manipulative behavior coincides with advanced neocortical development of primates and is not organized at subcortical levels in lower species (Noback and Moskowitz, 1963). Decreases in speed and accuracy of complex manipulatory behavior with aging, a prominent manifestation in old human subjects, may be demonstrable only in primates. Man and non-human primates have the highest brain/body ratio. The brain may play a "pacemaker" role in aging. Significant correlations have been established in phylogeny between brain weight and maximum life-span. This correlation is most unique in primates. According to allometry studies, an increase in brain size, particularly the neopallium, occurs concurrently with an increase in life-span, particularly in higher diurnal primates and man (Sacher, 1973).

In the past, there has been almost an exclusive use of short-lived mammals in neurobiological research on aging. A variety of theoretical and logistical reasons have been cited for the continued use of short-lived mammals in gerontological research. Some major characteristics and sequences of brain development, maturity, and aging may be universal among all mammals. Other apparent reasons for use of short-lived mammals rather than primates in research on aging include: logistical considerations, cost, time course of longitudinal evaluations, use of invasive experimental procedures, delay in publication, and lack of information on availability and longevity of primates. Since there is a lack of dissemination rather than a lack of information on the characteristics, availability, and longevity of primates, an attempt has been made to record the maximum longevity of primates in captivity. The primate taxonomic order ranges from the lowest, taxonomically controversial tree shrew (*Tupaia glis*) to man. Figure 5 illustrates schematically the maximum recorded longevity of the primate order based on authenticated records that have been reported in the literature (Napier and Napier, 1967) and the records made available in zoological parks, primate centers, private sources, and various other institutions (Jones, 1962).

Two of the most likely nonhuman primate candidates or prospects for increasing future use in neurobiological studies on aging include the rhesus monkey (*Macaca mulatta*) and the squirrel monkey (*Saimiri sciureus*). A comprehensive study on the early appearance and on regional differences in intraneuronal and extraneuronal lipofuscin pigment accumulation with age in the brain of the rhesus monkey (*Macaca mulatta*) has been published recently (Brizzee, Ordy and Kaack, 1974). The maximum longevity of laboratory born and raised female rhesus monkeys has been reported as 32 years (van Wagenen, 1972). In an effort to introduce the rhesus monkey as a primate "model" for neurobiological studies on aging, attempts were made to examine life-span changes in visual acuity in relation to neurochemical and morphological changes in specific cortical and subcortical regions of the brain. In these life-span studies of the rhesus monkey, visual acuity reached asymptotic 1 minute of arc early during the first year, remained

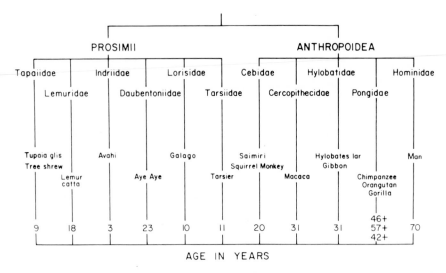

AGE IN YEARS

FIG. 5. The recorded maximum longevity of primates in captivity based on authenticated records cited in the literature, or records made available in zoological parks, primate centers, and primate laboratories.

unchanged until 18, and decreased to 2 minutes of arc after 18 years of age. Response latency and speed of locomotor performance also declined after 18 years. DNA, RNA, protein, cholinergic, adrenergic neurotransmitters, associated enzymes, and H_2O were examined in visual and somatosensory cortical regions, the caudate, and hypothalamus. Significant age and regional variations were observed in these neurochemical constituents (Ordy and Brizzee, 1974). Other studies of age and regional differences in chemical composition of the brain in the rhesus monkey have also reported changes in DNA, RNA, protein, cholinergic-adrenergic transmitters and enzymes, H_2O, and lipids in monkeys over 18 years of age (Samorajski and Rolsten, 1973; Sun and Samorajski, 1973). These multivariate studies with the rhesus monkey have indicated that major behavioral, neurochemical, and morphological life-span changes are comparable to those reported for man.

It seems likely that the unique advantages of primates for multivariate neurobiological research on aging will stimulate an increasing use of higher diurnal primates in future research. Essentially, in general support of this anticipation, the following points represent a summary of the unique contributions that can be made by the use of nonhuman primates in future research on neurobiology and aging: (1) If the brain does play a "pacemaker" role in aging, then molecular, subcellular, cellular, and regional age changes or differences are much more likely to be identified in higher diurnal primates where sensory-associative and motor regions have been more carefully defined according to specific functional and structural criteria. (2) Life-span changes in structure-function relations of the brain may be identified in visual and somatosensory systems of primates where neuronal contact specificity has been demonstrated to be uniquely precise. (3) Life-span changes in complex manipulative behavior are more likely to be identified in primates since advanced cortical control over manipulative behavior is not organized at subcortical levels in lower mammalian species. Consequently, age decreases in timing, speed, and accuracy in complex manipulatory behavior may be demonstrable only in higher diurnal primates and man. (4) If the ultimate concern of research on aging is man, results of experiments with primates are *a priori* more directly applicable to man since man and primates are of the same taxonomic order.

UNIVARIATE INTERPRETATIONS OF LIFE-SPAN NEUROCHEMICAL CHANGES IN MAN IN RELATION TO MULTIVARIATE INTEGRATION OF BEHAVIORAL, PHYSIOLOGICAL, CHEMICAL, AND MORPHOLOGICAL VARIABLES IN ANIMAL LIFE-SPAN STUDIES

Theoretical and social interest in neurobiology and aging is generally directed toward man. However, in contrast to the permissible noninvasive behavioral and many electrophysiological studies of the human brain in aging, normative neurochemical studies of major life-span changes in the chemical composition, energy metabolism, and neurotransmitters in the human brain are extremely scarce and fragmentary. This is due in part to the scarcity of human brain tissue and to the previously widely held belief that the rapid postmortem changes would preclude valid, sensitive, or reliable chemical evaluations at any age level. Since the major focus of this chapter has been on major life-span changes in chemical composition, metabolism, and neurotransmitters in the human brain, the concluding comments are obvious. They can be restricted to a recognition of the scarcity or extreme paucity of reliable data on the human brain and to an exhortation for future studies to reduce the glaring gaps in knowledge more selectively, particularly in these three central areas of "neurochemical gerontology."

It is obvious that the lack of availability of human brain tissue for normative chemical evaluations across the life-span is a very limiting factor to more rapid progress. Brain tissue availability is restricted to accident victims, or more frequently to autopsy material obtained from clinical cases. Although neurochemical findings from clinical cases were included only incidentally in this chapter, it is apparent that a considerably greater number of clinical studies than were cited have been reported in the literature on neurochemical aspects of many neurological disorders in man. However, it should be apparent that basic knowledge of the normal, normative neurochemistry of the human brain during development, maturity, and aging is an indispensable prerequisite for interpreting neuropathology throughout the life-span. It is also apparent that a more comprehensive interpretation of life-span neurochemical changes in man can be made if reference is made to concomitant behavioral, neurophysiological and neuroanatomical changes in human aging. Consequently, greater integration within and among neurobiological disciplines is not only desirable but highly essential.

Another major issue in neurobiology and aging that is also quite obvious in this chapter concerns the role of animal studies or "models" in past and future neurobiological research on aging to gain a broader phylogenetic insight into structural and functional changes in the human brain during development, maturity, and aging. In comparative perspective, it seems intuitively reasonable and plausible to assume that many behavioral, physiological, chemical, and morphological aspects of aging can be identified even more readily in lower short-lived mammalian species. Despite considerable controversy and conflicting findings, the reliance on short-lived lower mammalian species in biological gerontology has resulted in the following progress: the development of some highly sophisticated longitudinal and cross-sectional experimental designs; single-unit iontophoretic neurophysiological methods; sensitive and reliable chemical and microchemical techniques; and a substantial amount of basic data on major life-span changes in behavior, physiology, neurochemistry, and neuroanatomy that can serve as comparative points of reference for the interpretation of life-span changes in the human brain. However, the relevance of such animal studies has become considerably more limited for the investigation of life-span changes in more complex sensory, cognitive, and motor functions demonstrable only in man, unless increasing use is made of higher diurnal primates in future multivariate studies.

Finally, two contrasting theoretical views have and continue to influence neurobiological research on brain development, maturity, and aging. According to an extension of the Neuron Doctrine, or the so-called "cellular connection hypotheses," molecules, organelles, individual cells, and specific synaptic connections among cells in pathways and centers of the brain represent the basic units in neuronal coding, information, learning, memory, and loss of information in brain development, maturity, and aging. By contrast, neurophysiological or "aggregate field hypotheses" have proposed that molecules, organelles, single cells, and existing connections among groups of cells even in specific pathways and centers of the brain may have little or nothing to do with neuronal coding, learning, and memory in brain development, maturity, and aging. Both theoretical views probably accept to varying extents that the brain is uniquely characterized by tissue interdependence, organizational complexity, redundancy, and environmental modifiability. However, cellular hypotheses tend to emphasize life-span changes in molecules, organelles, cells, and groups of cells, whereas aggregate field hypotheses tend to emphasize tissue interdependence, network capacity, and organizational complexity of the brain. Some major current trends in life-span neurobiology include: (1) recognition of genetic and environmental interactions in the brain throughout the life-span, (2) environmental modifiability or a chemical and morphological "plasticity" of the brain throughout life, (3) a more inclusive focus on interrelationships among neurons, glia, neuropil, microenvironment or extracellular "space," and vascular elements in brain function, (4) multivariate attempts to bridge the gaps from behavioral to electrical, neurochemical and morphological levels of observation, and (5) an increasing or inevitable recognition that biological gerontology in general and a neurobiology of aging in particular not only will receive increasing attention in neurobiology and in biomedical research but that they will probably become major areas of biology.

REFERENCES

Agrawal, H. C., and Himwich, W. A. (1970): Amino acids, proteins and monoamines of developing brain. In: *Developmental Neurobiology*, edited by W. A. Himwich, pp. 287–310. Charles C Thomas, Springfield, Illinois.

Altman, P. L., and Dittmer, D. S., editors (1973): *Biological Handbook*. Federation of the American Society of Experimental Biology, Bethesda.

Andres, R. (1967): Relation of physiological changes in aging to medical change of disease in the aged. *Mayo Clin. Proc.*, 42:674–684.

Andrew, W. (1971): *The Anatomy of Aging in Man and Animals*, pp. 218–237. Grune and Stratton, New York.

Arendt, A. (1972): Altern des Zentralnervensystems. In: *Handbuch der Allegemeiner Pathologie*, edited by H. Gottfried, pp. 490–542. Springer, New York.

Aures, D., Hakanson, R., and Clark, W. G. (1970): Histidine decarboxylase and DOPA decarboxylase. In: *Handbook of Neurochemistry, Vol. 4: Control Mechanisms in the Nervous System*, edited by A. Lajtha, pp. 165–196. Plenum Press, New York.

Bachelard, H. S. (1969): Carbohydrates. In: *Handbook of Neurochemistry, Vol. 1: Chemical Architecture of the Nervous System*, edited by A. Lajtha, pp. 25–32. Plenum Press, New York.

Bachelard, H. S. (1970): Control of carbohydrate metabolism. In: *Handbook of Neurochemistry, Vol. 4: Control Mechanisms in the Nervous System*, edited by A. Lajtha, pp. 1–12. Plenum Press, New York.

Bakay, L. (1972): Alteration of the brain barrier system in pathological states. In: *Handbook of Neurochemistry, Vol. 7: Pathological Chemistry of the Nervous System*, edited by A. Lajtha, pp. 417–428. Plenum Press, New York.

Balazs, R. (1970): Carbohydrate metabolism. In: *Handbook of Neurochemistry, Vol. 3: Metabolic Reactions in the Nervous System*, edited by A. Lajtha, pp. 1–36. Plenum Press, New York.

Balis, M. E. (1969): Nucleic acids and proteins. In: *Aging Life Processes*, edited by S. Bakerman, pp. 23–51. Charles C Thomas, Springfield, Illinois.

Barondes, S. H., and Dutton, G. R. (1972): Protein metabolism in the nervous system. In: *Basic Neurochemistry*, edited by R. W. Albers, G. J. Siegel, R. Katzman, and B. W. Agranoff, pp. 229–244. Little, Brown and Co., Boston.

Baxter, C. F. (1970): The nature of γ-aminobutyric acid. In: *Handbook of Neurochemistry, Vol. 3: Metabolic Reactions in the Nervous System*, edited by A. Lajtha, pp. 289–354. Plenum Press, New York.

Bender, A. D. (1970): The influence of age on the activity of catecholamines and related therapeutic agents. *J. Am. Geriatr. Soc.*, 18:220.

Bertler, A. (1961): Occurrence and localization of catechol amines in the human brain. *Acta Physiol. Scand.*, 51:97–107.

Bhargava, P. M. (1970): Intercellular control of intracellular metabolic activity. In: *Control Processes in Multicellular Organisms: A Ciba Foundation Symposium*, edited by G. E. W. Wolstenholme and J. Knight, pp. 158–173. Churchill, London.

Birren, J. E. (1965): Age changes in speed of behavior: Its central nature and physiological correlates. In: *Behavior, Aging and the Nervous System,* edited by A. T. Welford and J. E. Birren, pp. 191–216. Charles C Thomas, Springfield, Illinois.

Bloom, F. E. (1974): Introduction: Dynamics of synaptic modulation. In: *The Neurosciences: Third Study Program,* edited by F. O. Schmitt and F. G. Worden, pp. 903–904. The M.I.T. Press, Cambridge, Massachusetts.

Bondareff, W., and Narotzky, R. (1972): Age changes in the neuronal microenvironment. *Science,* 176:1135–1136.

Brante, G. (1949): Studies on lipids in the nervous system with special reference to quantitative chemical determination and topical distribution. *Acta. Physiol. Scand. (Suppl.),* 18(63):1–189.

Brizzee, K. R., Ordy, J. M., and Kaack, B. (1974): Early appearance and regional differences in intraneuronal and extraneuronal lipofuscin accumulation with age in the brain of a nonhuman primate (*Macaca mulatta*). *J. Gerontol.,* 29:366–381.

Brody, H. (1955): Organization of the cerebral cortex. III. A study of aging in the human cerebral cortex. *J. Comp. Neurol.,* 102:511–556.

Buetow, D. E. (1971): Cellular content and cellular proliferation changes in the tissues and organs of the aging mammal. In: *Cellular and Molecular Renewal in the Mammalian Body,* edited by I. L. Cameron and J. D. Thrasher, pp. 87–106. Academic Press, New York.

Burton, R. M. (1971): The turnover of lipids. In: *Handbook of Neurochemistry, Vol. 5, Pt. A: Metabolic Turnover in the Nervous System,* edited by A. Lajtha, pp. 199–214. Plenum Press, New York.

Busse, E. W., and Pfeiffer, E., editors (1969): *Behavior and Adaptation in Late Life.* Little, Brown and Co., Boston.

Callaway, E. (1965): Response speed, the EEG alpha cycle, and the autonomic cardiovascular cycle. In: *Behavior, Aging and the Nervous System,* edited by A. T. Welford and J. E. Birren, pp. 217–234. Charles C Thomas, Springfield, Illinois.

Calloway, N. O. (1971): Senescence: Identical rates of water loss in various species. *J. Am. Geriatr. Soc.,* 19:773–780.

Chiarelli, A. B. (1973): Cranial capacity and its growth from primates to man: The differentiation and evolution of the brain. In: *Evolution of the Primates,* pp. 305–326. Academic Press, New York.

Clausen, J. (1969): Gray-white matter differences. In: *Handbook of Neurochemistry, Vol. 1: Chemical Architecture of the Nervous System,* edited by A. Lajtha, pp. 273–300. Plenum Press, New York.

Comfort, A. (1972): Measuring the human ageing rate. *Mech. Ageing Dev.,* 1:101–110.

Comfort, A., Youhotsky-Gore, I., and Pathmanathan, K. (1971): Effect of ethoxyquin on the longevity of C3H mice. *Nature (Lond.),* 229:254–255.

Cook, S. F. (1972): Aging of and in populations. In: *Developmental Physiology and Aging,* edited by P. S. Timiras, pp. 581–606. Macmillan Co., New York.

Cooper, J. R., Bloom, F. E., and Roth, R. H. (1970): *The Biochemical Basis of Neuropharmacology.* Oxford University Press, New York.

Costa, E., and Neff, N. H. (1970): Estimation of turnover rates to study the metabolic regulation of the steady-state level of neuronal monoamines. In: *Handbook of Neurochemistry, Vol. 4: Control Mechanisms in the Nervous System,* edited by A. Lajtha, pp. 45–90. Plenum Press, New York.

Cote, L. J., and Fahn, S. (1969): Some aspects of the biochemistry of the substantia nigra of the rhesus monkey. In: *Progress in Neuro-genetics,* edited by A. Barbeau and A. Burnette, pp. 311–317. Excerpta Medica Foundation, Amsterdam.

Cote, L. J., and Kremzner, L. T. (1974): Changes in neurotransmitter systems with increasing age in human brain. *Abstracts of the American Society of Neurochemistry,* p. 83.

Coxon, R. V. (1970): Glycogen metabolism. In: *Handbook of Neurochemistry, Vol. 3: Metabolic Reactions in the Nervous System,* edited by A. Lajtha, pp. 37–52. Plenum Press, New York.

Cremer, J. E. (1971): Body temperature and drug effects. In: *Handbook of Neurochemistry, Vol. 6: Alterations of Chemical Equilibrium in the Nervous System,* edited by A. Lajtha, pp. 311–324. Plenum Press, New York.

Cristofalo, V. J., and Sharf, B. (1973): Cellular senescence and DNA synthesis; Thymidine incorporation as a measure of population age in human diploid cells. *Exp. Cell Res.,* 76:419–427.

Curtis, D. R., and Johnston, G. A. R. (1970): Amino acid transmitters. In: *Handbook of Neuro-chemistry, Vol. 4: Control Mechanisms in the Nervous System*, edited by A. Lajtha, pp. 115–134. Plenum Press, New York.

Curtis, H. J. (1966): *Biological Mechanisms of Aging*. Charles C Thomas, Springfield, Illinois.

Davison, A. N. (1968): Lipid metabolism of nervous tissue. In: *Applied Neurochemistry*, edited by A. N. Davison and J. Dobbing, pp. 178–221. F. A. Davis, Co., Philadelphia.

Davison, A. N., and Dobbing, J. (1968): The developing brain. In: *Applied Neurochemistry*, edited by A. N. Davison and J. Dobbing, pp. 253–286. F. A. Davis, Co., Philadelphia.

Davison, P. F. (1970): Axoplasmic transport: Physical and chemical aspects. In: *The Neuro-sciences: Second Study Program*, pp. 851–857. The Rockefeller University Press, New York.

Dayan, A. D. (1972): The brain and theories of ageing. In: *Ageing of the Central Nervous System*, edited by H. M. Van Praag and A. F. Kalverboer, pp. 58–75. DeErven F. Bohn, Haarlem.

Dellweg, H., Gerner, R., and Wacker, A. (1968): Quantitative and qualitative changes in ribo-nucleic acids of rat brain dependent on age and training experiments. *J. Neurochem.*, 15:1109–1119.

Dickerson, J. W. T. (1968): The composition of nervous tissue. In: *Applied Neurochemistry*, edited by A. N. Davison and J. Dobbing, pp. 48–115. F. A. Davis, Co., Philadelphia.

Dobbing, J. (1968): The blood-brain barrier. In: *Applied Neurochemistry*, edited by A. N. Davison and J. Dobbing, pp. 317–331. F. A. Davis, Co., Philadelphia.

Dobbing, J., and Sands, J. (1970): Timing of neuroblast multiplication in developing human brain. *Nature (Lond.)*, 226:639–640.

Dustman, R. E., and Beck, E. C. (1969): The effects of maturation and aging on the wave form of visually evoked potentials. *Electroencephalogr. Clin. Neurophysiol.*, 26:2–11.

Egana, E. (1971): Effects of ionizing radiation. In: *Handbook of Neurochemistry, Vol. 6: Al-terations of Chemical Equilibrium in the Nervous System*, edited by A. Lajtha, pp. 525–573. Plenum Press, New York.

Eisdorfer, C., and Fann, W. E., editors (1973): *Psychopharmacology and Aging*. Plenum Press, New York.

Embree, L. J., Bass, N. H., and Pope, A. (1972): Biochemistry of middle and late life dementias. In: *Handbook of Neurochemistry, Vol. 7: Pathological Chemistry of the Nervous System*, edited by A. Lajtha, pp. 329–369. Plenum Press, New York.

Epstein, M. H., and Barrows, C. H. (1969): The effects of age on the activity of glutamic acid decarboxylase in various regions of the brains of rats. *J. Gerontol.*, 24:136–139.

Feldman, M. L. (1974): Degenerative changes in aging dendrites. *Gerontologist*, 14:36. (Abstr.)

Fenstermacher, J. D., Patlak, C. S., and Blasberg, R. G. (1974): Transport of material between brain extracellular fluid, brain cells and blood. *Fed. Proc.*, 33:2070–2074.

Fillerup, D. L., and Mead, J. F. (1967): The lipids of the ageing human brain. *Lipids*, 2:295–298.

Finch, C. E., and Jonec, V. (1973): Catecholamine metabolism in the brains of ageing male mice. *Brain Res.*, 52:261–276.

Finch, C. E., and Jonec, V. (1974): Properties of synaptosomes from senescent mice. *Geron-tologist*, 14:38. (Abstr.)

Fried, R. (1971): Introduction. In: *Methods of Neurochemistry, Vol. 1*, edited by R. Fried, pp. III–IV. Dekker, New York.

Friedman, G., Green, M. F., and Sharland, D. E. (1969): Assessment of hypothalamic-pituitary-adrenal function in the geriatric age group. *J. Gerontol.*, 24:292–297.

Gainer, H., and Barker, J. L. (1974): Synaptic regulation of specific protein synthesis in an identified neuron. *Brain Res.*, 78:314–319.

Galambos, R. (1970): Prefatory remarks on determinants of neural and behavioral plasticity. In: *The Neurosciences: Second Study Program*, edited by F. O. Schmitt, pp. 161–162. The Rockefeller University Press, New York.

Gentleman, J. F., and Forbes, W. F. (1974): Cancer mortality for males and females and its relation to cigarette smoking. *J. Gerontol.*, 29:518–533.

Glassman, E. (1974): Macromolecules and behavior: A commentary. In: *The Neurosciences: Third Study Program*, edited by F. O. Schmitt and F. G. Worden, pp. 667–678. The M.I.T. Press, Cambridge, Massachusetts.

Glowinski, J. (1970): Storage and release of monoamines in the central nervous system. In: *Handbook of Neurochemistry, Vol. 4: Control Mechanisms in the Nervous System*, edited by A. Lajtha, pp. 91–114. Plenum Press, New York.

Goldberg, A. M., and McCaman, R. E. (1973): Determination of picomole-amounts of ACh in mammalian brain. *J. Neurochem.*, 20:1–8.

Granich, M. (1972): Factors affecting aging: Pharmacologic agents. In: *Developmental Physiology and Aging*, edited by P. S. Timiras, pp. 607–614. Macmillan Co., New York.

Gross, N. J., Getz, G. S., and Rabinowitz, M. (1969): Apparent turnover of mitochondrial deoxyribonucleic acid and mitochondrial phospholipids in the tissue of rat. *J. Biol. Chem.*, 244:1552–1562.

Guroff, G. (1972): Transport and metabolism of amino acids. In: *Basic Neurochemistry*, edited by R. W. Albers, G. J. Siegel, R. Katzman, and B. W. Agranoff, pp. 191–206. Little, Brown and Co., Boston.

Hahn, P. von (1971): Failure of regulation mechanisms as causes of cellular ageing. *Adv. Gerontol. Res.*, 3:1–38.

Hall, Z. W., Hildebrand, J. G., and Kravitz, E. A. (1974): *Chemistry of Synaptic Transmission.* Chiron Press, Newton, Massachusetts.

Harman, D. (1956): Aging: A theory based on free radical and radiation chemistry. *J. Gerontol.*, 11:298–300.

Hayflick, L. (1973): The biology of human aging. *Am. J. Med. Sci.*, 265:432–445.

Herrmann, R. L. (1971): Aging. In: *Handbook of Neurochemistry, Vol. 5, Pt. B: Metabolic Turnover in the Nervous System*, edited by A. Lajtha, pp. 481–488. Plenum Press, New York.

Hess, H., and Pope, A. (1972): Quantitative neurochemical histology. In: *Handbook of Neurochemistry, Vol. 7: Pathological Chemistry of the Nervous System*, edited by A. Lajtha, pp. 289–328. Plenum Press, New York.

Hess, R., and Riegl, J. (1970): Pituitary ACTH, adrenal and plasma corticosterone responses to stress in old subjects. *J. Gerontol.*, 25:354–365.

Himwich, H. E. (1959): Biochemistry of the nervous system in relation to the process of aging. In: *The Process of Aging in the Nervous System*, edited by J. E. Birren, H. A. Imus, and W. F. Windle, pp. 101–126. Charles C Thomas, Springfield, Illinois.

Himwich, H. E. (1970): Historical review. In: *Developmental Neurobiology*, edited by W. A. Himwich, pp. 22–44. Charles C Thomas, Springfield, Illinois.

Ho, B. T., Taylor, D., Fritchie, G. E., Englert, L. F., and McIsaac, W. M. (1972): Neuropharmacological study of Δ9- and Δ8-L-tetrahydrocannabinols in monkeys and mice. *Brain Res.*, 38:163–170.

Hochschild, R. (1971): Effect of membrane stabilizing drugs on mortality in *Drosophila melanogaster*. *Exp. Gerontol.*, 6:133–151.

Hodos, W. (1970): Evolutionary interpretation of neural and behavioral studies of living vertebrates. In: *The Neurosciences: Second Study Program*, edited by F. O. Schmitt, pp. 26–38. The Rockefeller University Press, New York.

Hollander, C. F. (1972): Possibilities to delay the ageing process. In: *Ageing of the Central Nervous System*, edited by H. M. van Praag and A. F. Kalverboer, pp. 183–189. De Erven F. Bohn, Haarlem.

Hollander, J., and Barrows, C. H. (1968): Enzymatic studies in senescent rodent brains. *J. Gerontol.*, 23:174–179.

Holliday, R. (1969): Errors in protein synthesis and clonal senescence in fungi. *Nature (Lond.)*, 221:1224–1228.

Holliday, R., and Tarrant, G. M. (1972): Altered enzymes in ageing human fibroblasts. *Nature (Lond.)*, 238:26–30.

Holloway, R. L. (1966): Cranial capacity, neural reorganization, and hominid evolution: A search for more suitable parameters. *Am. Anthrop.*, 68:103–121.

Holloway, R. L. (1967): The evolution of the human brain: Some notes toward a synthesis between neural structure and the evolution of complex behavior. *Gen. Systems*, 12:3–19.

Hornykiewicz, O. (1972): Neurochemistry of parkinsonism. In: *Handbook of Neurochemistry, Vol. 7: Pathological Chemistry of the Nervous System*, pp. 465–501. Plenum Press, New York.

Hubel, D. H., and Wiesel, T. N. (1968): Receptive fields and functional architecture of the monkey striate cortex. *J. Physiol. (Lond.)*, 195:215–243.

Hyden, H. (1967*a*): RNA in brain cells. In: *The Neurosciences: A Study Program,* edited by G. C. Quarton, T. Melnechuk, and F. O. Schmitt, pp. 248–266. The Rockefeller University Press, New York.

Hyden, H. (1967*b*): Biochemical changes accompanying learning. In: *The Neurosciences: A Study Program,* edited by G. C. Quarton, T. Melnechuk, and F. O. Schmitt, pp. 765–771. The Rockefeller University Press, New York.

Hyden, H., and Lange, P. W. (1970): Protein changes in nerve cells related to learning and conditioning. In: *The Neurosciences: Second Study Program,* edited by F. O. Schmitt, pp. 278–288. The Rockefeller University Press, New York.

Iverson, L. L. (1970): Metabolism of catecholamines. In: *Handbook of Neurochemistry, Vol. 4: Control Mechanisms in the Nervous System,* edited by A. Lajtha, pp. 197–220. Plenum Press, New York.

Jacobson, M. (1970): *Developmental Neurobiology,* pp. 1–344. Holt, Rinehart and Winston, New York.

John, E. R. (1972): Switchboard versus statistical theories of learning and memory. *Science,* 177:850–864.

Johnson, H. A., and Erner, S. (1972): Neuron survival in the aging mouse. *Exp. Gerontol.,* 7:111–117.

Johnston, P. V., and Roots, B. I. (1972): *Nerve Membranes.* Pergamon Press, New York.

Jones, M. L. (1962): Mammals in captivity—primate longevity. *Lab. Primate Newsletter,* 3:3–13.

Kandel, E. R., and Spencer, W. A. (1968): Cellular neurophysiological approaches in the study of learning. *Physiol. Rev.,* 48:65–134.

Katzman, R. (1970): Ion movement. In: *Handbook of Neurochemistry, Vol. 4: Control Mechanisms in the Nervous System,* edited by A. Lajtha, pp. 313–328. Plenum Press, New York.

Katzman, R. (1972): Blood-brain-CSF barriers. In: *Basic Neurochemistry,* edited by R. W. Albers, G. J. Siegel, R. Katzman, and B. W. Agranoff, pp. 327–340. Little, Brown and Co., Boston.

Katzman, R., and Schimmel, H. (1969): Water movement. In: *Handbook of Neurochemistry, Vol. 2: Structural Neurochemistry,* edited by A. Lajtha, pp. 11–22. Plenum Press, New York.

Keevil-Rogers, P., and Schnore, M. M. (1969): Short-term memory as a function of age in persons of above average intelligence. *J. Gerontol.,* 24:184–188.

Kety, S. S. (1967): The central physiological and pharmacological effects of the biogenic amines and their correlations with behavior. In: *The Neurosciences: A Study Program,* edited by G. C. Quarton, T. Melnechuck, and F. O. Schmitt, pp. 444–451. The Rockefeller University Press, New York.

Kety, S. S. (1970): The biogenic amines in the central nervous system: Their possible roles in arousal, emotion and learning. In: *The Neurosciences: Second Study Program,* edited by F. O. Schmitt, pp. 324–335. The Rockefeller University Press, New York.

Kirsch, W. M., and Leitner, J. W. (1967): Glycolytic metabolites and co-factors in human cerebral cortex and white matter during complete ischemia. *Brain Res.,* 4:358–368.

Kohn, R. R. (1971): *Principles of Mammalian Aging,* Prentice-Hall, Englewood Cliffs, New Jersey.

Kormendy, C. G., and Bender, A. D. (1971): Chemical interference with aging. *Gerontologia,* 17:52–64.

Lajtha, A., editor (1969–72): *Handbook of Neurochemistry, Vols. 1–7.* Plenum Press, New York.

Lewis, C. M., and Tarrant, G. M. (1972): Error theory and ageing in human diploid fibroblasts. *Nature (Lond.),* 239:316–318.

Liu, Y. K., Wickstrom, J. K., Saltzberg, B., and Heath, R. G. (1973): Subcortical EEG changes in rhesus monkeys following experimental whiplash. *26th* Annual Conference on Engineering in Medicine and Biology, Minneapolis, Minn., p. 404.

Lloyd, K., and Hornykiewicz, O. (1970): Occurrence and distribution of L-DOPA decarboxylase in the human brain. *Brain Res.,* 22:426–428.

Maas, J. W., Dekirmenjian, H., Garver, D., Redmond, D. E., and Landis, E. (1973): Excretion of catecholamine metabolites following intraventricular injection of 6-hydroxydopamine in the *Macaca speciosa. Eur. J. Pharmacol.,* 23:121–130.

Maher, H. S., and Lehrer, G. M. (1972): Carbohydrate chemistry of brain. In: *Basic Neuro-*

chemistry, edited by R. W. Albers, G. J. Siegel, R. Katzman, and B. W. Agranoff, pp. 169–189. Little, Brown and Co., Boston.

Mahler, H. R. (1972): Nucleic acid metabolism. In: *Basic Neurochemistry,* edited by R. W. Albers, G. J. Siegel, R. Katzman, and B. W. Agranoff, pp. 245–268. Little, Brown and Co., Boston.

Mandell, A. J., editor (1973): *New Concepts in Neurotransmitter Regulation.* Plenum Press, New York.

Marks, N., and Lajtha, A. (1971): Protein and polypeptide breakdown. In: *Handbook of Neurochemistry, Vol. 5, Pt. A: Metabolic Turnover in the Nervous System,* edited by A. Lajtha, pp. 49–139. Plenum Press, New York.

Marx, J. L. (1974*a*): Aging research. I. Cellular theories of senescence. *Science,* 186:1105–1107.

Marx, J. L. (1974*b*): Aging research. II. Pacemakers for aging? *Science,* 186:1196–1197.

McCay, C. M., Sperling, L. S., and Barnes, L. L. (1943): Growth, aging and chronic diseases and life span in the rat. *Arch. Biochem.,* 2:469–477.

McGeer, E. G., Fibiger, H. C., McGeer, P. L., and Wickson, V. (1971): Aging and brain enzymes. *Exp. Gerontol.,* 6:391–396.

McGeer, E. G., and McGeer, P. L. (1973): Some characteristics of brain tyrosine hydroxylase. In: *New Concepts in Neurotransmitter Regulation,* edited by A. J. Mandell, pp. 53–68. Plenum Press, New York.

McGeer, E. G., McGeer, P. L., and Wada, J. A. (1971*a*): Distribution of tyrosine hydroxylase in human and animal brain. *J. Neurochem.,* 18:1647–1658.

McGeer, P. L., McGeer, E. G., and Fibiger, H. C. (1973): Choline acetylase and glutamic acid decarboxylase in Huntington's chorea. *Neurology (Minneap.),* 23:912–917.

McGeer, P. L., McGeer, E. G., and Wada, J. A. (1971*b*): Glutamic acid decarboxylase in Parkinson's disease and epilepsy. *Neurology (Minneap.),* 21:1000–1007.

McIlwain, H., and Bachelard, H. S. (1971): *Biochemistry and the Central Nervous System.* Williams and Wilkins Co., Baltimore.

McLennan, H. (1970): *Synaptic Transmission.* Saunders, Philadelphia.

Minckler, T. M., and Boyd, E. (1968): Physical growth. In: *Pathology of the Nervous System, Vol. 1,* edited by J. Minckler, pp. 120–137. McGraw-Hill, New York.

Mokrash, L. C. (1969): Myelin. In: *Handbook of Neurochemistry, Vol. 1: Chemical Architecture of the Nervous System,* edited by A. Lajtha, pp. 171–194. Plenum Press, New York.

Moore, C. L., and Strasberg, P. M. (1970): Cytochromes and oxidative phosphorylation. In: *Handbook of Neurochemistry, Vol. 3: Metabolic Reactions in the Nervous System,* edited by A. Lajtha, pp. 53–86. Plenum Press, New York.

Napier, J. R., and Napier, P. H. (1967): *A Handbook of Living Primates.* Academic Press, New York.

Nies, A., Robinson, D. S., Davis, J. M., and Ravaris, C. L. (1973): Changes in monoamine oxidase with aging. In: *Psychopharmacology and Aging: Advances in Behavioral Biology,* edited by C. Eisdorfer and W. E. Fann, pp. 41–54. Plenum Press, New York.

Nies, A., Robinson, D. S., and Ravaris, C. L. (1971): Amines and monoamine oxidase in relation to aging and depression in man. *Psychosom. Med.,* 33:470.

Noback, C. R., and Moskowitz, N. (1963): The primate nervous system: Functional and structural aspects in phylogeny. In: *Evolutionary and Genetic Biology of Primates,* edited by J. Buettner-Janusch. Academic Press, New York.

Norris, A. H., and Shock, N. W. (1966): Aging and variability. In: *The Biology of Human Variation, Vol. 134,* edited by E. M. Weyev, H. Hutchins, and P. E. Van Reyen, pp. 591–601. New York Academy of Sciences, New York.

Obrist, W. D. (1963): The electroencephalogram of healthy aged males. In: *Human Aging: A Biological and Behavioral Study,* edited by J. E. Birren, R. N. Butler, S. W. Greenhouse, L. Sokoloff, and M. R. Yarrow, pp. 79–93. Publication No. 986. U.S. Government Printing Office, Washington, D.C.

Obrist, W. D. (1965): Electroencephalographic approach to age changes in response speed. In: *Behavior, Aging and the Nervous System,* edited by A. T. Welford and J. E. Birren, pp. 259–271. Charles C Thomas, Springfield, Illinois.

Ochs, S. (1973): Effect of maturation and aging on the rate of fast axoplasmic transport in mammalian nerve. In: *Progress in Brain Research, Vol. 40: Neurobiological Aspects of Maturation and Aging,* edited by D. H. Ford, pp. 349–362. Elsevier, Amsterdam.

Oeriu, S. (1964): Proteins in development and senescence. In: *Advances in Gerontological Research, Vol. 1*, edited by B. L. Strehler, pp. 23–85. Academic Press, New York.

Okumura, N., Otsuki, S., and Kameyama, A. (1960): Studies on free amino acids in human brain. *J. Biochem.*, 47:315–320.

Ordy, J. M., and Brizzee, K. R. (1974): Life span changes in visual acuity, neurochemistry and morphology in the brain of a non-human primate, *Macaca mulatta. Gerontologist*, 14:38. (Abstr.)

Ordy, J. M., Samorajski, T., Hershberger, T. J., and Curtis, H. J. (1971): Life-shortening by deuteron irradiation of the brain in C57BL/10 female mice. *J. Gerontol.*, 26:194–200.

Ordy, J. M., Samorajski, T., Zeman, W., and Curtis, H. J. (1967): Interaction effects of environmental stress and deuteron irradiation of the brain on mortality and longevity of C57BL/10 mice. *Proc. Soc. Exp. Biol. Med.*, 126:184–190.

Ordy, J. M., and Schjeide, O. A. (1973): Univariate and multivariate models for evaluating long-term changes in neurobiological development, maturity and aging. In: *Progress in Brain Research, Vol. 40: Neurobiological Aspects of Maturation and Aging*, pp. 25–51. Elsevier, Amsterdam.

Orgel, L. E. (1963): The maintenance of the accuracy of protein synthesis and its relevance to aging. *Proc. Natl. Acad. Sci.*, 49:517.

Orgel, L. E. (1973): Ageing of clones of mammalian cells. *Nature (Lond.)*, 243:441–445.

Page, I. H., and Carlsson, A. (1970): Serotonin. In: *Handbook of Neurochemistry, Vol. 4: Control Mechanisms in the Nervous System*, edited by A. Lajtha, pp. 251–262. Plenum Press, New York.

Pappius, H. M. (1969): Water spaces. In: *Handbook of Neurochemistry, Vol. 2: Structural Neurochemistry*, edited by A. Lajtha, pp. 1–10. Plenum Press, New York.

Pelc, S. R. (1970): Metabolic DNA and the problem of ageing. *Exp. Gerontol.*, 5:217–226.

Pocchiari, F. (1971): Some aspects of carbohydrate metabolism in the developing brain. In: *Chemistry and Brain Development: Advances in Experimental Medicine and Biology, Vol. 13*, edited by R. Paoletti and A. N. Davison. Plenum Press, New York.

Potter, L. T. (1970): Acetylcholine, choline acetyltransferase and acetylcholinesterase. In: *Handbook of Neurochemistry, Vol. 4: Control Mechanisms in the Nervous System*, edited by A. Lajtha, pp. 263–284. Plenum Press, New York.

Pscheidt, G. R., and Himwich, H. E. (1963): Reserpine, monoamine oxidase inhibitors, and distribution of biogenic amines in monkey brain. *Biochem. Pharmacol.*, 12:65–71.

Quastel, J. H. (1970): Amine oxidases. In: *Handbook of Neurochemistry, Vol. 4: Control Mechanisms in the Nervous System*, edited by A. Lajtha, pp. 285–312. Plenum Press, New York.

Rappoport, D. A., and Daginawala, H. F. (1970): Changes in RNA and proteins induced by stimulation. In: *Protein Metabolism in the Nervous System*, edited by A. Lajtha, pp. 459–489. Plenum Press, New York.

Rappoport, D. A., Fritz, R. P., and Myers, J. L. (1969): Nucleic acids. In: *Handbook of Neurochemistry, Vol. 1: Chemical Architecture of the Nervous System*, edited by A Lajtha, pp. 101–120. Plenum Press, New York.

Robins, E., Robins, J. M., Croninger, A. B., Moses, S. G., Spencer, S. J., and Hudgens, R. W. (1967): The low level of 5-hydroxytryptophane decarboxylase in human brain. *Biochem. Med.*, 1:240–251.

Robinson, D. S., Nies, A., Davis, J. N., Bunney, W. E., Davis, J. M., Colburn, R. W., Bourne, H. R., Shaw, D. M., and Coppen, A. J. (1972): Ageing, monoamines and monoamine-oxidase levels. *Lancet*, 1(7745):290–291.

Robinson, N., and Phillips, B. M. (1964): Glycolytic enzymes in human brain. *Biochem. J.*, 92:254–259.

Robinson, N., and Williams, C. B. (1965): Amino acids in human brain. *Clin. Chim. Acta*, 12:311–317.

Rose, S. P. R. (1970): Neurochemical correlates of learning and environmental change. In: *Short-Term Changes in Neural Activity and Behaviour*, edited by G. Horn and R. A. Hinde, pp. 517–550. Cambridge University Press, Cambridge, England.

Rouser, G., and Yamamoto, A. (1968): Curvilinear regression course of human brain lipid composition changes with age. *Lipids*, 3:284–287.

Rouser, G., and Yamamoto, A. (1969): Lipids. In: *Handbook of Neurochemistry, Vol. 1:*

Chemical Architecture of the Nervous System, edited by A. Lajtha, pp. 121–170. Plenum Press, New York.

Ryan, J. M., Duda, G., and Cristofalo, V. J. (1974): Error accumulation and aging in human diploid cells. *J. Gerontol.,* 29:616–621.

Sacher, G. A. (1959): Relation of life span to brain weight and body weight in mammals. In: *Ciba Foundation Colloquin on Ageing. V. The Life Span of Animals,* edited by G. E. W. Wolstenholme and M. O'Connor, pp. 1–250. Churchill, London.

Sacher, G. A. (1968): Molecular versus systemic theories on the genesis of ageing. *Exp. Gerontol.,* 3:265–271.

Sacher, G. A. (1973): Maturation and longevity in relation to the expansion of cranial capacity in hominid evolution. Proceedings of the 9th International Congress on Anthropology and Ethological Sciences, Chicago.

Sacks, W. (1969): Cerebral metabolism *in vivo.* In: *Handbook of Neurochemistry, Vol. 1: Chemical Architecture of the Nervous System,* edited by A. Lajtha, pp. 301–324. Plenum Press, New York.

Samorajski, T. S., and Rolsten, C. (1973): Age and regional differences in the chemical composition of brains of mice, monkeys and humans. In: *Progress in Brain Research, Vol. 40: Neurobiological Aspects of Maturation and Aging,* edited by D. H. Ford, pp. 253–266. Elsevier, Amsterdam.

Schaie, K. W. (1968): *Theory and Methods of Research on Aging,* pp. 1–6. West Virginia University, Morgantown.

Schaie, K. W. (1970): A reinterpretation of age related changes in cognitive structure and functioning. In: *Life-Span Developmental Psychology,* edited by L. R. Goulet and P. B. Baltes, pp. 486–507. Academic Press, New York.

Schmitt, F. O. (1967): Molecular neurobiology in the context of the neurosciences. In: *The Neurosciences: A Study Program,* edited by G. C. Quarton, T. Melnechuk, and F. O. Schmitt, pp. 209–219. The Rockefeller University Press, New York.

Shock, N. W., and Yiengst, M. J. (1955): Age changes in basal respiratory measurements and metabolism in males. *J. Gerontol.,* 10:31–40.

Sinex, F. M. (1966): Biochemistry of aging. *Perspect. Biol. Med.,* 9:208–224.

Sokoloff, L. (1959): Circulation and metabolism of brain in relation to the process of aging. In: *The Process of Aging in the Nervous System,* edited by J. E. Birren, H. A. Imus, and W. F. Windle, pp. 113–126. Charles C Thomas, Springfield, Illinois.

Sokoloff, L. (1972): Circulation and energy metabolism of the brain. In: *Basic Neurochemistry,* edited by R. W. Albers, G. J. Siegel, R. Katzman, and B. W. Agranoff, pp. 299–325. Little, Brown and Co., Boston.

Solyom, L., Enesco, H. E., and Beaulieu, C. (1967): The effect of RNA on learning and activity in old and young rats. *J. Gerontol.,* 22:1–7.

Sparks, D., and Travis, R. (1967): Single unit activity during behavioral conditioning: Arousal effects. *Life Sci.,* 6:2497–2503.

Sperry, R. W. (1968): Plasticity of neural maturation. *Dev. Biol. (Suppl.),* 2:306–327.

Strehler, B. L. (1967): Environmental factors in aging and mortality. *Environ. Res.,* 1:46–88.

Strehler, B. L., Hirsch, G., Gusseck, D., Johnson, R., and Bick, M. (1971): Codon-restriction theory of aging and development. *J. Theor. Biol.,* 33:429–474.

Sun, G. Y., and Samorajski, T. S. (1973): Age differences in the acyl-group composition of phosphoglycerides in myelin isolated from the brain of the rhesus monkey. *Biochim. Biophys. Acta,* 316:19–27.

Surwillo, W. W. (1968): Timing of behavior in senescence and the role of the central nervous system. In: *Human Aging and Behavior,* edited by G. A. Talland. Academic Press, New York.

Suzuki, K. (1972): Chemistry and metabolism of brain lipids. In: *Basic Neurochemistry,* edited by R. W. Albers, G. J. Siegel, R. Katzman, and B. W. Agranoff, pp. 207–227. Little, Brown and Co., Boston.

Timiras, P. S. (1972): *Developmental Physiology and Aging.* Macmillan Co., New York.

Timiras, P. S., Hudson, D. B., and Oklund, S. (1973): Changes in central nervous system free amino acids with development and aging. In: *Progress in Brain Research, Vol. 40: Neurobiological Aspects of Maturation and Aging,* edited by D. H. Ford, pp. 267–276. Elsevier, Amsterdam.

Tiplady, B. (1972): Brain protein metabolism and environmental stimulation: Effects of forced exercise. *Brain Res.,* 43:215–225.

Tomasch, J. (1972): Is there a continuous loss of neurons due to aging? *Wien. Klin. Wochenschr.,* 84:169–170.

Tower, D. B. (1958): Origins and development of neurochemistry. *Neurology (Minneap.)* *(Suppl.),* 8(1):3–31.

Tryding, N., Tufvesson, G., and Ilsson, S. (1972): Aging, monoamines and monoamine oxidase levels. *Lancet,* 1:489.

Tyler, A., and Tyler, B. S. (1970): Informational molecules and differentiation. In: *Cell Differentiation,* edited by O. A. Schjeide and J. deVellis, pp. 42–118. Van Nostrand Reinhold, New York.

van den Berg, C. J. (1970): Glutamate and glutamine. In: *Handbook of Neurochemistry, Vol. 3: Metabolic Reactions in the Nervous System,* edited by A. Lajtha, pp. 355–379. Plenum Press, New York.

van Wagenen, G. (1972): Vital statistics from a breeding colony. *J. Med. Primatol.,* 1:3–28.

Vernadakis, A. (1973): Comparative studies of neurotransmitter substances in the maturing and aging central nervous system of the chicken. In: *Progress in Brain Research, Vol. 40: Neurobiological Aspects of Maturation and Aging,* edited by D. H. Ford, pp. 231–243. Elsevier, Amsterdam.

Verzar, F. (1968): Intrinsic and extrinsic factors of molecular aging. *Exp. Gerontol.,* 3:69–75.

Vogel, W. H., Orfei, V., and Century, B. (1969): Activities of enzymes involved in the formation and destruction of biogenic amines in various areas of human brain. *J. Pharmacol. Exp. Ther.,* 165:196–203.

Walford, R. L. (1969): *The Immunological Theory of Aging.* Munksgaard, Copenhagen.

Wallgren, H. (1971): Alcohol. In: *Handbook of Neurochemistry, Vol. 6: Alterations of Chemical Equilibrium in the Nervous System,* edited by A. Lajtha, pp. 509–524. Plenum Press, New York.

Wang, H. S. (1969): Organic brain syndromes. In: *Behavior and Adaptation in Late Life,* edited by E. W. Busse and E. Pfeiffer, pp. 263–287. Little, Brown and Co., Boston.

Wang, H. S., and Busse, E. W. (1974*a*): Heart disease and brain impairment among aged persons. In: *Normal Aging II,* edited by E. Palmore, pp. 160–167. Duke University Press, Durham.

Wang, H. S., and Busse, E. W. (1974*b*): Brain impairment and longevity. In: *Normal Aging II,* edited by E. Palmore, pp. 263–268. Duke University Press, Durham.

Wang, H. S., Obrist, W. D., and Busse, E. W. (1974): Neurophysiological correlates of the intellectual function. In: *Normal Aging II,* edited by E. Palmore, pp. 115–125. Duke University Press, Durham.

Weil-Malherbe, H. (1972): The biochemistry of affective disorders. In: *Handbook of Neurochemistry, Vol. 7: Pathological Chemistry of the Nervous System,* edited by A. Lajtha, pp. 371–415. Plenum Press, New York.

Weinbach, E. C., and Garbus, J. (1959): Oxidative phosphorylation in mitochondria from aged rats. *J. Biol. Chem.,* 234:412–417.

Wilson, A. C., and Sarich, V. M. (1969): A molecular time scale for human evolution. *Proc. Natl. Acad. Sci.,* 63:1088–1093.

Wilson, J. (1968): Chemical and metabolic aspects of heredodegenerative neurological disorders. In: *Applied Neurochemistry,* edited by A. N. Davison and J. Dobbing, pp. 401–423. F. A. Davis, Co., Philadelphia.

Winick, M., and Rosso, P. (1969): Head circumference and cellular growth of the brain in normal and marasmic children. *J. Pediatr.,* 74:774–778.

Woodruff, D. S., and Birren, J. E. (1972): Biofeedback conditioning of the EEG alpha rhythm in young and old subjects. *Proc. Am. Psychopathol. Assoc.,* 673–674.

Aging. Volume 1, edited by H. Brody,
D. Harman, and J. M. Ordy. Raven
Press, New York © 1975.

Multiple Forms of Monoamine Oxidase and Aging

Jean C. Shih

School of Pharmacy, University of Southern California at Los Angeles, California 90033

Monoamine oxidase (MAO) levels in the brain and heart increase with age in a number of species (Novick, 1961; Horita, 1967; Prange, White, Lipton, and Kirkead, 1967; Horita and Lowe, 1972). Robinson, Davis, Nies, Colburn, Davis, Bourne, Bunney, and Shaw (1972) first studied MAO in humans and showed that there was a marked increase in the MAO level with age in the human brain, platelet, and plasma using benzylamine as a substrate. However, McGeer, Fibiger, McGeer, and Wickson (1971) found that MAO activity in rat brains was not changed with age in rat brains using tryptamine as a substrate. Also, Wurtman, Axelrod, and Barchas (1964) showed that there was no significant difference in the MAO activity in human pineal glands among the four age groups (ranging from 3 to 70 years) they studied. The information on the relation of multiple forms of MAO with aging is lacking.

Compelling evidence has now been presented that MAO exists in multiple forms. It can be demonstrated by column chromatography (Shih and Eiduson, 1973, 1974) and electrophoretic techniques (Youdium, 1973; Shih and Eiduson, 1974). Selective inhibition by certain drugs (Johnston, 1968; Fuller, 1972) and substrate specificity (Hall, Logan, and Parsons, 1969; Yang and Neff, 1973) has represented another line of evidence for the existence of multiple MAOs. Therefore, if one would like to study MAO and aging, one must keep in mind that it exists in multiple forms.

MULTIPLE FORMS OF MAO AND DEVELOPMENT

We had previously reported (Shih and Eiduson, 1969) that the multiple forms of MAO derived from newborn chick brains differed from that of the adult. Later on, we extended these studies with regard to tissue, age, and substrate specificities. Figure 1 shows the gel electrophoretic patterns of MAO we have obtained in different tissues of the infant and adult rat (Shih and Eiduson, 1971). Tryptamine was used as substrate. In this experiment the infant or adult rats were decapitated, and various tissues (liver, heart, or brain) were removed and homogenized in phosphate buffer. MAO was solubilized by sonication and then centrifuged, and an equal amount of supernatant was applied to each gel. MAO was revealed by the appearance

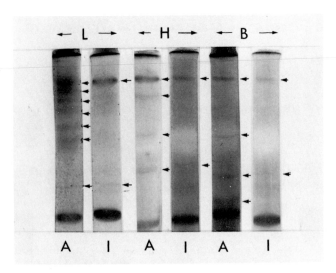

FIG. 1. MAO patterns comparing liver (L), heart (H), and brain (B) obtained from adult (A) and newborn (I) rats. Tryptamine was used as substrate for the enzyme. Arrows indicate MAO bands clearly visible on the gel. The dark bands at the bottom (anode) of the gel are dye markers.

of purple-colored bands, after incubation with a nitroblue tetrazolium staining solution and substrate (tryptamine) for MAO.

From these data, it is apparent that there are multiple forms of MAO in the brain, heart, and liver. Furthermore, it is clear that the MAO pattern for the newborn infant is different from that of the adult in all tissues studied.

The results of serotonin used as a substrate for the enzyme are shown in Fig. 2. From this figure, we obtained a similar pattern of age dependency. However, each gel shows different bands, suggesting substrate specificity. We can clearly see the substrate specificity of MAO derived from adult rat brains (Fig. 3). The slower (upper) moving band can use both benzylamine and tryptamine as a substrate, but not serotonin. The faster (bottom) moving band can utilize both serotonin and tryptamine, but not benzylamine.

Because the technique of gel staining may lead to artifacts (Glenner, Burtner, and Brown, 1957; Boadle and Bloom, 1969), we have employed radioactive substrate incubated with segments of the gel to check the authenticity of the stained bands that are presumed to be MAO. A comparison of the MAO activity on the gels, as seen by the staining technique and as determined by assay with ^{14}C-labeled serotonin, is shown in Fig. 4. The stained gel, with serotonin as substrate, showed the bands as indicated in the figure. This was compared with the radioactivity exhibited by a duplicate gel run at the same time. It can clearly be seen that the bands, which stained for MAO activity, also exhibited MAO activity by conversion of the labeled

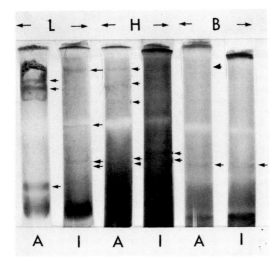

FIG. 2. MAO patterns comparing liver (L), heart (H), and brain (B) obtained from adult (A) and newborn (I) rats. Serotonin was used as substrate for the enzyme. Same illustration as Fig. 1.

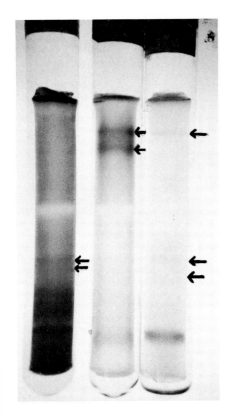

FIG. 3. MAO patterns obtained from adult rat brain with three different substrates: *Left:* serotonin; *middle:* benzylamine; *right:* tryptamine.

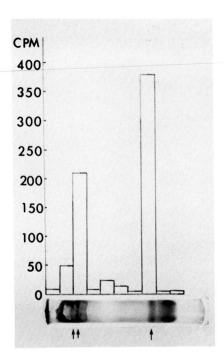

FIG. 4. A comparison of radioactivity obtained from a segmented unstained gel with the pattern of a gel stained for MAO activity, with the use of serotonin as substrate for each gel. Patterns were derived from adult rat liver.

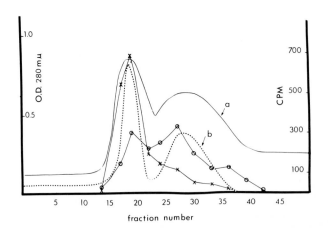

FIG. 5. Separation of MAO by Sephadex-electrophoresis and MAO activity determined with ^{14}C-serotonin or ^{14}C-benzylamine as substrate. The counts per minute have been corrected for background. Key to plots: curves a and b = patterns of protein content derived from two different experiments; O——O = MAO activity measured with ^{14}C-benzylamine; X——X = MAO activity measured with ^{14}C-serotonin. Enzyme activity was assayed on samples taken from curve a.

substrate to the product. It would appear from these results that the multiple forms of MAO we see on the gels do indeed possess MAO activity.

Then we proceeded to separate and isolate the multiple forms of MAO in order to characterize them further. In this experiment, MAO from rat brain mitochondria was solubilized by Triton X-100, followed with 20 to 40% ammonium sulfate cut, treated with calcium phosphate gel, and then subjected to Sephadex-electrophoresis (Fig. 5) Agarose (Bio-Gle Al. 5m) column chromatography (Shih and Eiduson, 1973). By either column, two MAO active fractions were obtained. As indicated in Fig. 5, fraction 1 has higher MAO activity than that of fraction 2, when serotonin was used as a substrate. On the other hand, when benzylamine was used as a substrate, fractions 1 and 2 have about the same enzymic activity.

MULTIPLE FORMS OF MAO AND AGING

According to Johnston (1968), Hall et al. (1969), and Yang and Neff (1973), the drug clorgyline could be used *in vitro* to identify two forms of MAO in rat brains. They called them enzymes A and B. Type A preferred serotonin as a substrate, type B preferred benzylamine as a substrate, whereas tyramine and tryptamine are common substrates for both types. From our own work (Shih and Eiduson, 1973) we were able to separate rat brain mitochondrial MAO into two fractions (1 and 2) by Sephadex-electrophoresis or Agarose column chromatography. These two fractions possess different substrate specificities (Fig. 5). With this information in mind, the MAO activity in 2-month-, 4-month-, and 24-month-old rats was determined using radioactive-labeled benzylamine, serotonin, tyramine, and tryptamine. The radioactive product was extracted and measured according to the method described previously (Shih and Eiduson, 1973). The result shows that in liver (Table 1) there is no significant difference in 2-month-, 4-month- and 24-month-old rats.

In the heart, when tyramine, serotonin, or benzylamine were used as a substrate, the MAO activity increased significantly with age as shown in

TABLE 1. *Relationship between age and MAO activity[a] in liver*

Substrates for Mao	Age (month)			p^b value
	2	4	24	
^{14}C-Tyramine	139.8 ± 17.7	128.6 ± 4.8	122.0 ± 6.0	ns
^{14}C-Serotonin	20.0 ± 2.7	10.9 ± 1.1 ↓	11.9 ± 1.8	ns
^{14}C-Benzylamine	169.8 ± 19.9	230.8 ± 13.1	205.5 ± 2.8	ns
^{14}C-Tryptamine	9.2 ± 0.4	—	4.0 ± 1.2 ↓	—

[a] MAO activity is presented as mean value ± SE from six samples in nanomole product formed per milligram protein per hour.
[b] p value is determined between 4- and 24-month-old rats.

TABLE 2. *Relation between age and MAO activity[a] in heart*

Substrates for MAO	Age (month)			p[b] value
	2	4	24	
¹⁴C-Tyramine	33.3 ± 3.9	48.8 ± 8.1	96.2 ± 9.5[b] ↑	< 0.01
¹⁴C-Serotonin	23.8 ± 2.7	22.7 ± 0.9	43.6 ± 3.6[b] ↑	< 0.01
¹⁴C-Benzylamine	7.9 ± 0.4	8.1 ± 0.9	13.7 ± 0.9[b] ↑	< 0.01
¹⁴C-Tryptamine	8.1 ± 1.0	—	2.9 ± 0.5 ↓	—

[a] MAO activity is presented as mean value ± SE from six samples in nanomole product formed per milligram protein per hour.
[b] p value is determined between 4- and 24-month-old rats.

Table 2. This finding agrees in part with Novick's (1961) work in which he reported that Osborn and Mendel rats exhibited an increase in cardiac MAO activity with age: Activity appeared about 4 weeks of age (about 50 g) and increased progressively over the ranges studied (up to 600 g). Similarly, Horita (1967) reported that the heart MAO, but not that of the liver, intestines, kidney, spleen, aorta, skeletal muscles, or brain, increased both with age (2 to 24 weeks) and weight (50 to 500 g) in male and female Sprague-Dawley rats.

Horita (1967) indicated that in the male rat heart, MAO concentration reached a plateau at about 20 to 24 weeks of age, but that other myocardial enzymes (succinic dehydrogenase, cytochrome oxidase, and aldehyde dehydrogenase) and total proteins did not increase in parallel fashion. From data reported here using benzylamine, serotonin, and tryptamine as a substrate, it can be seen that cardiac MAO increases from the 4-month-old to 24-month-old rats, but that decreased activity is apparent using tryptamine. Increased MAO activity with aging has also been observed by Gey, Burkard, and Pletscher (1965), but the cause is not clear.

In the brain, the MAO activity increases in the 4-month-old rat compared to the 2-month-old rat when serotonin was used as a substrate (Table 3). On the other hand, when tyramine or benzylamine was used as a substrate, MAO activity decreased in the 4-month-old rat compared with that of the

TABLE 3. *Relation between age and MAO activity[a] in brain*

Substrates for MAO	Age (month)		
	2	4	24
¹⁴C-Tyramine	41.1 ± 2.3	14.4 ± 1.5 ↓	—
¹⁴C-Serotonin	17.3 ± 0.9	23.3 ± 4.5 ↑	—
¹⁴C-Benzylamine	58.7 ± 3.9	42.3 ± 3.0 ↓	—

[a] MAO activity is presented as mean value ± SE from six samples in nanomole product formed per milligram protein per hour.

2-month-old rat. Whether these data suggest that type A of MAO increases with age and type B of MAO decreases with age, needs to be investigated.

SUMMARY AND DISCUSSION

These data demonstrated that MAO shows tissue and substrate change specifically with age. In general, activity is increased in the heart when serotonin, tyramine, or benzylamine were used as a substrate. On the other hand, using tryptamine as a substrate, hepatic and cardiac MAO activity decrease with age. In the brain, MAO activity increases when serotonin was used as a substrate, but decreases when tyramine and benzylamine was used as a substrate. However, it is not as yet clear which forms of MAO are important for aging.

Available physiological and pharmacological information suggests that brain biogenic amines are important for a variety of brain functions such as alertness, thermo-regulation, sexual activity, sleep, and depression. All these functions show changes with age and it thus seems to be a reasonable hypothesis that changes in the turnover of the biogenic amines in the brain may be a vital factor in aging of the central nervous system. It appears useful, therefore, to measure some enzymes controlling amine turnover in the brain areas from animals or humans of various ages. The role of multiple forms of MAO in this regard needs to be carefully studied.

ACKNOWLEDGMENTS

Support from the Grant Foundation is gratefully acknowledged. This work was also supported in part by U.S. Public Health Service Grant MH 19734–03.

REFERENCES

Boadle, M. C., and Bloom, F. E. (1969): A method for the fine structural localization of monoamine oxidase. *J. Histochem. Cytochem.*, 17:331–340.

Fuller, R. W. (1972): Selective inhibition of monoamine oxidase advances. *Biochem. Psychopharmacol.*, 5:339–354.

Gey, K. F., Burkard, W. P., and Pletscher, A. (1965): Variation of norepinephrine metabolism of the rat heart with age. *Gerontologia*, 11:1–11.

Glenner, G. G., Burtner, H. J., and Brown, G. W. (1957): The histochemical demonstration of monoamine oxidase activity by tetrazolium salts. *J. Histochem. Cytochem.*, 5:591–600.

Hall, D. W. R., Logan, B. W., and Parsons, G. H. (1969): Further studies on the inhibition of monoamine oxidase by M & B 9302 (clorgyline). I. Substrate specificity in various mammalian species. *Biochem. Pharmacol.*, 18:1447–1454.

Horita, A. (1967): Cardiac monoamine oxidase in rat. *Nature (Lond.)*, 215:411–412.

Horita, A., and Lowe, M. C. (1972): On the extraneuronal nature of cardiac monoamine oxidase in the rat. *Adv. Biochem. Psychopharmacol.*, 5:227–242.

Johnston, J. P. (1968): Some observations upon a new inhibitor of monoamine oxidase in brain tissue. *Biochem. Pharmacol.*, 17:1285–1297.

McGeer, E. G., Fibiger, H. C., McGeer, P. L., and Wickson, V. (1971): Aging and brain enzymes. *Exp. Gerontol.*, 6:391–396.

Novick, W. J. (1961): The effect of age and thyroid hormones on the monoamine oxidase of rat heart. *Endocrinology,* 69:55–59.

Prange, A., Jr., White, J., Lipton, M., and Kirkead, A. M. (1967): Influence of age on monoamine oxidase and catechol-O-methyl-transferase in rat tissues. *Life Sci.,* 6:581–586.

Robinson, D. S., Davis, J. M., Nies, A., Colburn, R. W., Davis, J. N., Bourne, J. R., Bunney, W. E., and Shaw, D. M. (1972): Aging, monoamines and monoamine-oxidase level. *Lancet,* 1:290.

Shih, J. C., and Eiduson, S. (1969): Multiple forms of monoamine oxidase in the developing brain. *Nature (Lond.),* 224:1309–1310.

Shih, J. C., and Eiduson, S. (1971): Multiple forms of monoamine oxidase in developing brain: Tissue and substrate specificities. *J. Neurochem.,* 18:1221–1227.

Shih, J. C., and Eiduson, S. (1973): Monoamine oxidase (E C 1.4.3.4.) isolation and characterization of multiple forms of the brain enzyme. *J. Neurochem.,* 21:41–49.

Shih, J. C., and Eiduson, S. (1974): Some interrelated properties of brain monoamine oxidase. In: *Advances in Biochemical Psychopharmacology, Vol. 12,* edited by E. Usdin, pp. 29–35. Raven Press, New York.

Wurtman, R. J., Axelrod, J., and Barchas, J. D. (1964): Age and enzyme activity in the human pineal. *J. Clin. Endocrinol.,* 24:299–301.

Yang, H.-Y. T., and Neff, N. H. (1973): B-Phenylethylamine: A specific substrate for type B monoamine oxidase of brain. *J. Pharmacol. Exp. Ther.,* 187:365–371.

Youdium, M. B. H. (1973): Multiple forms of mitochondrial monoamine. *Br. Med. Bull.,* 29:120–122.

Aging. Volume 1, edited by H. Brody,
D. Harman, and J. M. Ordy. Raven
Press, New York © 1975.

Age-Related Changes in Brain Biogenic Amines

T. Samorajski

*Biological Gerontology Research Section Texas Research Institute of Mental Sciences,
Houston, Texas 77025*

There are many basic differences in the brain during development, maturity, and senescence. Although the brain may be especially vulnerable during the early developmental stage, important changes may occur throughout the life-span which may affect the functional capacity of the brain in a variety of ways during aging. Aging has been defined as a universal, progressive, intrinsic, and deleterious decline after reproductive maturity (Strehler, 1962).

The fundamental mechanisms involved in the complex process of aging are just beginning to be understood. The three major categories of change that have been considered in relation to human aging of the brain have been morphological, behavioral, and more recently, neurochemical. Studies with human subjects have indicated an overall decrease in modifiability of behavior and "neural" plasticity of the brain with age. At the same time, there may be an increasing vulnerability to disease, drugs, harmful metabolites, and various toxic agents. There may also be a progressively slower recovery of brain function with age subsequent to brain damage. These changes in the brain with age may be associated with a progressive and cumulative loss of nerve cells which would ultimately lead to important modifications in the "microenvironment" and "synaptic organization" of the surviving neurons (Ordy and Schjeide, 1973).

Although the significance of the cumulative loss of neurons and other structural and functional changes during maturity and senescence for learning, motor coordination, and sensory processes is unclear, there seems to be some agreement that chemical and structural changes at the synaptic level may have important consequences for brain function. According to current concepts, the amines norepinephrine (NE), serotonin (5-HT), dopamine, and acetylcholine (ACh), among others, act as transmitters of nerve impulses at central synaptic junctions (Weil-Malherbe, 1972). The present state of investigations in this field indicates that the levels of biogenic amines in the brain may be variable and correlated also with changes in behavior.

The role of stress on brain chemistry has been particularly exploited in recent laboratory studies correlating aggressive behavior in mice and rats with changes in brain biogenic amine levels (Bennett and Rosenzweig, 1971). Several other studies have associated the effects of stress on brain catecholamines with activation of the hypothalamic-pituitary-adrenal axis (Ganong, 1963). Additional studies have suggested that brain and endocrine changes in response to stress may vary at different age levels (Bowman and Wolf, 1969; Friedman, Green, and Sharland, 1969; Samorajski, Rolsten, and Ordy, 1971; Ordy and Schjeide, 1973). Striking results on the functions of NE and 5-HT on sleep mechanisms have also been reported (Jouvet, 1967; Jouvet, Bobillier, Pujol, and Renault, 1967). Finally, a number of age-related neuropathological disease entities and mental disorders have been associated with changes in circulating biogenic amines, their metabolites, and associated enzymes. These relationships are considered in greater detail in subsequent paragraphs.

From the evidence presented, it is apparent that the importance of the biogenic amines in the brain depends on their putative role as CNS neurotransmitters involved in the central control of a wide variety of functions associated with human behavior. Inasmuch as the biogenic amines—NE, dopamine, and 5-HT—have been found to be correlated with more specific aspects of behavior, they will be considered in greater detail than ACh whose effects on behavior may be more general and diffuse. It is presently felt that a better understanding and treatment of mental disorders depends on a clarification of the related alterations in the distribution, biosynthesis, and metabolism of the biogenic monoamines. This chapter is a selective presentation of some of the information available in this area in relation to aging.

MENTAL DISORDERS, DISEASE, AND THE BIOGENIC AMINES

Recent studies of circulating catecholamine and indolamine levels in mental disorders strongly suggest that measures of various amines and their metabolites and associated enzymes can provide important information about the activity of the CNS (Carlson, Levi, Ryd, and Tord, 1970; Maas, Fawcett, and Dekirmenjian, 1972). It has been reported that the brain biogenic amine levels may be decreased in depression and increased in mania (Schildkraut, 1965; Schildkraut and Kety, 1967; Coppen, 1967, 1968; Coppen, Prange, Whybrow, and Noguera, 1972; Weil-Malherbe, 1972). Most clinical studies seem compatable with the hypothesis that drugs that are antidepressants may increase one or another of the amines at the receptor sites in the brain, whereas drugs that cause depression and are effective in the treatment of manias may decrease the activity of amines at the receptors (Schildkraut, 1970). The affective disorders as a group occur with greater frequency and become progressively more resistant to treatment with advancing age (Rawnsley, 1968).

Changes in monoamine metabolism in the brain were shown to occur also in senile dementia and Alzheimer's disease (Gottfries, Gottfries, and Roos, 1969a). There was a significantly lower concentration of homovanillic acid

(HVA) in the basal ganglia of a senile dementia group compared with a control group. Also, levels of HVA and 5-hydroxyindole acetic acid in cerebrospinal fluid were highest in a group of healthy volunteers and decreased in order for senile dementia, presenile dementia, and parkinsonism (Gottfries, Gottfries, and Roos, 1969b). Idiopathic parkinsonism is age-related in that onset is usually late in life, and increases in severity with time (Brain, 1969). The dementias, often associated with changes in memory, alertness, brain wave activity, and desynchronization of some physiological rhythms, are also seen more frequently in old age (McMenemey, 1963). A recent study showed that there was an inverse relationship between excretion of 3-methoxy–4-hydroxyphenylglycol, a metabolite of NE, and the amount of time spent in desynchronized sleep, particularly in the manic-depressive disorders (Schildkraut, Keeler, Papousek, and Hartmann, 1973). It is apparent, therefore, that changes in brain biogenic amines may be an important aspect of aging, particularly during the later periods of life when disease, cell death, and other conditions may further alter neurotransmitter activity in the brain.

The fact that it is possible to correlate abnormalities in catecholamine metabolism with depressive states and some age-related conditions in the human brain makes it appear probable that at least some forms of mental illness may involve the accumulation of a toxic intermediate which is normally further metabolized to a harmless one, or to the production of a toxic substance that does not normally occur (McIsaac, 1961). In the former case, a catecholamine enzyme would be lacking or inhibited, or might be hyperactive; in the latter case, an enzyme not normally present would occur, which might have a fundamental significance in the etiology of a psychosis.

Recently, it has been shown that monoamine oxidase levels increased with age in human, rhesus monkey, and mouse brain (Nies, Robinson, Davis, and Ravaris, 1973; Samorajski and Rolsten, 1973). Catechol-O-methyltransferase levels in various regions of monkey brain have also been studied, but no consistent trend occured with age (Samorajski and Rolsten, 1973). The highest levels of acetylcholinesterase (AChE) activity are found predominantly in structures associated with extrapyramidal function. Consequently, changes in ACh metabolism in nervous tissue might lead to severe mental and physical disturbances. However, levels of AChE activity in whole brain homogenates of mouse were found to decline only slightly at extreme old age (Samorajski et al., 1971). Analysis of some rhesus monkey and human brain regions did not reveal any significant changes with age within the intervals studied (Samorajski and Rolsten, 1973).

From a clinical point of view, the possibility of a change in neurotransmitter enzyme activity in aged human brain may have a significant bearing on the etiology and neurochemistry of mental disorders and neurological diseases affecting older individuals. The response of patients with Parkinson's disease to large doses of L-DOPA has focused attention on the importance of catecholaminergic processes to extrapyramidal functions.

CHANGES WITH AGE IN BIOGENIC AMINES OF MAMMALIAN BRAIN

Aging and Regional Distribution of Biogenic Amines

Table 1 lists the regional and age differences in the distribution of NE, dopamine, and 5-HT for various regions of the brain of mouse, rhesus monkey, and man. The basal ganglia complex contains a major portion of the total brain dopamine. The hypothalamus and brainstem contain most of the total brain 5-HT and NE. The functional significance of the interregional difference in biogenic amine content is not yet fully established. Using the technique of histochemical fluorescence developed largely by the Scandinavian investigators (Anden, Dalström, Fuxe, Larsson, Olson, and Ungerstedt, 1966), it has been found that fairly specific ascending and descending monoamine systems exist in the CNS (Fig. 1). Parkinson's disease, which usually occurs late in life, appears to be a disorder of the basal ganglia characterized morphologically by a degeneration of melatonin-containing cells in the substantia nigra and neurochemically by a marked decrease in the concentration of dopamine in the nigro-striato-pallidal system (Hornykiewicz, 1973). It is an interesting question as to whether other conditions

TABLE 1. *Regional distribution of NE, dopamine, and 5-HT in brain of mouse, monkey, and man in relation to age*

Region	NE (μg/g)			Dopamine (μg/g)			Serotonin (μg/g)		
	Dev.	Mat.	Sen.	Dev.	Mat.	Sen.	Dev.	Mat.	Sen.
Mouse[a]									
Whole brain	0.52	0.45	0.43						
Forebrain		0.89					0.91	1.14	1.08
Caudate		0.02			6.77				
Rhesus monkey[a]									
Hypothalamus	2.81	1.14	1.29				5.30	4.43	4.33
Brainstem	0.67	0.35	0.22						
Man[b]									
Caudate		0.05	0.04		4.21	2.93		0.25	0.29
Globus pallidus		0	0.04		0.55	0.24		0.08	
Putamen		0.04	0.02		5.54	3.27		0.22	0.23
Hypothalamus		0.85	0.51		0.19	0.23		0.44	0.31
Red nucleus		0.22	0.17		0.10	0.19			
Substantia nigra		0.08	0.05		0.51	0.42			

[a] From Samorajski et al. (1971) and Samorajski and Rolsten (1973). The results are based on mean values for five subjects at three different age levels, i.e., 3, 8, and 21 months for mouse and 3 to 5, 6 to 10, and 12 to 18 years for rhesus monkey representing the periods of late development (Dev.), maturity (Mat.), and senescence (Sen.), respectively.

[b] From Bertler (1961). Values for man are based on three mature subjects (43, 52, and 60 years) and eight at senescence (73 to 87 years).

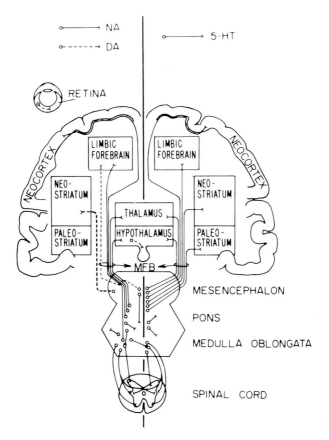

FIG. 1. Schematic drawing illustrating the dopaminergic, noradrenergic, and serotoninergic systems in the CNS (reprinted with permission from Andén et al., 1966).

associated with mental deterioration might not reflect a "deficiency syndrome" subsequent to the loss of cells in one or more of the other monoaminergic systems.

Table 1 also lists age differences in regional distribution of NE, dopamine, and 5-HT in the brain of mouse, rhesus monkey, and man. The levels of NE in the brain of mice maintained under controlled laboratory conditions decreased slightly with age. NE levels in the hypothalamus and brainstem of rhesus monkey and hypothalamus of man also decreased significantly with age. 5-HT in mouse forebrain increased slightly with age and decreased in the hypothalamus of rhesus monkey and man between the periods of development and senescence. These data further indicate that the levels of dopamine in the striata of older human populations may be reduced. Reduced levels of dopamine in the striata of senescent mice have also been reported (Finch, 1973).

Although the data are incomplete and do not include the extremes of old age in the rhesus monkey, which is the most important animal model for human aging, they do suggest that significant changes may occur in various regions of mammalian brain as a consequence of advancing age.

Aging and Metabolism of Biogenic Amines

Preliminary studies of the effect of aging on monoamine metabolism in the brains of mature and senescent mice has shown that aging has some significant effects on cerebral catecholamine metabolism (Finch, 1973). These include reduced levels of striatal dopamine in the brain of senescent male mice and also a reduced conversion of L-^{3}H-tyrosine and L-^{3}H-DOPA to catecholamines in several different regions of the brain. In addition, there was a slowed catabolism of total NE in the hypothalamus and of total dopamine in the striatum of senescent mice.

Information about age-related changes in monoamine metabolism in the brain has not been carefully examined in normal humans and subhuman primates of older age groups. At the present time, most of the available data is converging in support of hypotheses implicating the synaptic processes. One line of evidence points to alterations in membrane composition with age as a possible cause of change in the turnover of neuronal catecholamine stores. Synaptosomal membranes contain a high proportion of polyunsaturated fatty acids and may be particularly vulnerable to lipid peroxidation from free radical attack during aging. Lipid peroxidation might alter the permeability properties of the plasma membrane (Bishayee and Balasubramanian, 1971). In support of this concept is the recent finding by Sun and Samorajski (1970, 1975) that ethanol at various concentrations inhibits membrane-bound synaptosomal Na-K ATPase to a significantly higher extent in nerve-ending fractions isolated from older human brain. This deterioration of the plasma membrane and increasing vulnerability to attack by exogenous agents with age may be a major factor in the age-related incidences of Parkinson's disease and other conditions associated with alterations in catecholamine metabolism. However, it should be pointed out that the above results do not relate exclusively to turnover of neuronal catecholamines. Changes in intracellular compartments and distribution of the monoamines and their precursors in the various intracellular pools may also contribute to the changes noted. Information on these issues is of importance because of the potentially critical role changes in brain amine metabolism may have on cell activities within the brain and elsewhere in the body.

EFFECTS OF STRESS, IRRADIATION, AND CHLORPROMAZINE ON ADAPTATION AND BRAIN BIOGENIC AMINE LEVELS

The physical, chemical, and physiological development of the brain and its subsequent adaptation to the challenges of advancing age in all species of higher animals evolve from the continuous interaction of genetic and numerous environmental factors. Among the later are disease, nutrition, stress, irradiation, and various psychological, learning, and cultural variables of ranging complexity. Of these, stress, irradiation, and disease may be concerned more directly with age changes in the distribution, synthesis, and metabolism of biogenic amines. In addition, drugs may be used to produce more rapid and specific changes in catecholamine metabolism and consequent functional and behavioral alterations. The effects of suboptimal nutrition may be more important for development than for maturity and aging, while the relevance of the other environmental variables for changes in catecholamine metabolism in relation to aging is largely unknown at the present time.

A unified concept of how genetic and environmental factors might affect the brain, behavior, and aging is expressed in Fig. 2. This diagram also shows that the factors associated with aging in the brain may operate as feedback regulators of the genetic and environmental input. If so, the brain may play an important role as a "regulator" or "pacemaker" of the aging process as proposed by Still (1969). The following paragraphs provide some examples of the critical relationship between the biogenic amines and some major environmental variables including stress, irradiation, and long-term treatment with the "antipsychotic" drug chlorpromazine (CPZ).

Brain Amines, Stress, and Aging

It is generally accepted that genetic factors must play an important role in aging and in determining the life-span of an organism. However, since life-span in a selected population can vary in accordance with some extreme environmental fluctuations, it has seemed equally plausible that the external environment may also exert an important influence on the rate of aging and mortality. From the evidence available, it appears that the ac-

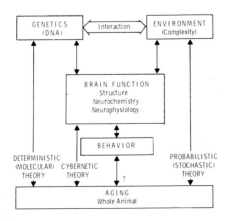

FIG. 2. Conceptual scheme depicting interrelationships between genetic and environmental influences on brain function, behavior, and aging.

cumulated biochemical, physiological, and behavioral impairments from repeated stress with aging may be more directly associated with some breakdown or loss of nondividing neuronal cell populations in the brain and in integrative neuroendocrine structures and functions of the organism (Ordy, Rolsten, Samorajski, and Collins, 1964). A number of animal experiments have attempted to relate biochemical changes in the brain to various types and periods of stress. States of stress may be expected to increase brain activity and release of neurotransmitters from the synapse.

In general, the effects of stress on endogeneous brain amines may be influenced by the severity and duration of the stress applied and the age, sex, and species of the animal tested (Ordy and Schjeide, 1973). A decrease of NE level in the brain is usually found after conditions of short-term and severe stress, whether induced by physical, pharmacological or emotional stimuli, whereas the application of more moderate stress over a longer period of time may result in an increase of NE levels. The levels of 5-HT, on the other hand, remain unchanged with stress or, in some cases, may be slightly increased. Stress does not appear to significantly alter dopamine levels and AChE activity.

More recently, studies using adult subjects at different age levels have examined age and stress effects with emphasis on concurrent changes at several different levels of observation. A summary of results obtained from one such experiment is shown in Table 2. These experimental findings revealed that the changes in NE content were variable across age. Moreover, it was shown that the effects of stress on brain biogenic amines may be associated with some morphological and behavioral changes. A recent application of multivariate evaluations has provided an even better correlation between various behavioral, morphological, and chemical components associated with "plasticity" of the brain and neuroendocrines in response to stress throughout maturity and senescence (Ordy and Schjeide, 1973).

Brain Amines, Irradiation and Aging

There has been repeated experimental confirmation of the fact that sublethal whole-body or partial-body irradiation from external sources can cause an increased mortality rate or life shortening in mammals. Consequently, irradiation is a useful tool for altering and studying the aging phenomena. However, the variable radiosensitivity of organs with a preponderance of cell types with a high rate of renewal appears considerably greater than that of an organ, such as the brain which is composed primarily of postmitotic cells. Therefore, it is logical to assume that irradiation of the brain can more accurately simulate some of the more specific effects of aging in cells as well as accelerate many of the more obvious structural and functional changes observed normally with aging.

We have recently found that deuteron irradiation of the brain at dose

TABLE 2. Statistical summary of group means of age and stress effects on behavior, morphology, and neurochemistry of C57BL/10 control (C) and stress (S) male mice

| | Age in months | | | | | | ANOVA | p^a | |
| | 3 | | 9 | | 28 | | | | |
Variables	C	S	C	S	C	S	units	A	S
Behavior									
Activity	2,366	2,383	2,409	2,397	1,907	1,931	rev	0.01	ns
Exploration	161	164	182	167	128	102	e/t	0.01	ns
Morphology									
Brain	0.419	0.419	0.426	0.425	0.435	0.433	g	0.05	ns
Body	22.6	21.4	29.0	28.1	28.0	26.9	g	0.01	ns
Pituitary	1.30	1.10	1.51	1.25	1.16	1.11	mg	0.05	0.01
Adrenals	3.11	3.19	3.28	3.43	3.34	3.44	mg	ns	ns
Neurochemistry									
AChE	13.0	13.7	13.6	13.6	12.4	12.5	IU/g	0.01	ns
NE	0.406	0.593	0.442	0.644	0.413	0.456	µg/g	0.01	0.01
5-HT	1.09	1.06	1.21	1.16	1.10	1.24	µg/g	0.01	ns

From Samorajski et al. (1971).
^{a} Age (A) and stress (S) effects on control (C) and stress mice were evaluated by separate (2×3) analyses of variance (ANOVA) and then by Newman-Keul's multiple range test ($p < 0.05$ or ns = not significant). Stress consisted of a 15 day period of intermittent electric shock.

levels below 25,000 rad produced significant life-span shortening which was proportional to the dose. A plot of the cumulative percentage of mortality distribution revealed a negatively skewed curve, suggesting that ionizing radiation of the brain can approximate an idealized representation of the Gompertz curve of the probability of death with increasing age (Ordy, Samorajski, Hershberger, and Curtis, 1971; Samorajski and Ordy, 1972). Since nerve cells are not replaced by cell division, the radiation-induced changes in mortality observed in these studies indicate that biological aging may be determined to a significant extent by cell loss or damage in the brain. Several efforts have been made to investigate biogenic amine levels in the brain in relation to cell loss resulting from an interaction between irradiation and aging. There is some indication that the consequences of irradiation and aging on brain catecholamine levels may be similar (Samorajski, Ordy, Zeman, and Curtis, 1970).

Proton irradiation of striate area 17 of the visual cortex of the squirrel monkey resulted in a decrease of NE in several areas of the brain far removed from the site of irradiation (Table 3). Changes in biogenic amine levels have also been investigated in mice at 18 months after focal irradiation of the brain at dose levels ranging from 0 to 10 krad (Samorajski, Rolsten, and Curtis, 1970). Significant biochemical changes were observed in neuro-

TABLE 3. Changes in endogenous NE and dopamine in different regions of the brain after proton irradiation of striate area 17 of the visual cortex

Brain region	Controls (4)		10,000 rd (4)		20,000 rd (4)	
	Right	Left	Right	Left	Right	Left
	NE (μg/g wet wt.)[a]					
Hypothalamus	6.93 ± 0.26	6.37 ± 0.51	4.06 ± 0.93	4.36 ± 0.71	3.15 ± 0.22	3.44 ± 0.46
Caudate	0.30 ± 0.03	0.27 ± 0.04	0.18 ± 0.01	0.24 ± 0.06	0.22 ± 0.03	0.18 ± 0.02
Brainstem	0.63 ± 0.04	0.65 ± 0.07	0.50 ± 0.04	0.51 ± 0.06	0.50 ± 0.05	0.49 ± 0.06
Hippocampus	0.58 ± 0.06	0.47 ± 0.08	0.40 ± 0.02	0.37 ± 0.02	0.44 ± 0.05	0.37 ± 0.06
Putamen	0.28 ± 0.03	0.27 ± 0.02	0.15 ± 0.01	0.19 ± 0.01	0.20 ± 0.01	0.24 ± 0.01
Cerebellum	0.13 ± 0.02	0.12 ± 0.02	0.11 ± 0.02	0.10 ± 0.02	0.10 ± 0.02	0.11 ± 0.02
	Dopamine (μg/g wet wt.)[b]					
Caudate	11.6 ± 0.8	13.1 ± 2.1	14.7 ± 2.1	12.1 ± 1.6	12.9 ± 1.8	14.2 ± 0.6
Putamen	9.4 ± 1.29	10.7 ± 1.0	10.6 ± 1.6	13.0 ± 0.6	10.0 ± 1.1	12.3 ± 2.1

From Hsu et al. (1971).

Results are expressed as means $\pm$ SEM. The values in parentheses are the number of animals analyzed. For statistical analyses, the samples from the left and right side were treated as separate samples in each case.

[a] Significance of differences in NE levels: between left and right sides, ns; between control and irradiated brains, excluding cerebellum, $p < 0.005$; and between brain regions, $p < 0.005$.

[b] Significance of differences in dopamine levels: between left and right sides, ns; between control and irradiated brains, ns; and between brain regions, $p < 0.05$.

transmitter and enzyme content in whole-brain homogenates. Significant changes in Na^+, K^+, MG^{2+} ATPase activity in nerve-ending particles were also observed at 6 hr after 50 krad. We and others have already shown that NE and striatal dopamine may be reduced in human as well as mouse and monkey brain during the course of aging. Such findings and those from the irradiation studies cited, indirectly point to a major involvement of the monoamines both in normal aging and life-shortening consequent to partial brain irradiation. Although the direction of change in some of the amines was at variance with changes noted in relation to aging alone, these results taken together may be interpreted as an indication that the synapse may be particularly vulnerable to both ionizing radiation and aging.

In summary, these findings indicate that changes in the brain must play a more critical role than in other organs in mortality and aging, particularly since it can be assumed that changes in the brain may ultimately influence directly or indirectly all other organs of the body. Available evidence points to an important role for the biogenic amines in life-shortening, both in aging and after irradiation. However, the mechanism involved remains unclear at the present time.

Brain Amines, CPZ, and Aging

To further test the possible interrelationship between environmental influences and certain related variables associated with aging, a study was undertaken to consider the possibility that the "antipsychotic" drug CPZ may also modify the rate of aging in the brain. CPZ was selected for testing because of its ability to deplete NE stores in the brain and block dopamine receptors (Gabay, 1971; Horn and Snyder, 1971).

Mice of a highly inbred strain raised and maintained in a carefully regulated environmental chamber were selected for the study. The variables selected for measure included: (1) body and brain weight changes, (2) mortality rates, (3) locomotor activity at intervals preceeding and following CPZ administration, (4) hexobarbital and sodium barbital narcosis for liver and brain "cortical" function, respectively, (5) endogenous biogenic amine content, and (6) brain DNA, RNA, and total protein content for estimating possible cell loss. Procedural information may be found in an earlier report from our laboratory (Samorajski et al., 1971).

The data for body weight, brain weight, and survival in 20-month-old control and CPZ-treated mice is shown in Table 4. There was a significant difference in body weight between the control and CPZ-treated groups. The cause and significance of this difference is unknown at the present time. Food and water intake, which was monitored during the treatment period, did not indicate any significant difference in consumption between the control and two experimental groups. At the time of sacrifice, survival was

TABLE 4. *Statistical summary of neurobiological changes in 20-month-old C57BL/10 female mice after 7 months of CPZ administration*

Observation on:	Experimental groups			Analyses	
	Control (N = 11)	CPZ, 5 mg/kg (N = 9)	CPZ, 10 mg/kg (N = 8)	ANOVA units	p[a]
Body weight	33.0	30.8	29.2	g	0.025
Brain weight	0.423	0.417	0.425	g	ns
Survival (Fr 15 Ss/Gp)	88	82	62	%	
Biochemistry					
(1) Protein and nucleic acids (cerebellum)					
Total protein	114.11	120.02	109.63	mg/g	ns
DNA	8.15	8.94	7.98	mg/g	ns
RNA	5.31	5.54	5.30	mg/g	ns
(2) Biogenic amines					
5-HT (L. forebrain)	1.43	1.46	1.46	μg/g	ns
NE (R. forebrain)	1.21	1.03	0.94	μg/g	0.025
Dopamine (caudate)	7.65	7.81	8.42	μg/g	ns
Locomotor activity[b]					
Pre-CPZ	1,384	1,472	1,314	$\bar{X}$ rev/h	ns
Post-CPZ	1,517	1,328	1,580	$\bar{X}$ rev/h	0.05
Barbital narcosis[c]					
(1) Barbital sodium duration	314.7	313.4	252.9	min	0.05
(2) Hexobarbital duration	112.3	115.7	102.6	min	ns

[a] Values not underscored by a common line are significantly different by analysis of variance (ANOVA) and multiple range test. ns = not significant.

[b] Locomotor activity data represent the mean value for 5 days of testing before CPZ administration (Pre-CPZ) at 12 months of age and at 10 days after the last treatment (Post-CPZ) when the animals were 20 months of age.

[c] These tests were conducted when the mice were 17 months of age and had received 4 months of placebo or CPZ treatment. Narcosis was determined by 250 mg/kg, i.p., of barbital sodium and 120 mg/kg, i.p., of hexobarbital.

88% for the control group, 82% for the 5 mg/kg CPZ group, and 62% for the 10 mg/kg CPZ group.

The concentration of total protein, RNA, and DNA in the cerebellum of control and CPZ-treated mice is also shown in Table 4. There was no significant difference between the three groups in these measures, indicating that there was no major change in glial-neuronal relationships subsequent to 7 months of CPZ administration. Likewise, the levels of 5-HT and dopamine in the forebrain and caudate nuclei, respectively, did not differ between the control and two CPZ-treated groups. However, there was a significant decrease in NE levels in the forebrain of the two CPZ-treated groups compared with the control group. A comparison of locomotor activity (Table 4) revealed contradictory results. The 5 mg/kg CPZ group compared to the control group had a significantly lower score, whereas the 10 mg/kg CPZ group had a slightly higher score than the control group, due perhaps to a bias introduced by a higher death rate in the 10 mg/kg CPZ group.

The results of the barbital narcosis study are also shown in Table 4. Sodium barbital sleeping time was lower in the CPZ-treated groups compared with the control group after 4 months of CPZ treatment, and achieved statistical significance in the 10 mg/kg CPZ-treated group. Hexobarbital sleeping time did not differ significantly between the control and two experimental groups. These data may be interpreted as an indication that a change occurred in the metabolic activity of the brain as a consequence of the long-term CPZ administration.

One of the purposes of this study was to focus attention on a selected "extrinsic" or "environmental" variable such as CPZ which is known to have a specific neurochemical and behavioral effect. The use of CPZ as a means of testing a model system for aging resulted not only in a significant decrease of NE in the brain as late as 2 weeks after the last treatment, but also produced significant differences in behavior, barbital narcosis, and mortality. Admittedly, the data is preliminary in nature and requires additional confirmation. If, however, this data is corroborated by additional studies, then it must be assumed that altering brain chemistry by "antipsychotic" agents may have some important consequences for aging in the brain.

SUMMARY AND CONCLUSIONS

The role of environment in changing both behavior and the levels of brain biogenic amines has been particularly exploited in recent years. Interest in the possible relationship between the biogenic amines and behavior derives in part from the hope that studies of emotional behavior in laboratory animals may ultimately lead to human application. Unfortunately, information concerning changes in biogenic amine levels in the brain of aged animal and human populations is sparse and frequently controversial. Although it has been possible to relate Parkinson's disease to changes in dopamine metabolism in human brain, a major difficulty in elucidating biochemical mechanisms in aging is that of disentangling the effects of gene expression from a variety of environmental influences that may be imposed during development, maturity, and senescence. Also, the problem of devising proper controls for biochemical effects in aging is almost unsurmountable. Other controversies in neurobiology are attributable in part to the arbitrary selection of time intervals across age and the lack of appropriate experimental designs for evaluating long-term changes in the brain. The recent development and application of multivariate statistical techniques may make it possible to bridge the gap between some of the various behavioral, biochemical, and morphological variables involved.

The second section of this chapter described studies aimed at elucidating the relationship between circulating levels of biogenic amines, neurological diseases, and mental disorders. Although it has not been possible to relate human behavior with amine levels in brain, there seems to be much promise that measures of various amines, their metabolites, and associated enzymes in body fluids may provide some information about the activity of the CNS. Furthermore, the concepts arising from this research may help clarify the relationship between mental disease, cell death, and changes in neurotransmitter activity in the brain.

The third section dealt with studies relating to changes in the regional distribution and metabolism of the biogenic amines NE, 5-HT, and dopamine in relation to age. These studies, although far from complete, indicate that the levels of biogenic amines may decrease in the mammalian brain with advancing age. There is some evidence from studies of human and rhesus monkey brain that a decrease in the monoamines may be associated with a concomitant increase in monoamine oxidase activity and possibly other enzymes associated with neurotransmission.

Although monoamine metabolism in the brain in normal humans of older age groups has not been carefully examined, there is some information available from studies of senescent mice, suggesting that brain monoamine metabolism may be reduced during the course of aging. By analogy with human data relating to the increased incidence and severity of idiopathic Parkinson's disease and phenothiazine-induced parkinsonism with increasing age, it may be hypothesized that striatal dopamine may be reduced in human brain as well as in mouse brain during the course of aging.

The final section focused on the influences of several environmental factors on brain biogenic amine levels and some possible behavioral and morphological correlates in relation to advancing age. A concept unifying these interrelationships is presented on the basis of tests conducted following exposure of laboratory animals to stress, irradiation, and treatment with the antipsychotic drug CPZ. The two major categories that were considered in relation to each other were changes in cumulative mortality and levels of various biogenic amine substances which might reflect alterations at the level of the synapse. Activity of AChE and the levels of the neurotransmitters NE, 5-HT, and to a lesser extent dopamine, were altered in many instances, and behavioral performance was affected in a variety of ways, suggesting that the aging process in the brain may be accelerated or retarded in response to some of the environmental conditions tested. These data provide further support for the concept that these monoamines may be important for the brain in its role as a "regulator" or "pacemaker" of the aging process.

ACKNOWLEDGMENTS

I wish to thank Miss Carolyn Rolsten and Mrs. Jo Ann Broussard for able technical assistance and Dr. J. M. Ordy, Delta Primate Center, for helpful discussions.

REFERENCES

Andén, N.-E., Dahlström, A., Fuxe, K., Larsson, K., Olson, L., and Ungerstedt, U. (1966): Ascending monoamine neurons to the telencephalon and diencephalon. *Acta Physiol. Scand.,* 67:313–326.

Bennett, E. L., and Rosenzweig, M. R. (1971): Chemical alterations produced in brain by environment and training. In: *Handbook of Neurochemistry, Vol. 6: Alterations of Chemical Equilibrium in the Nervous System,* edited by A. Lajtha, pp. 173–201. Plenum Press, New York.

Bertler, A. (1961): Occurrence and localization of catechol amines in the human brain. *Acta Physiol. Scand.,* 51:97–107.

Bishayee, S., and Balasubramanian, A. S. (1971): Lipid peroxide formation in rat brain. *J. Neurochem.,* 18:909–920.

Bowman, R. E., and Wolf, R. C. (1969): Plasma 17-hydroxycorticosteroid response to ACTH in *M. mulatta:* Dose, age, weight, and sex. *Proc. Soc. Exp. Biol. Med.,* 130:61–64.

Brain, Lord (1969): *Brain's Diseases of the Nervous System* (7th ed.), edited by J. N. Walton, pp. 522–534. Oxford University Press, London.

Carlson, L. A., Levi, L., Ryd, E., and Tord, I. (1970): Reports from the Lab for Clinical Stress Research, No. 18.

Coppen, A. (1967): The biochemistry of affective disorders. *Br. J. Psychiatry,* 113:1237–1264.

Coppen, A. (1968): Depressed states and indolealkylamines. In: *Advances in Pharmacology, Vol. 6, Pt. B,* edited by S. Garattini and P. A. Shore, pp. 283–291. Academic Press, New York.

Coppen, A., Prange, A. J., Jr., Whybrow, P. C., and Noguera, R. (1972): Abnormalities of indoleamines in affective disorders. *Arch. Gen. Psychiatry,* 26:474–478.

Finch, C. E. (1973): Catecholamine metabolism in the brains of ageing male mice. *Brain Res.,* 52:261–276.

Friedman, M., Green, M. F., and Sharland, D. E. (1969): Assessment of hypothalamic-pituitary-adrenal function in the geriatric age group. *J. Gerontol.,* 24:292–297.

Gabay, S. (1971): Phenothiazines: Neurochemical aspects of their mode of action. In: *Handbook of Neurochemistry, Vol. 6: Alterations of Chemical Equilibrium in the Nervous System,* edited by A. Lajtha, pp. 325–347. Plenum Press, New York.

Ganong, W. F. (1963): The central nervous system and the synthesis and release of adreno-corticotrophic hormone. In: *Advances in Neuroendocrinology,* edited by A. V. Nalbandov, pp. 92–157. University of Illinois Press, Urbana.

Gottfries, C. G., Gottfries, I., and Roos, B. E. (1969a): The investigation of homovanillic acid in the human brain and its correlation to senile dementia. *Br. J. Psychiatry,* 115:563–574.

Gottfries, C. G., Gottfries, I., and Roos, B. E. (1969b): Homovanillic acid and 5-hydroxy indoleacetic acid in the cerebrospinal fluid of patients with senile dementia, presenile de-mentia and parkinsonism. *J. Neurochem.,* 16:1341–1345.

Horn, A. S., and Snyder, S. H. (1971): Chlorpromazine and dopamine: Conformational similarities that correlate with the antischizophrenic activity of phenothiazine drugs. *Proc. Natl. Acad. Sci.,* 68:2325–2328.

Hornykiewicz, O. (1973): Metabolism of dopamine and L-DOPA in human brain. In: *Frontiers in Catecholamine Research,* edited by E. Usdin and S. H. Snyder, pp. 1101–1107. Pergamon Press, Inc., New York.

Hsu, L. L., Samorajski, T., Ordy, J. M., Bose, H., and Curtis, H. J. (1971): Regional changes in brain catecholamines after proton irradiation of the striate cortex in the squirrel monkey. *J. Neurochem.,* 18:1719–1724.

Jouvet, M. (1967): Mechanisms of the states of sleep: A neuropharmacological approach. In: *Sleep and Altered States of Consciousness,* edited by S. S. Kety and E. Evarts, pp. 86–126. Williams and Wilkins, Baltimore.

Jouvet, M., Bobillier, P., Pujol, J. F., and Renault, J. (1967): Suppression du sommeil et dim-inution de la sérotonine cérébrale par lésions du système du raphé. *C. R. Acad. Sci. [D] (Paris),* 264:360–362.

Maas, J. W., Fawcett, J. A., and Dekirmenjian, H. (1972): Catecholamine metabolism, de-pressive illness, and drug response. *Arch. Gen. Psychiatry,* 26:252–262.

McIsaac, W. M. (1961): A biochemical concept of mental disease. *Post-grad. Med.,* 30:111–118.

McMenemey, W. H. (1963): The dementias and progressive diseases of the basal ganglia. In: *Greenfield's Neuropathology,* edited by W. Blackwood, W. H. McMenemey, A. Meyer, R. M. Norman, and D. S. Russell, pp. 520–580. Edward Arnold Ltd., London.

Nies, A., Robinson, D. S., Davis, J. M., and Ravaris, C. L. (1973): Changes in monoamine oxidase with aging. In: *Advances in Behavioral Biology, Vol. 6: Psychopharmacology and Aging,* edited by C. Eisdorfer and W. Fann, pp. 41–54. Plenum Press, New York.

Ordy, J. M., Rolsten, C., Samorajski, T., and Collins, R. L. (1964): Environmental stress and ageing. *Nature (Lond.),* 204:724–727.

Ordy, J. M., Samorajski, T., Hershberger, T. J., and Curtis, H. J. (1971): Life-shortening by deuteron irradiation of the brain in C57 BL/10 female mice. *J. Gerontol.,* 26:194–200.

Ordy, J. M., and Schjeide, O. A. (1973): Univariate and multivariate models for evaluating long-term changes in neurobiological development, maturity and aging. In: *Progress in Brain Research, Vol. 40: Neurobiological Aspects of Maturation and Aging,* edited by D. H. Ford, pp. 25–51. Elsevier, New York.

Rawnsley, K. (1968): Epidemiology of affective disorders. Recent developments in affective disorders. *Br. J. Psychiatry,* Special Publication No. 2: pp. 27–36.

Samorajski, T., and Ordy, J. M., (1972): Neurochemistry of aging. In: *Aging and the Brain,* edited by C. M. Gaitz, pp. 41–61. Plenum Press, New York.

Samorajski, T., Ordy, J. M., Zeman, W., and Curtis, H. J. (1970): Brain irradiation and aging. *Interdiscipl. Topics Gerontol.,* 7:72–86.

Samorajski, T., and Rolsten, C. (1973): Age and regional differences in the chemical composition of brains of mice, monkeys and humans. In: *Progress in Brain Research, Vol. 40: Neurobiological Aspects of Maturation and Aging,* edited by D. H. Ford, pp. 253–265. Elsevier, New York.

Samorajski, T., Rolsten, C., and Curtis, H. J. (1970): Changes in neurochemistry and neuronal morphology after exposure of the mouse brain to lethal levels of focal irradiation. *Anat. Rec.,* 168:203–220.

Samorajski, T., Rolsten, C., and Ordy, J. M. (1971): Changes in behavior, brain and neuroendocrine chemistry with age and stress in C57 BL/10 male mice. *J. Gerontol.,* 26:168–175.

Schildkraut, J. J. (1965): The catecholamine hypothesis of affective disorders: A review of supporting evidence. *Am. J. Psychiatry,* 122:509–522.

Schildkraut, J. J. (1970): *Neuropsychopharmacology and the Affective Disorders,* pp. 15–37; 43–48. Little, Brown and Co., Boston.

Schildkraut, J. J., Keeler, B. A., Papousek, M., and Hartmann, E. (1973): MHPG excretion in depressive disorders: Relation to clinical subtypes and desynchronized sleep. *Science,* 181:762–764.

Schildkraut, J. J., and Kety, S. S. (1967): Biogenic amines and emotion. *Science,* 156:21–30.

Still, J. W. (1969): The cybernetic theory of aging. *J. Am. Geriat. Soc.,* 17:625–637.

Strehler, B. L. (1962): Definitions, criteria, categories, and origins of age changes. In: *Time, Cells, and Aging,* pp. 4–32. Academic Press, New York.

Sun, A. Y., and Samorajski, T. (1970): Effects of ethanol on the activity of adenosine triphosphatase and acetylcholinesterase in synaptosomes isolated from guinea pig brain. *J. Neurochem.,* 17:1365–1372.

Sun, A. Y., and Samorajski, T. (1975): The effects of age and alcohol on Na-K ATPase activity of whole homogenate and synaptosomes prepared from mouse and human brain. *J. Neurochem.,* 24:161–164.

Weil-Malherbe, H. (1972): The biochemistry of affective disorders. In: *Handbook of Neurochemistry, Vol. 7: Pathological Chemistry of the Nervous System,* edited by A. Lajtha, pp. 371–416. Plenum Press, New York.

Subject Index

A

Activity, aging rate and, 8
Aging
  activity and, 8
  amyloid and, 60-72
  arteriosclerosis and, 3
  behavior and, 138
  blood-brain barrier in, 121,
    151-152
  brain weight and, 136-138
  calendar age and, 23
  carbohydrates in, 147, 161-162
  chemical composition and,
    141-144
  clinical aspects of, 1-8
  depression and, 4-5
  DNA and, 145-146, 151-160
  EEG in, 138, 150, 170
  enzyme activity in, 164-170
  error accumulation theory of,
    155-157
  genetic factors in, 171-172
  glucose utilization and, 149-151
  histology of, 11-35
  intelligence and, 6
  leukocytes in, 2-3
  lipids in, 119-130, 160, 161
  lipofuscin and, 12-13, 39-60
  memory and, 2, 153-154,
    164-165
  mental disorders in, 3-4, 175-
    176
  morphological changes and, 1-8
  neuromelanin and, 79-112

Aging *(contd.)*
  neurofibrillary tangles and, 17-18,
    68-69
  neuronal loss in, 2, 6, 13, 33-34,
    163
  neurotransmitters and, 163-170,
    179-181, 199-213
  oxygen uptake and, 148-151
  personality and, 1
  physical illness in, 5-6
  in primates, 176-179
  proteins and, 141, 146
  RNA and, 145-146, 156-160
  sex differences and, 3
  slowing and, 6-7
  stress and, 199-200, 204-211
  theories of, 155-157
  threshold model of, 1-2
  turnover rate and, 153-155
  water content and, 141-144
Alzheimer's disease
  amyloid and, 61
  histology of, 14-15
  neurofibrillary changes in, 16-19,
    61
  pyramidal cells in, 23-25
Amino acids
  aging and, 159-160
  free, in brain, 146-147
Amyloid
  aging and, 60-61, 69-72
  characterization of, 61-64, 69-70
  classification of, 62-63
  clinical aspects of, 62, 70, 72